THE SUPREME COURT
AND "POLITICAL QUESTIONS":
A STUDY IN JUDICIAL EVASION

by
Philippa Strum

The University of Alabama Press
University, Alabama

Contents

CHAPTER 1

THE NATURE OF THE
POLITICAL QUESTION

. . . The definition of a political question can be expanded or
contracted in accordion-like fashion to meet the exigencies of the
times. A juridical definition of the term is impossible, for at root
the logic that supports it is circular: political questions are matters
not soluble by the judicial process; matters not soluble by the judicial
process are political questions. As an early dictionary explained,
violins are small cellos, and cellos are large violins.[1]

Speaking in 1940, a federal court defined political questions
as "such as have been entrusted by the sovereign for decision to
the so-called political departments of governments, as distinguished
from questions which the sovereign has set to be decided by the
courts." [2] Two months later, the same court wrote: "It would be
difficult to draw a clear line of demarcation between political and
nonpolitical questions. . . ." [3] If these two statements, treading on
each other's heels as they do, seem to indicate some confusion
in the minds of the judges as to the nature of a political question,
then the members of this court were surely not alone in their
perplexity. Justices of the Supreme Court and of lower courts, as
well as commentators who are members of the bar and those who
practice the occult art of political "science," have floundered in
the quagmire of definition.[4] One scholar finally threw up his hands
in despair and decided that the Court utilized the phrase "as a
term of exclusion, rather than as one of positive definition." [5] In
most cases, the bewilderment has resulted from an attempt to define
the category as a function of political institutions—that is, as political
dogma or a constitutional doctrine such as separation of powers—
rather than of the political process—that is, the struggle to obtain
and retain power.[6]

The phrase appears in American constitutional law when the
Supreme Court refuses to decide a case on the grounds that the

power to make the kind of decision involved was constitutionally delegated to one of the "political" branches of the federal government—the legislature or the executive. On occasion, the term is extended to include those power areas given to the states rather than the federal government, but this occurs less frequently—and, as we shall see, less correctly. Thus the political question is differentiated from that of jurisdiction; where the procedure is legitimate but the particular issues which constitute the substance of the case prevent the Court from deciding it, it is labeled a political question. If, for example, the Court feels that a case does not represent an actual controversy between litigants who are personally involved in the proceedings, it can refuse to hear it on the grounds of lack of jurisdiction.[7] Where an actual controversy between litigants with a substantial interest involves an issue which the Court feels it cannot decide—for example, whether or not a state's government is republican in form—the Court calls it a political question. The effect is not the same, because presumably in the first case other litigants might persuade the Court to hear the case; in the second, were the political question category as absolute as the Court would have us believe, the problem could never be adjudicated. It is the Court itself, however, which has cast suspicion on the category, by adjudicating the same question in one case and not in the next.

The key concept in all of this is "political branches." It is an interesting one, primarily because it reflects a desire on the part of both rulers and ruled to ignore the actual function of the judiciary under a system of separation of powers and judicial review. The interpretative power of the courts serves as a methodology by which a supposedly neutral third force can arbitrate between the government and its citizens when a difference of purpose or of understanding arises between them. Although most American children are taught in the fifth grade and again in high school that the "founding fathers" thoughtfully provided them with a government composed of three branches, American adults seem to visualize their government as a two-pronged entity, with a disinterested and unconnected judiciary somehow established on the sidelines. "Politics" to these Americans means "elections," and since there is no apparent relation between the federal judiciary and polling places, a negative syllogism concludes that the courts are apolitical and therefore non-governmental. Pupils learn that the independence of the judges enables them to remain above the corrupting tensions of the political process. The lesson further states that instead of making their decisions on the basis of party or personal interest, judges rely upon an inanimate and impartial body of precedents, which may sometimes be misinterpreted but which can never be manipulated. If this theory is inaccurate, it is not only the schools which are to blame. The courts themselves seemingly attest to its veracity by proclaiming a rigid adherence to *stare decisis*—and the only strange element in this situation is that they occasionally appear to believe their own propaganda. Popular belief in an independent judiciary enables the courts to place a final stamp of legitimacy upon all governmental acts, including those which might otherwise come under direct attack in the form of disobedience.

Popular myths do not exist in a vacuum; unless they serve some useful social purpose, they disappear. The benefits of this particular myth are threefold: it permits the legislature and executive, operating as power groups and/or sincere guardians of the public interest, to function within the confines of an amorphously limited constitution; it clothes the judiciary in robes of neutrality, thus adding to the power of that body while maintaining the kind of respect for law necessary in a stable society; and it absolves the citizen from what might otherwise be the uncomfortable necessity of participating in an unending re-examination of political actions and assumptions. As Franklin D. Roosevelt belatedly discovered, the veneration felt by Americans for their judges can be so great and so irrational as to approach the mystical, and it undoubtedly stems from the common belief that only the justices possess the key to those universal truths whose existence is the underlying supposition of American democracy.[8]

This unenlightened esteem is indispensable to the courts, for it constitutes their only independent resource. The Court can hand down opinion after opinion—scholarly, thoughtful, realistic—but unless it parallels public feeling, or unless the "political" branches and particularly the executive are willing to undertake its enforcement, a Court decree becomes a meaningless piece of paper. The Court, of course, has no police officials of its own, and its independence is therefore of a limited kind. This might not be too significant in an individual case, but the Court's publication of worthless decisions has a cumulative effect. If one decree is ignored the Court loses some of its immense prestige, and each unenforced decision increases the possibility that the next will also go unheeded. Proportionately to the ineffectiveness of its rulings, the operational validity of the Court disappears, and it can eventually cease to exist as a body performing a valuable function. Disrespect for the Court means that it fails in its job of legitimation. Unfortunate from the viewpoint of a stable society, this development would be equally obnoxious to the Court-cum-interest group. And so it is an axiom of constitutional justice that any decision which the Court thinks will not be enforced will probably not be made.

Hence the Court becomes a team of Delphic oracles, making educated guesses as to what the future will bring. Usually the problem is not great. If the Court is asked to mediate between the government and a citizen and finds the governmental action legal, there is no problem; the enforcement agencies will effect the Court's decree. Should the government attempt to run too far ahead of its constituents, passing a statute before the groundwork for social acceptance has been laid, the Court can negate it without danger and add to its own prestige in the bargain. The Court thus operates in accordance with its estimation of two factors: executive enforcement of judicial decisions, and the existence of a societal consensus. Beyond this, of course, the Court's own view of political policy will be a major factor in the determination of what it says; but we are concerned here with the situations in which the Court cannot make policy decisions because these would be ignored.

The Supreme Court decrees that a case involving domestic policy embodies a political question whenever a particular kind of situation develops. The fact pattern differs, but the typology does not. Where the Court can make one of two choices, with the first certain to go unenforced, and the second likely to be enforced but at the same time depending on a negation of an existing or emerging American "truth," the Court is forced to utilize the political question device. With either choice, the Court would suffer a loss of prestige and power. The situation is frequently complicated by a lack of social consensus.

In the ordinary course of events, enforcement of the Court's decisions is a function of the executive branch of the federal government. This is usually not a hindrance to the workings of the Court, whose *raison d'être* is the validation of actions and laws performed or approved by the executive. Occasionally, however, the Court takes its disguise seriously, and acts as a third body in striking down contested legislation. At such times the government, including the executive branch thereof, becomes the victim of its more frequently self-serving judicial mystique. It may denounce the Court's action and thunder with outraged oratory, but a combination of the Frankenstein it has created and the Court's knowledge of how far it can and cannot safely go almost inevitably defeats any suggested punitive measures or any threats of noncompliance. Such decisions add to the success of the judicial myth, for they live indefinitely as instances of the fearlessness and neutrality of the Court. And should they be reversed by a measure as serious as a Constitutional amendment, this is taken as further evidence that the judiciary was only doing its job of interpreting the original, very slightly imperfect document. So here, too, the enforcement problem does not exist. The government ceases to do whatever it was it wanted to do, and the Court continues on its incorruptible way.

When the Court does not agree with the government, then, a negative kind of enforcement is usually called for; a previously legitimate act is not performed. But there are occasions on which the Court, in negating one governmental act, implicitly asserts that another one is necessary; for example, if the Court nullifies a state's latest apportionment act, it is in effect asking that another be enacted. But the state legislature may refuse to reapportion, and where does that leave the Court? Unless it has reason to believe that the federal government will insist upon the enforcement of its decision, it leaves the Court with three choices: it can ask for reapportionment, and consent to appear both silly and impotent when no new law is forthcoming; it can uphold the apportionment act, denying the principle of individual equality for purposes of representation when the majority of Americans are coming to believe that they have a personal stake in the promulgation of this great truth,[9] and thus agree to accept a loss of prestige and the epithet "undemocratic"; or it can choose not to encounter such dangers and take a harmless road: it can virtuously admit that the power to decide the case was delegated elsewhere by the Constitution. Some crotchety people may call this ducking the situation, but many other observers will point to it as yet another indication of the Court's uncorrupted wisdom. In reality, this is no more than another example of that human instinct for self-preservation which, at the institutional level, becomes a partiality towards power.

This kind of judicial dilemma cannot exist where there is a strong societal consensus, for such an agreement would inevitably force the executive to uphold a Court order reflecting it. Thus the Court's discovery of a political question in the murky depths of a case is based upon its evaluation of the existence of a consensus. The 1954 Court thought it discerned a social agreement that the time had come to end legalized, overt Southern segregation.[10] In 1946 it perceived no social accord concerning reapportionment and representative equality; by 1962 it had changed its mind. It could be argued that there was something myopic about the Court's vision in 1946, but its view at that time led it to follow the third road. Its guessing was better in 1954 and 1962.[11]

Political Questions and the
Judicial Educative Function

Alexander Bickel has suggested that a prudent Court will occasionally utilize the political question as an educational device when to do otherwise would be foolhardy.[12] It would be difficult to think of more than one occasion on which a political question decision can be shown to have educated anyone outside of the legal profession. Certainly the opinions in *Colegrove v. Green,*[13] in effect upholding malapportionment while criticizing it, led neither a state legislature to reapportion nor Congress to reject Representatives from overrepresented districts. *Luther v. Borden*[14] taught no lesson other than that the Court would not strike down operative governments. The only case in this category which might be interpreted as educational is *Coleman v. Miller,*[15] Chief Justice Hughes' hint that Congress might legitimately set a seven-year ratification limit on proposed Constitutional amendments having been accepted by that body. But even there, if an educational role was played by the opinion, it was not the reason for the writing of that opinion. It is evident from the concurring opinions, subscribed to by four justices, that a majority of the Court believed it did not have jurisdiction; and it is equally clear that Justice Black's concurrence originated as a reaction to Hughes' attempt to combine an educational with a judicial function.[16] A power group does not expend its energy on educational efforts when it can be exerting power, and therefore any educational overtone which can be detected in Court opinions must be understood as an incidental result rather than cause. The Court does perform an educational function, but this is not the primary purpose of its majority opinions, which are written to establish legal guidelines. Dissents are great educators; anyone who doubts this need only glance at a few of Justice Holmes' better efforts. And the twentieth century's contribution in this area is indicated by the growing importance of the concurring opinion. John Marshall's court attempted to stand united behind one document which could serve as the indisputable Law, but that was an effort possible only in a society whose legal scholars proclaimed the absolute nature of discovered legal principles. The twentieth century has—at least on a theoretical level—pried off the mask of Justice and discovered behind it the occasionally uncertain, sometimes wicked, and unerringly human faces of nine different men. Cognizant of the doctrines of sociological jurisprudence and legal realism, the justices have poured out a proliferation of concurrences (and dissents) in the hope of living to fight more successfully with more allies another day. But this, along with an occasional obiter dictum, is the self-imposed boundary of the judicial educational system; certainly, it does not extend to the creation of political questions.

Assuming that the justices work with a conscious or semiconscious knowledge of the power struggle, "educational" concurrences and dissents can be written only when the concurring and dissenting members of the Court are certain that their opinions will not prevent the majority's publication of a political question decision. Or, of course, they can be written with the presupposition that the rest of the Court guessed incorrectly. For instance, Justices Black, Douglas and Murphy dissented in *Colegrove* v. *Green;* [17] Justices Black and Douglas dissented in *Cook* v. *Fortson* [18] and *Turman* v. *Duckworth* [19] and in *South* v. *Peters;* [20] Justice Rutledge concurred in *Colegrove* and apparently concurred in the *Cook* and *Turman* cases.[21] Justices Black, Douglas, and Murphy, who must have been aware of the Court's need for the political question category and yet rejected its application in these instances, could only have been operating on one of two rationales: either they disagreed with the majority's evaluation of the enforcement problem; or they agreed with it, and utilized the opportunity to educate the public while the majority of the justices kept the Court out of jeopardy. Justice Rutledge's contribution to *Colegrove* is quite explicit in its disagreement with the political question basis of the Court's opinion, while it makes clear that he supported the Court's decision because he considered it the only expedient one.[22] His motive in adding an additional opinion to the confusion called *Colegrove* v. *Green* was obviously that of hinting to the plaintiffs that, as far as he was concerned, they might retry their suit successfully at a later date.[23] Here, then, lies the educational function of the Court—not in its majority statements.

Political Questions and Equity

A number of red herrings have been dragged across the trail of political questions with tiresome frequency. A court's inability to decide what is and is not a "republican form of government" is one of these; another is "separation of powers." If a red herring can be presumed to have a ghost, then these particular spirits deserve to be laid to an undisturbed rest. And with them should go their odoriferous colleague, the inapplicability of equity to the preservation of political rights.

Equity proceedings originated in response to the rigid character of the early common law. The English courts became so concerned with precedent that by the thirteenth century they refused to issue new kinds of writs, even when such writs became a matter of social necessity. Citizens turned away by the law courts could appeal to the King as a last resort; and if he found their cause worthy of his grace, the monarch would administer justice. Such applications eventually were delegated to the Chancellor, whose discretion was great. With the passage of time, a system of rules developed and equity proceedings became somewhat systematized, but they remained more fluid than actions at law:

> . . . [Equity's] jurisdiction enlarges constantly to meet the needs of a growing civilization, finding new remedies as new wrongs are developed. It is and always has been an expanding jurisprudence.[24]

> As the expansive tendencies of the common law are thus confined within certain limits, and as its power to administer justice and to grant the variety of remedies needed in the manifold relations of society is incomplete, the English and American system of equity is preserved and maintained to supply the want, and to render the national jurisprudence as a whole adequate to the social needs.[25]

A number of equity "maxims" came into existence. Among these was the doctrine that equity will not act where there is a remedy at law. If an early suitor could receive relief from a court of law, there was no need for him to solicit the king's grace; hence the development of that particular maxim. It has no doubt served its function, but when, as in some of the cases described below, it was utilized as an excuse for the courts' refusal to consider social problems, its legitimacy became doubtful. Another axiom, never entirely unchallenged, was that equity could protect only rights of property. In a 1702 case which has since become a favorite source of quotations for Supreme Court justices, Lord Holt, a minority of one, stated his belief that the plaintiff should have been allowed a cause of action for the deprivation of his right to vote:

> ... the plaintiff had a right to vote, and that in consequence thereof the laws give him a remedy, if he is obstructed. . . . It is a vain thing to imagine, there should be a right without a remedy . . .[26]

The case went to the House of Lords on a writ of error, where, impressed by Holt's reasoning, the majority of the Lords voted to reverse the judgment. His thinking was later to be echoed by Justices Black and Douglas. Nevertheless, the idea of equity as the protector of property only was firmly entrenched, and it became the basis for the Court's pronouncement that equity could not handle disputed claims to political office.[27] "Property" took on an expanded meaning, most notably in 1818, when invasion of privacy was brought under its purview.[28] And although Black and Douglas were to argue that it should be expanded to include the right to vote, the Supreme Court generally held that equity could not protect political rights.

Like popular myths, historical dogmas do not exist in a vacuum; their genesis depends upon a particular need, whether social, scholarly, or personal. The political question grew out of such a "felt necessity," [29] and so, undoubtedly, did the very expedient concomitant that equity and political rights could never meet. Most Supreme Court justices of the twentieth century, and certainly those on the bench during the last two decades, have been aware of the extremely contingent and therefore changing nature of the law. When they rely on an old legal saw as a means of avoiding decision, it is safe to guess that this reliance on clichés reflects their heartfelt unwillingness to involve the court in the matter. And they are in danger of doing what other courts were once accused of:

> The common law courts paid such deference to forms and precedents that they became slaves to them.[30]

Perhaps, to speak more nearly correctly, the Court knows very well how to turn forms and precedents into serviceable slaves.

It is possible that the expansion of equity jurisprudence constitutes a legal acknowledgment of a social consensus. Until it is sure that such a consensus has come into being, the Court can insist that the rules of equity forbid it to decide certain dangerous cases. And when the time is ripe for a decision, the previously restrictive rules can be found to have expanded miraculously. Judicial cries of "no equity!" in reapportionment cases have suddenly disappeared. Lord Haldane summed it all up quite neatly, back in 1913:

> The moral of the whole story is the hopelessness of attempting to study Anglo-Saxon jurisprudence apart from the history of its growth and of the characters of the judges who created it.[31]

In this essay, which focuses only on political question cases involving domestic (as opposed to foreign) policy, the Court has been treated much as if it were a continuing entity with unchanging personnel. In a sense, this is no more than poetic justice, for if such a treatment illuminates inconsistencies in the Court's tradition, it also reflects the way in which the Court's announcements ask that it be regarded. But it does not necessarily render any less tangled the web that is constitutional law. *Baker* v. *Carr* [32] can and should be explained, at least partially, in terms of the enforcement problem. However, Professor Fred Rodell of the Yale Law School, writing before that decision was handed down, correctly predicted seven out of eight votes. The bases for his guess were the personal predilections of the justices.[33] A study that attempted to present the whole truth about various Court decisions would have to take into account the philosophical (and perhaps the psychological) system of every justice—and, of course, the extent to which the system includes final reliance on legal formulae. Such an examination may be impossible; at any rate, it would have made this essay far too lengthy, and so it has not been undertaken. What has been explored is the close relation between the enforcement problem and the proclamation that a particular domestic societal difficulty constitutes a political question.

CHAPTER 2

A REPUBLICAN FORM OF GOVERNMENT

Article IV Section 4 of the United States Constitution reads:

The United States shall guarantee to every State in this Union a Republican Form of Government, and shall protect each of them against Invasion; and on Application of the Legislature, or of the Executive (when the Legislature cannot be convened) against domestic Violence.

The Court has consistently refused to decide questions which have arisen under either the Republican Form of Government or the domestic Violence sections of this paragraph. The motivation for this refusal becomes quite clear upon examination of the relevant cases.

In 1827, the Court was confronted with a situation relating to the court-martial of a militiaman.[1] The details of the case and the major portion of Justice Story's opinion for a unanimous Court are not relevant here. What is important is Story's refusal to decide when a state of invasion exists.

We are all of the opinion, that the authority to decide whether the exigency has arisen, belongs exclusively to the President, and that his decision is conclusive upon all other persons. We think that this construction necessarily results from the nature of the power itself.[2]

Part of the reason given by Story was the necessity for immediate action in the case of invasion, and his unwillingness to subvert military discipline through providing a judicial opening for the questioning of orders. There was also the question of secret matters relating to security—an issue which was to arise more frequently in the twentieth century. For present purposes, the importance of the case lies in Story's decision that the Constitution permitted presidential discretion in the interpretation of "invasion," one of the terms employed in Article IV Section 4.

Martin v. *Mott* became a much relied-upon precedent in the best known instance of the Court's refusal to apply or interpret this section of the Constitution.[3] *Luther* v. *Borden,* in turn, was to be the precedent most frequently cited in subsequent decisions. This is no more than just, for *Luther* is an extremely illuminating example of the Court's inevitable involvement in American political affairs.

In 1663, Charles the Second granted a charter to the freemen of Rhode Island, establishing the laws of the colony. It extended suffrage to freeholders, limited officeholding to the same men, and made no mention of any amendment procedure. Unlike most other states, when Rhode Island announced her independence on July 4, 1776, she retained her colonial charter as her constitution. This meant that suffrage was still confined to freeholders, and that there was no constitutional methodology for altering this provision. In addition, the charter apportioned representation in the General Assembly (state legislature) as follows: six deputies from Newport, four each from Portsmouth, Warwick, and Providence; two each from all other towns. These figures were based on the population of the towns in the seventeenth century, and of course they quickly became outdated—but the apportionment could not constitutionally be changed. By 1824, Providence County contained three-fifths of Rhode Island's population and only twenty-two out of seventy-two representatives. The town of Providence, with more than double the population of Newport, had half as many representatives as did Newport. Occasional attempts to change the provisions got nowhere.

It was commonly assumed in the seventeenth century that only freeholders—men who owned their land—were deserving of the vote and capable of using it. They represented respectability and, sometimes, education, and by virtue of their landed property they possessed a valid interest in the way the government was run. This assumption, however, could not last long in post-Revolutionary America. It was challenged not only by non-land-owning laborers but, more important, by the growing class of non-land-owning merchants and others engaged in commerce. Rhode Island began to industrialize during the first half of the nineteenth century. Under the constitution, freeholders and their oldest sons could vote, and so between fifty and seventy-five per cent of the white adult males in Rhode Island had the vote at the time of the Revolution. As industrialization proceeded and increased its pace, this proportion changed. Disenfranchised citizens began petitioning the legislature for an extension of the suffrage in 1790. This was of no avail; the landowners in the legislature saw no reason to limit or eliminate their monopoly over political power in the state. An attempt to allow all taxpayers to vote was defeated by the legislature in 1811. By that time, it had become clear that non-freeholding taxpayers would include immigrants and Catholics, and so a bit of strait-laced Protestant bigotry was added to the power drive as a motivation for retaining the suffrage limitation. In 1841, 11,239 out of 26,000 males in Rhode Island had the vote; had the only qualification been the payment of taxes, voters would have numbered 18,139.[4] Even within the limited vote structure inequalities existed; for instance, younger non-freeholders were occasionally allowed to vote if they promised to cast their ballots as directed (secret balloting was unheard of in Rhode Island, so the promises were kept). The freehold qualification remained on the books, however, making Rhode Island the only state in the Union with such a limitation.

Following the repeated waves of egalitarianism generated by the Jacksonian era, and the suffrage agitation in England, the disenfranchised of Rhode Island decided to do something about their plight. Earlier reformers—extremely "respectable" citizens such as merchants and professionals—had been banded together under the name of "Constitutionalists." They had made no progress, so in 1840 they disbanded, and a new kind of organization came into being. The Democratic Party was agitating for suffrage reform throughout the country, and the new Suffrage Associations throughout the state decided to demand universal manhood suffrage. The demand attracted not only the former Constitutionalists, but less "respectable" elements—that is, laborers—as well. Its leaders, however, were eminent men; one of them had studied at Exeter and Harvard and had read law under Kent. An extremely successful lawyer, his advocacy of reform led to his being considered a traitor to his class. His name, soon to become famous, was Thomas Dorr.

The new, louder demands frightened the General Assembly, which decided to call a constitutional convention. Delegates to the convention, however, were to be chosen only by those qualified to vote for general officers; that is, freeholders. The constitution was to be submitted to the same voters for ratification, and each voter was to write his name clearly on his ballot. This did not satisfy the Suffrage Associations, representatives of which convened in May, 1841, to call for their own constitutional convention. All free white males of twenty-one or over were invited to vote for delegates. Apparently they did so, for the convention met, drafted a constitution, submitted it to the people, counted the votes, declared the new People's Constitution to be in effect, and organized elections for governmental officials. Copies of the constitution and the count of the vote for it were forwarded to the Governor along with a request that he communicate them to the Geveral Assembly. He did so, but the General Assembly postponed consideration of the constitution indefinitely. Instead, it went ahead with its own constitutional convention.

Dorr was to be elected Governor under the People's Constitution. Both he and his movement were warmly supported by much of the Northern half of the Democratic Party. Michigan and Maryland had each elected a constitutional convention without the consent of existing legislatures and had remodeled their state governments. The federal government had not intervened in these cases, and it was well known that President Tyler was a states-rights man unlikely to interfere where he was not wanted. The Rhode Island situation became a national issue, carefully played upon by politicians throughout the country. It was discussed in Congress and received widespread newspaper coverage. The question was considered to be that of whether or not might was right, as well as that of suffrage. All states were interested in the outcome, because if Rhode Islanders had a right to overthrow their government, no state in the Union could be considered safe from a similar proceeding. Public mass meetings were held in large cities, with all classes of men and all political parties participating. Dorr seems to have had the support of Democrats in Congress,[5] although Congress was eventually to refuse to aid him.

A great deal of jockeying back and forth took place, and it was probably as confusing to Rhode Islanders as it has been to subsequent historians. The conservative Freemen's Constitution was not ratified by the freeholders. Elections under the more liberal People's Constitution were held on April 18, 1842, two days before those under the old Constitution. In the latter election, Governor

King and his Assembly were returned to office, but a great many freeholders refused to cast their ballots. There thus existed two governments, side by side.

The Dorr government insisted that it and it alone was entitled to control public places, offices, records, arsenals, etc., but the General Assembly was not inclined to give them up. A private request, made to the Rhode Island Supreme Court in March of 1842, had yielded the opinion that the People's Constitution was invalid. Dorr may not have known this or may have decided to disregard it. At any rate, the only way for him to get what he wanted seemed to be through the use of force, and he and a number of followers began to arm themselves. Governor King hesitated to call out the militia because he knew that it, like the remainder of the citizenry, was split in its allegiance, and he could not be sure that his arms would not be turned against him. He quietly appealed to President Tyler for help under the "domestic Violence" clause of the Constitution. Tyler refused immediate aid, but said in effect that he would come to King's assistance if violence broke out in the state. This pronouncement was published in Rhode Island, inducing many Dorr supporters to return to the legal fold. Dorr and his government convened and were sworn in on May 3, but quickly adjourned, never to reassemble.

The King government was encouraged to activity. It issued a proclamation naming Dorr as the leader of a rebellion, warning against intercourse with him or his followers, and commanding him and his adherents to disperse immediately. Not unexpectedly, they didn't. A warrant was issued for Dorr's arrest; martial law was declared. After a series of futile military skirmishes, followed by a number of arrests, Dorr's government handed him their resignations, and his movement began to collapse. He continued to move in and out of the state, both avoiding arrest and pleading elsewhere for aid.

A group of Dorr's stauncher supporters, including one named Luther, planned an attack on the town of Warren for the purpose of seizing its arsenal. On June 29, 1842, a group of militiamen led by one Borden broke into Luther's house, armed with a warrant for his arrest, but Luther had been warned and had escaped to Massachusetts. He was arrested in April of 1843, when he returned to Rhode Island. He promptly sued Borden for trespass. The question of the old government's legitimacy thus reached the courts: if it was legitimate, Borden was within his rights in breaking in to arrest Luther; but if the Dorr government was legitimate, then Borden had no official capacity and could be punished for trespassing. It was impossible for the courts to decide the case without first declaring one or the other of the governments to be illegal.

Before the case could reach the Supreme Court, Thomas Dorr was brought to trial. He had been arrested in October of 1843, and was tried before the Rhode Island Supreme Court. In June, he was sentenced to hard labor and solitary confinement for life. The court thus indicated its acceptance of the King government, to whose existence it owed its own.[6] That government had caused its proposed constitution to be redrafted. Although the new consitution did not give urban areas more representation, it did include a personal property qualification for native-born non-free-holding citizens. It limited the vote of naturalized citizens, and explicitly rejected the secret ballot. In a completely corrupt referendum highlighted by voter intimidation, violence, and a campaign which played on religious, anti-urban, and anti-immigrant fears, Rhode Islanders accepted this constitution, and elections were held under it in April, 1843. Political apathy ensued in Rhode Island; 15,000 people voted in the 1843 election, 4,000 in that of 1850. But the new constitution and the government elected under it possessed legal importance when *Luther* v. *Borden* reached the Supreme Court.

The case for Luther was presented before the Court by Benjamin F. Hallett. Referring to his oral argument, the Court Reporter wrote:

> It has already been said that Mr. Hallett alone argued the case on behalf of the plaintiff in error, but the Reporter is much at a loss how to give even a skeleton of the argument, which lasted for three days, and extended over a great variety of matters.[7]

Hallett cited, among others, Jefferson, Locke, the *Federalist,* the Declaration of Independence, Burke, Roger Williams, Paine, and Washington's Farewell Address.[8] His argument was couched in Jeffersonian terms, and his most important point was that a constitution which had no provisions for amendment violated the principle "that government is instituted by the people" and that "a majority of the community hath an indubitable, inalienable, and indefeasible right to reform alter, or abolish" a government which it finds to be inadequate.[9] In addition, he claimed that those voting for the People's Constitution included not only a large majority of white males over twenty-one, but a majority of those men entitled to vote under the old constitution as well.[10] For all of his citations of Burke and the *Federalist* and Washington, Hallett's argument typified the more radical form of Jeffersonian democracy, relying heavily on Jefferson's theory of the living generation's right to reconstitute its government without reference to the wishes or laws of previous generations. Democratic newspapers agreed that Jeffersonian democracy was the central issue involved in the case. One such paper declared that the Court's decision would "settle or overthrow the whole doctrines of the Declaration of Independence . . . [it would] determine whether the American doctrine proclaimed in the Declaration of Independence or the doctrine of the divine right of rulers avowed in the manifests of the holy allies of Europe is the real theory of our institutions." [11] The *Boston Post* agreed that the "great doctrine of popular sovereignty" was itself on trial.[12]

Borden's counsel was none other than the eloquent Daniel Webster. His argument, as expected, turned out to be a solidly conservative one. His main point was that even under a democratic government, the sovereign people carefully prescribe the way in which their government may be changed, so as to "secure themselves against sudden changes by mere majorities."[13] Said Webster, "Our American mode of government does not draw any power from tumultuous assemblages." These are too much like "a stormy South American liberty, supported by arms to-day and crushed by arms tomorrow," which yields only a government "of the strongest and most numerous." [14] Continuing his analogy, he pointed out that the Dorr government was actually in operation for only two days:

> Even the French revolution rapid as it was, required three.[15]

The only way to find out the will of the people was through legislative action.[16]

Webster then examined the justiciability of the case much as Taney and subsequent justices were to do in this and later instances of political questions. In deciding which government was legitimate, Webster said, the Court had to look to the Constitution and laws, and acts of the government of the United States. How did the President of the United States treat this question? . . . [His decision] is obligatory upon this court, which always follows an executive recognition of foreign government.[17]

It would be impossible for the Court to consider Luther's claim that the Dorr constitution was adopted by a majority of the people:

> But how could a court judge of this? Can it know how many persons were present, how many of them qualified voters, and all this to be proved by testimony? Can it order to be brought before it the minutes and registers of unauthorized officers, and have them proved by parol? [18]

Lack of competence, or nonjusticiability, was to become a major argument in political question cases, up to and including the dissenting opinions in *Baker* v. *Carr* and *Gray* v. *Sanders.*[19]

Response to Webster's appearance in the Court ran along party lines. The *Philadelphia North American,* a Whig paper, wrote:

> If anything was left of Dorrism and all its abominable Jacobin doctrines, it has, this day, been swept from the face of existence. . . . In the whole range of political controversy, there was no one subject better calculated to call forth all the powers of that giant intellect than this, involving as it did an investigation of the whole character of the Constitution, the relations between the Federal and State Governments, and a philosophical analysis of what really constituted government at all. The occasion and the man were worthy of each other.[20]

The Democratic *Boston Post* cried that Webster's speech was worthy of a monarchist and a despiser of everything democratic or republican:

> It is in the very face and eyes of the institutions of this country. . . . The sentiments breathed in that comment are infamous.[21]

And the *New York Evening Post:*

> It is nothing unusual that Mr. Webster and the Whigs generally should undertake to convince the public that the institutions of government, with all their offices and honors and emoluments and the distinction that attaches to its ministers, is far above and supreme over the plain, simple and humble mass of the people. . . . Are the people sovereign?[22]

This, then, was the issue before the Court, and as the Chief Justice said, it was both a new and a very grave one.[23] In his opinion, Taney spent some time reviewing the background material, noting that both governments claimed to be supported by a majority of the state's citizens.[24] He mentioned that the "old" government had provided a constitutional convention which wrote a new constitution, under which a government had been functioning since May, 1843.[25] This was of primary importance:

> . . . if . . . it should be decided that the Charter government had no legal existence during the period of time above mentioned,—if it had been annulled by the adoption of the opposing government,—then the laws passed by its legislature during that time were nullities; its taxes wrongfully collected; its salaries and compensation to its officers illegally paid; its public accounts improperly settled; and the judgments and sentences of its courts in civil and criminal cases null and void, and the officers who carried their decisions into operation answerable as trespassers, if not in some cases as criminals.
>
> When the decision of this court might lead to such results, it becomes its duty to examine very carefully its own powers before it undertakes to exercise jurisdiction.[26]

As part of that examination, Taney stated that questions of political legitimacy had never been recognized as judicial ones; the "political department" of a government had always determined when a constitution or amendment had been ratified.[27] This tradition had been recognized by the Rhode Island courts. In deciding the trials of various Dorrists, the courts had said that they were compelled by the decision of the "political power," which had chosen not to recognize the Dorr government.[28] Without really meaning to, Taney went on to imply that the state courts had not really left the question of legitimacy to the "political power," after all: by the very act of sitting, he pointed out, they had recognized the legitimacy of the government under whose authority they sat. This decision of the state courts was binding upon the Supreme Court, which followed "the well settled rule" of adopting rulings of the state courts in questions relating to state constitutions and laws.[29]

Taney had so far presented three arguments: negation in 1849 of the "old" government would have caused anarchy and confusion, and would perhaps have resulted in the declaration of irremediable wrongs which had been unknowingly committed by a government which had thought itself legitimate; the entire area had been regarded as outside the limited functioning of a court; the problem had already been solved in a manner which the Court had, for procedural reasons, to accept. The first of these judicial thoughts implicitly acknowledged the possibility of a decision based less upon legal axioms than upon considerations of social prudence, and Taney did not mention it again. An age which recognized sociological jurisprudence as a valid philosophy was later to accept this argument for precisely the pragmatic reasons which drove Taney from it. His third argument was shaky: *Fletcher* v. *Peck* had indicated the Court's willingness to interfere in purely state matters when it so desired and when the claim of unconstitutionality was raised.[30] Left with only his second idea, Taney followed the adroit footsteps of Marshall in *Marbury* v. *Madison*[31] and managed to retain his dignity while wriggling through the least immediately embarrassing exit.

A court, said Taney, agreeing with Webster, had no way of deciding whether or not voters were qualified to cast their ballots in a constitutional referendum; nor was it able to ascertain whether or not a majority had voted either way in such an election.[32] Such decisions were not properly judicial:

> It is the province of a court to expound the law, not to make it.[33]

In any case, the Constitution put such problems in the hand of the "political departments." By admitting the senators and representatives of a state to Congress, that body recognized the republican character and the legitimacy of the government under which they were appointed. Congress had not had a chance to make such a decision about the Dorr government, because no Congressional delegates had been elected under it. Nevertheless, the right to make this decision belonged to Congress rather than to the courts.[34] And a different political department *had* made a decision concerning the Rhode Island controversy. Under the Constitutional article guaranteeing the states protection against domestic violence, Congress had in 1795 passed an act which gave the President the power to call forth the militia upon application of the legislature or the executive of a state. Before calling the militia, the President necessarily decided whether the legislature or executive which had appealed to him was legitimate. In the instant case, the President had taken "measures to call out the militia to support [the old government's] authority if it should be found necessary for the general government to interfere."[35] The courts could not question the authority or the decision of the President:

> In the case of foreign nations, the government acknowledged by the President is always recognized in the courts of justice. And this principle has been applied by the act of Congress to the sovereign States of the union.[36]

Taney then discussed *Martin* v. *Mott*.[37] And finally specifically utilizing the concept of political questions, he concluded:

> Much of the argument on the part of the plaintiff turned upon political rights and political questions, upon which the court has been urged to express an opinion. We decline doing so.[38]

The sole dissenter in the case was Justice Woodbury, who did not disagree that a political question was involved, but who was not quite sure that the establishment of martial law had been entirely legal. Three justices did not sit.

The reaction to the decision was extremely interesting, especially as an indication of Taney's canniness. Some Whig papers rejoiced in the blow delivered to Dorrism; a New York journal reported that "Dorrism has at length received its quietus and in a form from which it can never hope to recover."[39] More arresting was the claim of Boston's leading Democratic newspaper that the decision both recognized "Dorrism and Dorrism alone to be the fundamental principle of the political institutions of the country" and sustained the right of the majority "to modify or change their constitutional form, without the concurrence or consent of the existing holders of political power."[40] The leading Democratic journal in Pennsylvania agreed that the Court had sanctioned this majority right, while holding that no court could "prescribe the rules under which the sense of the majority is to be ascertained. . . . It is, therefore, purely a political question, and must be determined by such public agents as are clothed with political authority."[41] What better testament to Taney's genius than an accolade from the side that stood to lose the most?

It is precisely this general acceptance of a potentially controversial decision which must be seen as the guiding motive behind Taney's legal prose. The Court would not declare the existing government to be illegal; Taney was fully aware of the confusion and loss of confidence to which this would lead, and it was only natural for a responsible statesman to shy away from it.[42] But what kept him from recognizing the Charter government as legal and stating simply that Dorr and Luther had acted illegally?

There are three answers to this question. One is the realization that if Dorr's government had never existed legitimately, then neither had the governments of Michigan and Maryland, both of which had been in existence for some time. Invalidation of governments long in office was an evil Taney specifically wished to prevent. If he chose to act in this case, he ran the danger of forcing himself to decide in others, and the Court could only lose by involving itself in such validation controversies. The second answer concerns the way in which Dorr's rebellion had become a party issue which aroused a good portion of the nation.[43] The democratic principles implicit in the Declaration of Independence may have been ignored by the writers of the Constitution, but social realities and Andrew Jackson had combined to preserve them as a rallying-cry for the Democratic (Loco-Foco) Party and as a moral philosophy for many citizens not otherwise concerned with political principles. Jefferson's theory of the sovereignty of the living generation could become an extremely impractical idea if pushed to its ultimate conclusion, but it retained a great deal of emotional appeal nonetheless. Add to this the determined strivings for social and political recognition of the commercial classes, the non-Protestant native American, the immigrant, the Northern non-white, the urban dweller; and what comes out is a situation in which it might not be quite politic for a suspiciously undemocratic institution to declare that Jefferson was really dead—and dead wrong, to boot. The problem is one of social acceptance; at the least, a highly unpopular decision might be ignored; at the worst, there was always the chance of Congress' eliminating this area of the Court's appellate jurisdiction.[44]

A fairly responsive government can move only as fast as the electorate is willing to go. This is rather obvious when Congress or the Executive is under consideration, but it is equally true for the judiciary.[45] Many writers have pointed out that the Supreme Court's most important asset is its high prestige. It would take gamblers less prudent than Supreme Court justices to risk the loss of this prestige in a highly-charged partisan atmosphere.

The third factor, precedent, is of equal importance. *Stare decisis* is *not* the rule of the Court, but it is a custom which continues to receive lip-service; and until a jurisprudence more realistic than that existing in the 1840's or the 1970's gains general recognition, the Court's own precedents will constitute a potentially embarrassing hurdle over which the justices must bound as gracefully as possible. Their great aid is the device of "distinguishing" one case from another, but in spite of this, they are careful not to accept now categories of cases which they may not want to accept in the future. There might well be subsequent cases [46] in which it was not entirely clear which side was in the right; or, more importantly, in which the Court stood to lose a great deal of prestige by having its decision ignored. Had the Court decided for the Charter government of Rhode Island, its decision would undoubtedly have been enforced.[47] In future cases, however, a contest might reach the Court before the issue had actually been settled by force of arms and six years of government under the victor, and there the Court's position would be more hazardous. And so the Court instituted its precedent of not deciding cases which involved the "republican government" clause of the Constitution.

Twenty years later, the Court avoided interpretation or application of this clause. In *Texas* v. *White* [48] it declared that the federal government, acting under the guaranty clause, had an obligation to reestablish a republican form of government in secessionist Texas. But the Court would not decide whether the provisional officials appointed by the President constituted a republican government, since Congress, by passing the Reconstruction Acts, had recognized such temporary governments as legitimate. This was the kind of problem presented by *Mississippi* v. *Johnson* [49] and *Georgia* v. *Stanton*.[50] There, as here, a refusal to pass judgment on the Reconstruction Acts kept the Civil War out of the Courtroom.

Like any other group interested in its own survival, the judiciary traditionally "protects its own." This penchant, as well as its pro-states-rights attitude, lay behind the willingness of the 1870 Court to venture as far into troubled waters as was necessary to declare the indispensability of judges in a republic. *The Collector* v. *Day* [51] was brought to the Court because J. M. Day, judge of the Court of Probate and Insolvency for the County of Barnstable, Massachusetts, paid a federal tax on his salary under protest, and sued to recover the money. During the course of his 7-1 decision holding that the federal government could not tax the salaries of state judicial officials, Justice Nelson said that no republican government "could long preserve its existence" without being permitted to enjoy its "sovereign and reserved rights, one of which is the establishment of the judicial department, and the appointment of officers to administer their laws." [52] The brethren in Washington would uphold the integrity of their brethren anywhere else, even if it meant a partial interpretation of "republican form of government." [53]

The Court issued another such interpretation of the clause in an 1874 case [54] involving a subject which at that time brought only smiles: the fight for women's suffrage. A small minority of radical females understood the Fourteenth Amendment as making all citizens legally equal; and to them, "all citizens" included women. There was no legal precedent for their claim. The first recorded demand for women's suffrage was made in Maryland in 1647 by the female heir of Lord Calvert and sister of Lord Baltimore. Her demand went unheeded. New Jersey tax-paying women were given the vote in 1776, but it was firmly taken away from them in 1807. The movement gained national attention and derision after Susan B. Anthony and Elizabeth Cady Stanton began organized work in New York in 1851, at which time suffragettes were looked upon much as anti-vivisectionists are today, with the added onus that the morals of such women were suspect. The close identification of the movement with the temperance drive did not add to its general appeal. In 1869, the first national suffrage association was formed; in the same year, Wyoming women were given the vote. The Wyoming heresy, however, was not expected to spread, and there were no indications that it would do so. Various communities and states presented women with the right to vote on school issues, but this was not considered a concession, woman's "place" extending beyond the home as far as the school and church. Far more typical of the times than the Wyoming practice was the Colorado Constitution of 1876, which specifically excluded female suffrage, and the 1874 rejection of a proposed women's suffrage amendment to the Michigan constitution. [55] By 1872, then, people were taking note of the suffrage movement, but only as the kind of temporary aberration which is good for a few off-color jokes.

Nonetheless, Mrs. Virginia Minor, a free native-born Missourian, tried to register as a voter in the 1872 presidential election. The registrar, acting under the section of the Missouri Constitution which permitted only males to vote,[56] refused to allow her to do so. She then sued him, charging a violation of the privileges and immunities clause of the Fourteenth Amendment. As expected, the lower courts decided in favor of Happersett, the registrar.

Chief Justice Waite, writing for a unanimous Court, chose to solve the problem by examining it historically. While it was true that a republican government clause existed, he said, the Court had to construe it in the light of the circumstances surrounding its creation. This was necessary because the Constitution itself yielded no clues as to what kind of government was considered republican by its framers. The answer was to be found in the kind of government which the various States possessed when the Constitution went into effect. Briefly mentioning the important idea that the guarantee "necessarily implies a duty on the part of the States themselves to provide such a government," Waite pointed out that the State governments in existence at the time of the Constitution's adoption remained in power after the Constitution went into effect, and therefore were presumed to have been those governments which "it was the duty of the States to provide"; that is, republican governments:

> Thus we have unmistakable evidence of what was republican in form, within the meaning of that term as employed in the Constitution.[57]

Waite found that the young States invested only males with suffrage, and not all males at that, and concluded:

> Under these circumstances it is certainly now too late to contend that a government is not republican, within the meaning of this guaranty in the Constitution, because women are not made voters.[58]

There was no reference to *Luther v. Borden.*

Waite's argument is not hard to demolish. The duty of the federal government under Article IV Section 4 implies a duty not to undertake any action which would deny a republican government to the states. This section has never been explicitly altered, nor has any Amendment ever been interpreted as having altered this duty. The Fifteenth Amendment, which forbids deprivation of the vote "on account of race, color, or previous condition of servitude," was declared ratified in 1870.[59] It then became the duty of the executive to enforce this law. It was also the duty of the executive to ensure a republican form of government in every state, and it has not been suggested that these two duties were incompatible. Negro slaves were not allowed to vote under the republican governments of the 1790's. The existence of the Fifteenth Amendment implies that deprivation of suffrage because of color or former condition of servitude was unrepublican; or, to put it differently, that Negro suffrage was not incompatible with republicanism. Therefore the suffrage laws in existence in the 1790's were at least partially unrepublican, as seen in the 1870's, or, to rephrase again, forms of suffrage unheard of in the 1790's were not necessarily unrepublican. This argument does not prove that a government is unrepublican unless it provides for female suffrage, but it does indicate that an historical interpretation is hardly sufficient here. Yet this is one of the only cases [60] in which the Court interpreted Article IV Section 4. Why?

There was little chance that anybody beyond a few powerless women would argue with the Court's decision. It would certainly be enforced. But the Court could just as easily have refused to decide the case, calling it a political question because it dealt with political rights. It chose instead to ignore the tradition of *Luther* v. *Borden* and *Texas* v. *White* and interpret an extremely controversial phrase. Part of the motivation for doing so must have been simple personal preference. There is evidence that very few people in the United States of 1874 thought that women should be given the vote, and it is not unlikely that the justices agreed with the majority view. They had a chance to humor their personal predilection while agreeing with the feelings of the vast majority, and they apparently thought that they had nothing to lose: no one of major political importance would argue with their decision. They might have hesitated to set a precedent for interpreting the phrase, but the issue was such a specialized and unique one and the popular sentiment was so clear that any second thoughts must have been quickly dismissed. The justices were merely performing their function of validating the view of the majority as expressed by their governments. Certainly they had no reason to think that the majority would overrule them in 1920.

The case of *United States* v. *Cruikshank* [61] was not primarily concerned with the republican form of government. It involved a small anti-black riot, or what the Court called the attempt of Cruikshank and other Louisiana stalwarts "to deprive" two Negroes "of their rights" by beating them. Chief Justice Waite and seven others struck down the case on the flimsy technical grounds of faulty counts (i.e., faulty charges brought by the government), and before he delivered this opinion Waite said:

> The very idea of a government, republican in form, implies a right on the part of its citizens to meet peaceably for consultation in respect to public affairs and to petition for a redress of grievances. [62]

This statement was hardly dangerous; while he defined this attribute of republicanism, the bulk of Waite's opinion made it unnecessary for him to determine whether or not such a state of affairs had existed in Louisiana. Knowing that he was about to hand down what amounted to an anti-Negro decision which could hardly hope to receive universal acclaim and which would not please the government which had brought the action, Waite paid long paragraphs of lip service to the great American verities. [63]

The Initiative and Referendum

In his Federalist Paper No. 10, Madison defined a republic as a system in which the functions of government were delegated by the citizenry to a small number of their fellows. A republican rather than a pure democratic form of government seemed to be dictated by the relatively large territory and large population encompassed by the United States. But, as Madison went on to indicate, questions of political philosophy could also be found behind the decision for republicanism. Motivated primarily by self-interest, the average citizen would not have the breadth of vision necessary to enable him to act for the good of the entire country. However, he presumably would have the sense to elect as his representatives men "whose wisdom may best discern the true interest of their country, and whose patriotism and love of justice will be least likely to sacrifice it to temporary or partial considerations." The decisions of these men would be "more consonant to the public good than if pronounced by the people themselves. . . ." Thus a strong strain of non-Jeffersonian mistrust of the average man's farsightedness reinforced the practical decision to institute a republican form of government. This strain is to be detected throughout the Constitution.

At the same time, however, the dominant political ideology—that under whose aegis the Revolution had supposedly been fought—was predicated on an acceptance of the sovereignty of the people. The tension between a mistrust of the people and a belief in their sovereignty appears throughout American history, most obviously in the idea of a Bill of Rights. At one stage in America's past— specifically, during the days of Progressivism and the muckrakers— mistrust of the people was exchanged for distrust of their representatives, and it appeared for an historical moment that this change would upset the American pattern of legislative government. The Supreme Court was called upon to decide whether or not the pattern could be amended legitimately, and announced once again that the best part of valor is discretion.

As early as 1647, Rhode Island established a system of initiatives, under which a majority of towns could enact temporary laws, whose acceptance by the entire electorate rendered them permanent. The entire procedure by-passed the legislature. A referendum procedure also existed, permitting the general court to propose laws which required the approval of a majority of towns in order to stand as temporary laws until the next meeting of the legislature.[64] The influence of this arrangement was limited, as was that of the New England town meetings. More important were the nineteenth century provisions of most state constitutions forbidding alterations in those constitutions unless the amendments had received majority approval in a referendum. While only three state constitutions adopted before 1800 were submitted to the voters for approval, all constitutions adopted between 1840 and 1860 were popularly ratified.[65] The referendum, however, was confined to constitutional acceptance and amendments, and was not extended to statutes.

By the late nineteenth century, agitation for "direct legislation" had begun as part of the general protest against legislative corruption and the overrepresentation of industry within the halls of government. It was supported especially by organized labor and by the predominantly agricultural regions of the country. The District Legislation League was formed in 1897, with the sole purpose of obtaining widespread initiative and referendum reforms.

It was aided by the National Farmers' Alliance, anxious for laws which it knew would not be permitted by the "vested interests" controlling many legislators. In 1898, South Dakota became the first state to ratify initiative and referendum amendments to its constitution. It was followed by Oregon in 1902; Nevada in 1904; Montana in 1906; Oklahoma in 1907; Missouri, Michigan, and Maine in 1908; Arkansas and Colorado in 1910; California, Arizona, and New Mexico in 1911. In almost all cases, the amendments were passed by extremely large majorities, and by 1912 the movement appeared to be one which would snowball endlessly. President William Howard Taft chose to veto the Arizona Admission Act in 1911, on the grounds that the proposed state constitution contained provisions for judicial recall, a measure much favored by the proponents of initiative and referendum. Arizona removed the offending passages, became the forty-eighth state, and promptly reinstated the provisions as amendments. Other politicians, however, were smart enough not to get in the way of the snowball. The movement was supported by Bryan, Woodrow Wilson, and Roosevelt:

. . . even the so-called conservative or reactionary statesmen with political ambitions seek to avoid expressing an adverse opinion on this popular tenet of the progressive faith.[66]

The movement was to lose much of its momentum after 1912 and to disappear by the 1920's, leaving a host of disillusioned reformers in its wake, but this was not foreseen in 1912.

Oregon had been caught up in the new ideas quite early. The Oregon Direct Legislation League was organized in 1892, and Oregon was the second state in the Union to pass initiative and referendum amendments.[67] It used the machinery more extensively than most states, adopting thirty-one pieces of legislation between 1902 and 1910,[68] and voting on thirty-seven measures in 1912 alone.[69] In 1906, Oregon citizens utilized the initiative to adopt an act requiring telephone and telegraph companies to pay a license fee of two per cent per annum on their gross receipts. The legislation included penalties to be imposed on any company which refused payment. The Pacific States Telephone and Telegraph Company, which stood to lose most from this enactment, was sued by Oregon when the Company refused to pay either the taxes or penalties. It retaliated by charging that not only the act but the entire Oregon government was unconstitutional, because the initiative and referendum violated the "republican form of government" clause. That clause was meant to establish the states as republics, the Company said, but the proceedings in question transferred power from the legislature to the people at large and thus transformed what had been a republic into a pure democracy. Thus the initiative and referendum were unconstitutional because they subverted republicanism, and the government under which this democratic power had been created was *ipso facto* unconstitutional, too.[70] Oregon had been admitted to the Union with an avowedly republican fundamental law. Any change in this constituted "an impairment of the obligation of the State to preserve a republican form of government." [71] For good measure, the Company also charged violations of equal protection, due process, and private property rights. Oregon replied by calling the entire matter a political one which could not be decided by any court, the power to determine whether a state has a republican form of government having been given to Congress. The state cited *Luther, Texas* v. *White, Taylor & Marshall* v. *Beckham*, and *In re Duncan*. In addition, it pointed out that Oklahoma had been admitted to the Union with a constitution which made provision for initiative and referendum proceedings, and that other states had adopted and employed such amendments.[72]

Various cases challenging the legality of the initiative and referendum had found their way to Oregon courts before the instant case reached the federal Supreme Court. The amendments had been upheld by the Oregon Supreme Court.[73] By the time the case got to the Supreme Court, other Oregon decisions had followed suit.[74] As if to emphasize the importance of the Court's potential decision, Oklahoma, California, Arkansas, Colorado, South Dakota, and Nebraska filed briefs as *amicus curiae*. In addition, while the Court was considering the case, its members were "swamped with a deluge of letters from a large number of people throughout the country demanding that the initiative and referendum law be declared valid." [75]

Chief Justice White wrote the opinion for a unanimous Court, and quickly indicated his intention of accepting Oregon's view of the matter. The question at issue was whether the state government was republican; and that was important but not novel, "as that question has long since been determined by this court conformably

to the practice of the Government from the beginning to be political
in character, and therefore not cognizable by the judicial power,
but solely committed by the Constitution to the judgment of Congress." [76] Then White got down to particulars, indicating as he did
so exactly why the Court could not possibly invalidate the law.
The corporation's contention,

> if held to be sound, would necessarily affect the validity, not only
> of the particular statute which is before us, but of every other statute
> passed in Oregon since the adoption of the initiative and refer-
> endum. And indeed the propositions go further than this, since in
> their essence they assert that there is no governmental function,
> legislative or judicial, in Oregon, because it cannot be assumed,
> if the proposition be well founded, that there is at one and the
> same time one and the same government which is republican in
> form and not of that character. [77]

As one wends one's way through Justice White's prose, it becomes
clear that the Company overplayed its hand in maintaining that
not only the particular law but the state government as well was
unconstitutional. The consequences of proclaiming ten years of
government in Oregon and as many in other states illegal was
too overwhelming for the justices, as it might well have been. But
Justice White was not finished. Mixing his fear of anarchy and
the loss of law and order with subsidiary arguments, he went on
to say that acceptance of the company's proposition would also
mean "the inconceivable expansion of the judicial power and the
ruinous destruction of legislative authority." [78] This is the kind of
separation-of-powers verbiage which one might expect, and the
good judge returned to this theme later on. But suddenly he saw
another spectre: if the Court acknowledged the company's suit as
a proper one for judicial decision, it would have given every citizen
the right to haul its government into Court as illegal in order to
avoid paying taxes. [79] The Court would have to decide if the government was indeed illegal, and what if it should feel that the suitor's
contention was justified?

> And as a consequence of the existence of such judicial authority,
> a power in the judiciary must be implied unless it is that anarchy
> is to ensure, to build by judicial action upon the ruins of the
> established government a new one, a right which by its very terms
> also implies the power to control the legislative department of the
> Government of the United States in the recognition of such new
> government and the admission of representatives therefrom, as well

as to strip the executive department of that government of its otherwise lawful and discretionary authority.[80]

The Court could not agree to ensure a state republican government by destroying a national republican government.[81] White carefully couched his thoughts in the language of separation of powers, but it seems clear that he was more concerned with judicial prestige than with theoretical principles. Had the Court accepted this case and agreed to decide on the legitimacy of the Oregon government, it would have opened the door to similar suits. In the present case it might easily decide that the initiative and referendum were constitutional measures, but what if a plaintiff whose case had obvious and undoubted merit should appear before the Court? If the Court ever invalidated a state government, the government in question might simply refuse to accept the Court's order. Congress, through seating the representatives elected under that government, might seriously embarrass the Court, as might the President, by pledging to recognize a particular government as Tyler did in the case of Dorr's rebellion. These thoughts must have been uppermost in the minds of the justices, and White's next remarks support this idea. He called *Luther* v. *Borden* "leading and absolutely controlling" [82] and devoted the next few pages to a thorough examination of that case.[83] Perhaps in the course of his examination Justice White began to wonder exactly what a political question was, in legal terms, and how it could be distinguished from the area in which the Court might legitimately function. His answer was not too helpful, attempting as it did to differentiate two "widely different things":

> ... the legislative duty to determine the political questions involved in deciding whether a state government republican in form exists, and the judicial power and ever-present duty whenever it becomes necessary in a controversy properly submitted to enforce and uphold the applicable provisions of the Constitution as to each and every exercise of governmental power.[84]

The instant case could not be classified as falling into the second category, because the attack was made "not on the tax as a tax, but on the State as a State." [85] This meant that the Oregon government as a political entity was being called to the bar "not for the purpose of testing judicially some exercise of power" supposedly unconstitutional, "but to demand of the State that it establish its right to exist as a State . . ." [86] What White really said was that a government which commits an unconstitutional act may be called before the bench, but a government faced with the charge that its very existence contravenes the constitution may not.

On the same day, the Court decided *Kiernan* v. *Portland*,[87] which also involved Oregon. An amendment to the Oregon constitution gave the powers of initiative and referendum to voters on the municipal level.[88] The plaintiff, a Portland taxpayer, attempted to have the city enjoined from issuing bonds to build a bridge, legislation for which was enacted through initiative proceedings. The Chief Justice, again speaking for a unanimous Court, called *Pacific Telephone and Telegraph* controlling.[89]

The issue arose four years later in the case of *Ohio ex. rel. Davis* v. *Hildebrant*.[90] In 1912, Ohio had added to its constitution an amendment which declared the legislative power of the state to be vested in the General Assembly and in the people.[91] The people specifically reserved the right of referendum to approve or disapprove any law passed by the General Assembly, if six per cent or more of the voters petitioned to have such a referendum. Acting under this amendment, Ohio voters disapproved a 1915 congressional redistricting law. The entire process was challenged on the grounds that under Article I Section 4 of the Constitution only the legislature can decide matters pertaining to elections.[92] Once again the Chief Justice wrote the opinion for a unanimous Court. He pointed out that the Congressional reapportionment statute of 1911 seemed to connote acceptance of referenda as entirely legitimate.[93] This being true, Davis' assumption must have been that the referendum was incompatible with republican government, but this was not a justiciable matter.[94] Congress had acted in this matter by passing the 1911 Act, and this was decisive for the Court, especially as the Constitutional article in question gave control of such issues to Congress.[95] White could merely have said that Congress had acted and that was that; instead, he reintroduced the political question, making it quite clear that the Court had no intention of treading on Congress' toes, even should that body pass a law in contradistinction to the Constitutional requirement of republican governments.

When the issue of the referendum reappeared in 1920, it did so under quite another guise.[96] An Ohio constitutional amendment passed in 1918 had extended the referendum to the General Assembly's ratification of amendments to the national Constitution.[97] In 1919, the General Assembly ratified the Eighteenth Amendment; shortly thereafter, the Secretary of State of the United States proclaimed the amendment ratified. Over six per cent of Ohio's voters petitioned to have the ratification submitted to a referendum. Hawke, a taxpayer, brought suit to enjoin the Secretary of State of Ohio from spending state funds in order to prepare the ballot which would be used in submitting the issue to a referendum. Here the question was not merely one of proceedings within a state; if Ohio could change its decision for ratification, an operative Constitutional amendment would have to be declared retroactively void. The Court was thus faced with a dilemma. If it chose to treat this as a political question, it would take the chance of throwing the Eighteenth and future constitutional amendments into the state of anarchy so feared by members of the bench. If it decided when and where referenda could be utilized, it would reopen a door which it had tried its best to close permanently. Justice Day, writing for all of his colleagues, deftly steered his way between Scylla and Charybdis. When a state legislature ratified a proposed amendment to the national Constitution, said Justice Day, its function was derived not from the state, but from the United States Constitution. The methodology promulgated by that Constitution could not be unilaterally changed by any state.[98] The framers of the Constitution, employing the word "legislature," meant "legislature" and nothing else; they did not mean the people acting as a legislature, but referred to a representative body.[99] It was therefore only the legislature of Ohio which could choose to ratify or reject Constitutional amendments, and referenda were not valid in this area. Day distinguished the *Davis* case by pointing out that there Congress had "recognized the referendum as part of the legislative authority of the State for the purpose stated." [100] Where Congress had not acted, the Constitution was the authority. Justice Day thus said that the Court would interpret "legislature" where it would not define "republican." The rationale behind arbitrarily placing these two words into different categories would seem to be less a function of their intrinsic dissimilarity than the result of the course into which the Court was forced in two problematic cases.[101]

The "republican form of government" clause is sometimes referred to as the keystone to the intervention, by any federal court, in a state's governmental affairs, and therefore as the clue to political questions.[102] After the above examination of cases, it should be quite apparent that the political question is not invoked in the name of federalism, but rather as a necessary concomitant to separation of powers. It is accepted legal theory and practice that the federal laws and Constitution are the supreme law of the land, and that a federal court will refuse to interfere in state matters only when a federal question has not been raised. Occasionally, of course, the justices will decline to concede the existence of a federal question when they have their own reasons for refusing a case; but where a federal question is recognized, the Court has never turned the case into a political question on the grounds of state sovereignty. As in *Luther* v. *Borden,* when a decision concerning a state's government may well bring the Court into conflict with Congress or the President, and where a social consensus strong enough to ensure a Court victory does not exist, the problem will be labeled political. And because it is Article IV Section 4 which has frequently threatened this kind of head-on collision, the Court refrains from accepting almost any claims involving that paragraph so as to avoid setting an embarrassing precedent. Once it is seen that the trouble with "republican form of government" is not that it refers to states but that the "political branches" possess the final power of decision, the political question can be understood as a judicial reaction to the enforcement problem.

CHAPTER 3

REAPPORTIONMENT

> Representatives shall be appointed among the several States according to their respective numbers, counting the whole number of persons in each State, excluding Indians not taxed.[1]

> The Actual Enumeration shall be made within three Years after the first Meeting of the Congress of the United States, and within every subsequent Term of ten Years, in such Manner as they shall by Law direct. The Number of Representatives shall not exceed one for every thirty Thousand.[2]

Following the 1910 national census, Congress passed the Reapportionment Act of 1911.[3] Two sections of this Act were to become especially important in the history of the reapportionment question. Section 3 said, in part, that members of the House of Representatives "shall be elected by districts composed of a contiguous and compact territory, and containing as nearly as possible an equal number of inhabitants." Realizing that the number of representatives from various states would grow with the population in the years to come, Congress added Section 4, providing for the election of additional representatives. Should the number of Representatives in any State be increased, the additional Representatives were to be elected at large until the State was redistricted "in accordance with the rules enumerated in section Three of this Act"; should the number of Representatives from a State remain stable, Section 4 decreed that until the State was redistricted "as herein prescribed" (i.e., in Section 3), Representatives were to be elected by existing districts. Presumably, this provision was included as a recognition of possible population shifts within states; or, more specifically, as a recognition of the farm-to-city movement that was to result in reapportionment controversies. The Act did not mention the possibility of a state's representation being decreased.

It should be noted that sections similar to Sections 3 and 4 had been included in similar Acts passed in 1842, 1872, 1882, 1891, and 1901.

The next reapportionment act was passed in 1929. It omitted Sections 3 and 4 of the 1911 Act, and specifically repealed those parts of the Act of 1911 which were inconsistent with the 1929 Act. The majority of state courts which were later faced with the question of whether the 1929 Act therefore included Sections 3 and 4 of the 1911 Act held that these two Sections were not inconsistent with the 1929 Act and so were not repealed by it.[4]

The problem of the continuing existence of Sections 3 and 4 first appeared before the Supreme Court in *Smiley* v. *Holm*.[5] Under the Census of 1930, Congress allotted Minnesota one representative less than she had previously had, bringing her delegation to the House to nine. The Minnesota Senate and House both passed a bill dividing Minnesota into nine districts, but the Governor did not sign it.[6] Although it was not repassed by the Minnesota legislature, as it should have been in order to have gone into effect under the Minnesota constitution, the bill was filed with the Secretary of State of Minnesota. Smiley, a citizen of the state, brought suit to declare invalid all filings for nomination for the office of representative under the law, and to enjoin the Secretary from giving notice of elections, on two grounds: the bill had not been repassed as required by law, and the proposed districts were not " 'compact' and did not 'contain an equal number of inhabitants as nearly as practicable' in accordance with the Act" of 1911.[7] Counsel for the State questioned the validity of the Act of 1911, claiming that it came into conflict with Article I, Section 4 of the United States Constitution.

Speaking for a unanimous Court,[8] Chief Justice Hughes ignored the Justices' usual rule that constitutional issues were to be considered only when unavoidable, and held that the Act of 1911 was consistent with the Constitution.[9] He may have done so because the charge that the Act was unconstitutional was so blatantly without merit. It any case, he quickly added that it was not necessary, in the context of the case, to decide whether the Act or sections of it remained in force in 1930.[10] Questions relating to Section 3, said Hughes, were "wholly abstract" because there was no statute in effect which did or did not have to comply with the provisions

of Section 3: the Minnesota bill had not been passed in accordance
with the Minnesota constitution and was therefore invalid.[11] This
left the question of what was to be done about electing representatives in Minnesota, and the Court's solution should be carefully
noted. Apparently trying to derive his answer from the guidelines
of Section 4, Hughes declared that where the number of representatives allotted to a state had been decreased, they would have
to be elected at large until new districts were created.[12] The specter
of elections at large, which seems to have filled later Courts with
fear and trembling, was accepted by Hughes and his colleagues
with a great deal of equanimity.

Subsequent cases dealing with the problem of reapportionment,
as well as cases involving the existence or nonexistence of state
acts, were treated as political questions by the Court. Later on,
it will be necessary to explain why these similar cases were labeled
political questions; here, it is more germane to consider why *Smiley*
v. *Holm* was not. The answer probably lies in the attitude of the
American people towards the law-making process. While Americans
can look upon a citizen with 104 unpaid traffic tickets as a minor
hero, they cannot tolerate the thought of *their* laws being brought
into existence in any but the most orthodox fashion. Corruption
in the state legislature bring cries of outrage and accusations during
the next campaign, even though constituents will cheer the man
who breaks *their* law after it was legitimately passed (unless, of
course, he is a "hippie" or a radical or otherwise threatens their
lifestyle). If they cannot decide what laws are to be passed, at least
American voters can insist that their representatives adhere rigidly
to procedural requirements. It was this kind of sentiment, directed
towards legislative corruption and bribe-taking, which led to the
initiative and referendum reforms discussed above. It was therefore
unlikely that the populace of Minnesota would wish to comply
with a "law" that was being promulgated in such obvious defiance
of Minnesota's own constitution, and so enforcement of the Court's
decision would not be a problem. Should the legislature be recalcitrant, it was to be ignored while elections were held at large. It
was the executive branch of the government, controlled by the
very governor the Court was in effect supporting, that would be
expected to carry out the Court's order. Enforcement of this order
would certainly take place, and there was no chance that the Court's

prestige would be diminished as a result of its decision; if anything, it would be somewhat enhanced. By validating constitutional government, the Court performed the task assigned to it, and did so in an area which held no room for controversy.

Koenig v. *Flynn* [13] was decided similarly, with a one-page opinion by Chief Justice Hughes citing *Smiley*. In 1929, New York's allotment of Representatives in the House was increased by two, to forty-five. The Republican-dominated legislature of New York then passed a reapportionment act which Governor Franklin Delano Roosevelt refused to sign. The act would have reduced New York City's traditionally Democratic representation, and it became an important party issue. Attorney General Bennett of New York State informed Secretary of State Flynn that he could legally disregard the bill. Three Republican Party leaders, led by one Samuel S. Koenig and acting in their capacity as voters, thereupon asked the Court to compel Flynn to certify that elections for Congressional representatives were to be carried out under the legislation in question. Flynn replied that the bill had not been approved by the governor, to whom, he claimed, it had never been submitted.[14] The New York Court of Appeals upheld the Secretary, which left the problem of the basis on which elections were to be held. Utilizing the provisions of Section 4 of the 1911 Act, the lower court decreed that in the absence of a valid redistricting statute forty-three representatives were to be elected in the old districts and two were to be elected at large. This decision was affirmed unanimously by the Supreme Court,[15] with Cardozo of course disqualifying himself. Hughes' opinion, which, with the exception of one sentence, is composed entirely of a presentation of the background of the case, does not explain his rejection of Koenig's contention that the Constitution gives the legislature rather than the executive the right to make this kind of law, and that provisions in the state constitution which conflict with Article I Section 4 by requiring executive involvement must be ignored.[16]

The argument was repeated by the plaintiff in *Carroll* v. *Becker*.[17] The circumstances were similar: under the Act of 1929, Missouri's representation in the House was reduced from sixteen to thirteen. The reapportionment bill subsequently passed by the state legislature was vetoed by the governor. Carroll asked the Court for a writ of mandamus, compelling the Secretary of State of Missouri to admit Carroll's candidacy in one of the districts created by the bill. The Missouri Supreme Court upheld the Secretary and directed that "since the number of representatives for Missouri has been reduced the former districts no longer exist and representatives must be elected at large." [18] In another one-page 8-0 opinion written by Hughes, the lower court's decision was affirmed on the basis of *Smiley*. Once again, the Court did not flinch at the prospect of elections at large.

The situation which led to *Wood* v. *Broom* [19] was somewhat different. Under the Act of 1929, Mississippi was given seven representatives, a loss of one. The Mississippi legislature divided the state into seven districts, and the bill was duly signed by the governor; thus there was no charge of illegal proceedings. Citizen Broom, however, charged that the redistricting act was an unconstitutional violation of Article I Section 4, and of the Fourteenth Amendment; and of the Act of 1911, Section 3. He asked that state officials be restrained from taking steps toward an election under the provisions of the new law. The District Court, agreeing that the districts were not contiguous and compact, granted a permanent injunction on the basis of Section 3.

Chief Justice Hughes again wrote the opinion of the Court. He omitted discussion of Article I Section 4 and the Fourteenth Amendment (this was consistent with the Court's policy of not deciding constitutional issues unless absolutely necessary), and concentrated his attention on the Act of 1911. Hughes asserted that the Act was meant to apply only to elections based on the 1910 census. He pointed out that provisions similar to Sections 3 and 4 had been proposed when the 1929 Act was being considered by Congress, and that they had been stricken out before passage. This, to Hughes, indicated that these sections were no longer effective; although they had not been specifically repealed, they had not been reenacted, and they had therefore expired.[20] So, Hughes concluded, there was no case before the Court.

It should be remembered that most state courts handling this question had reached the opposite conclusion.[21] Four justices of the Court felt that Hughes should not have touched the matter in reaching his decision. Mississippi had argued that the Court had no equity jurisdiction for three reasons: the plaintiff had a remedy at law, there was no probability of multiplicity of suits, and the deprivation of a political right was not a matter for a federal court of equity. It also hinted that "the decree of this Court would be inefficacious." [22] Broom replied that the right to vote was a legal one which equity would protect.[23] The four justices, in a concurring opinion, agreed with Wood, stating that the decree should have been reversed and "the bill dismissed for want of equity" without discussing the validity of Section 3, as that question had not been raised either by the parties or the lower courts, all of whom seemed to assume that it was controlling.[24] Thus the question of whether or not equity can protect political rights, which was to become both an important side issue and a convenient camouflage for judicial inactivity, was introduced in the reapportionment controversy.

From the dramatic point of view, the most exciting political question case of the first half of the twentieth century was *Colegrove* v. *Green*,[25] primarily because it was reversed sixteen years later. In it, the Court laid down the rule that it would not consider reapportionment cases because to do so would be to violate the boundary between Court and Congress. The questions of why it would not decide the cases and exactly what it was the Court said have led to a number of conflicting interpretations.

As of 1942, ten states required by their constitutions to redistrict after each census had not done so since 1930; seven had not done so since 1920; five had not done so since 1901.[26] This refusal to comply with constitutional provisions reflected the population shift from rural to urban areas, and the consequent fear on the part of rural legislators that to redistrict would be to legislate themselves out of their jobs. A study of the redistricting question in Illinois, the state from which *Colegrove* v. *Green* came, reported that "if the legislature could have found a way to redistrict to satisfy the constitutional mandate and yet preserve the seat of every member, it would have received virtually unanimous support." [27] An Oklahoma professor was quoted as saying:

> Some of my friends in the legislature point out that it is extremely difficult for one legislator to vote another legislator out of his job.[28]

The situation was particularly acute in Illinois. The census of 1900 indicated that Illinois was the first midwestern state whose population was more than 50 per cent urban. By 1950, only 22.5

per cent of the population would be living in rural areas. Over half lived in Cook County (51.7 per cent); three-quarters of these (41.6 per cent of the state's population) lived in Chicago.[29] Although Cook County's 1950 population was 4,508,792 and all of "downstate" had 4,203,384 people, Cook County had only nineteen of the state's fifty-one districts, each of which was entitled to one state senator and one representative.[30] Illinois urbanites did try to modify the situation. The proposed Constitution of 1922 would have permanently limited Cook County to one-third of the Senate seats but would have given it full representation in the House. To ensure reapportionment, three designated elective state officials were directed to act if the legislature did not. The Constitution was rejected, partly because of this section.[31] Between 1922 and 1952, twenty resolutions proposing constitutional amendments to equalize representation were submitted to the General Assembly; twenty resolutions died in the General Assembly.

The rurally-dominated Illinois legislature—and those of other states—thus refused to heed urban complaints, and the only possible solution for urban dwellers lay with the courts. But the judges had no desire to entangle themselves in a fight with the legislature, both because of enforcement difficulties and because they were all bound together by the same party machines. In 1926, the Illinois Supreme Court refused to issue a writ of mandamus, ordering reapportionment, on the grounds that the judiciary could not compel the legislature to act.[32] Two years later, the same court denied the right to file a bill in equity, asking the court to restrain the state Treasurer from paying the salaries and expenses of the General Assembly until it redistricted.[33] In 1930, the same plaintiff initiated *quo warranto* proceedings, used to correct the usurpation or misuse of public office, against various Senators and Representatives of the General Assembly, in an attempt to force them to show by what right and authority they held office. This attempt was also unsuccessful.[34] During the following year, a federal appeals court rejected the argument of a Chicagoan that the United States government had failed to guarantee a republican form of government in Illinois.[35] Some pressure was generated by these cases, however, and in 1931 the General Assembly passed a new apportionment bill, which was so minimal that its effects would scarcely have been noticed. In 1932, the Illinois Supreme Court enjoined elections under this act, holding that it violated the federal Act of 1911 and the Illinois Constitution in that its districts were not approximately equal.[36] This left the previous apportionment law of 1901 still in effect. *Wood* v. *Broom* prevented successful action against the 1901 Act; in 1942 the Illinois Supreme Court dismissed a suit to have that Act declared unconstitutional, holding that under the *Wood* doctrine it had no equity to hear the case.[37] Obviously, the state courts were not going to be of much use, and the situation continued to worsen: by 1946 one vote in Illinois' Fifth District was worth 8.1 votes in the Seventh. No corrective action could be expected from Congress, which had a vested interest in the preservation of unequal districts; the fourteen states suffering most severely from unequal apportionment elected nearly a majority of the House. In 1901 and again in 1910, the seating of a member in the House was challenged on the grounds that he represented a district which did not meet constitutional standards of equality. After *pro forma* hearings, both challenges were rejected, largely on practical grounds.[38] The urban dwellers of Illinois turned in desperation to the federal courts. The *Colegrove* case, which reached the Supreme Court in 1946, was brought by three voters[39] in over-sized Illinois congressional districts to restrain the Governor, Secretary of State, and Auditor from arranging a Congressional election. They charged that the districts drawn by the 1901 Act lacked compactness of territory and approximate equality of population, and were therefore in conflict with the Reapportionment Act of 1911 and the Constitution; that the guaranty clause of Article IV Section 4 was violated; and that the provision for "proportionate representation of the people in the legislature" of the Northwest Ordinance had been made a permanent part of Illinois' organic law and was not being heeded. They relied heavily on the precedents set by the *Smiley*, *Koenig*, and *Carroll* cases. The Attorney General of Illinois replied that the issue was a political one; that a federal court's acceptance of jurisdiction would violate the sovereign immunity of Illinois; that jurisdiction over such disputes belonged to the House of Representatives; and, as repeated by Justice Rutledge, that exercise of jurisdiction would disenfranchise more people than it could enfranchise. A three-judge trial court composed of members of the District Court dismissed the complaint, holding itself to be bound by *Wood* v. *Broom* contrary to its own sympathies.[40]

The members of the Supreme Court found themselves so completely unable to agree about the case that no majority opinion could be written. Justice Frankfurter "announced the judgment of the Court and an opinion in which Mr. Justice Reed and Mr. Justice Burton concur"; this opinion is listed in the Reports as "Opinion of Frankfurter, J.," rather than as "Opinion of the Court.' Chief Justice Stone had died in April (the opinion was handed down on June 10), and Justice Jackson did not sit. Justice Rutledge wrote an opinion which is not listed as either concurring or dissenting, although it concurs in the result; Justice Black wrote a dissenting opinion in which he was joined by Justices Douglas and Murphy. Justice Rutledge thus held the deciding vote.

Justice Frankfurter cited the decision in *Wood* v. *Broom* that the 1929 Act did not require compactness and equality, adding that the Court saw no reason to overrule that case, "the more so since seven Congressional elections have been held under the Act of 1929 as construed by this Court." [41] It should be noted that in accordance with the rule against deciding constitutional questions unless absolutely necessary, Justice Frankfurter could and should have ended right there. He chose to go on, probably to make quite clear what the Court (or, at least, three members thereof) thought about the whole problem. The Act of 1929 aside, said Justice Frankfurter, the Court had no jurisdiction over the apportionment issue:

> It must be resolved by considerations on the basis of which this Court, from time to time, has refused to intervene in controversies. It has refused to do so because due regard for the effective working of our Government revealed this issue to be of a peculiarly political nature and therefore not meet for judicial determination.[42]

This was not a case in which a plaintiff had been deprived of his rights by others; the wrong involved here was "suffered by Illinois as a polity." [43] The federal courts were being asked to "reconstruct the electoral process of Illinois," something which they could not do. All a court could do was invalidate the existing electoral system, which would leave Illinois undistricted. Should

the legislature choose not to pass a new law, members of the House
of Representatives would then have to be elected on a statewide
ticket, which would be undesirable as a violation of the principle
behind districting; i.e., giving local subdivisions a voice so as to
ensure minority representation. Justice Frankfurter was apparently
not sure that the Illinois legislature would go along with such a
mode of election, for his next sentence begins:

> Assuming acquiescence on the part of the authority of Illinois in
> the selection of its Representatives by a mode that defies the direc-
> tion of Congress for selection by districts . . .[44]

The enforcement problem would seem to have been foremost in
the justice's mind. He ended the sentence by saying,

> . . . the House of Representatives may not acquiesce. In the exercise
> of its power to judge the qualifications of its own members, the
> House may reject a delegation of Representatives-at-large.[45]

We have, then, two possible situations which could leave the Court
sitting high and dry and looking rather foolish. Either the Illinois
legislature or the national legislature might refuse to be bound
by the Court's decision, and there would be nothing any judge
could do about it. Acting in the grand judicial manner, however,
Justice Frankfurter went on to clothe the enforcement problem
in its traditional trappings. The entire problem, he said, brought
the Court into involvement with party contests, from which area
the Court had "traditionally held aloof":

> It is hostile to a democratic system to involve the judiciary in
> the politics of the people. And it is not less pernicious if such judicial
> intervention in an essentially political contest be dressed up in the
> abstract phrases of the law.[46]

It is difficult to believe that a man of Justice Frankfurter's intellectual prowess could be taken in by such rhetoric, even if he did
write it himself. It must have been axiomatic to the justice that
any decision of the Court necessarily affected the "politics of the
people." And if he was referring to the specific process by which
the people articulate their political desires, he was deliberately
ignoring the Court's multitudinous electoral decisions.[47] It is quite
easy to distinguish these cases from *Colegrove* v. *Green;* because
any two cases by definition involve two different sets of facts, it
is quite easy to distinguish any case from any other case. But the

fact of the matter remains: the Court has not hesitated to involve itself in the "politics of the people."

Citing Article I Section 4 of the Constitution, Justice Frankfurter went on to hold that the authority to secure fair representation rested exclusively with Congress, and that if Congress did not exercise the authority, "the remedy ultimately lies with the people." [48] It is totally impossible to believe that Justice Frankfurter did not realize how unrealistic he sounded—and was. What he was saying was that the Constitution demanded that a patently unfair situation be allowed to exist; but he didn't quite enunciate this. Two pages later he returned to this theme, saying that the Constitution included "many commands that are not enforceable by courts because they clearly fall outside the conditions and purposes that circumscribe judicial action." He cited *Kentucky* v. *Dennison*,[49] *Mississippi* v. *Johnson*,[50] and *Pacific Telephone & Telegraph Company* v. *Oregon* [51] —all cases in which the Court extracted itself from an embarrassing situation and exited through the door marked "jurisdiction." Justice Frankfurter did not think that courts ought to "enter this political thicket":

> The remedy for unfairness in districting is to secure state legislatures that will apportion properly, or to invoke the ample powers of Congress.[52]

He neglected to describe the way in which this could be done.

And finally, merely emphasizing the tenuous nature of his argument, Justice Frankfurter delved into the history of districting requirements in order to show that "glaring inequalities" in redistricting had always existed.[53] Or, to rephrase slightly, if an evil exists long enough, a conscientious judge must accept its continued existence, presumably in the pious hope that long life will mitigate its sting. This weakest of all arguments was extended to include two appendixes. The first, entitled "Disparities in Apportionment, Showing Districts in Each State Having Largest and Smallest Populations," included those disparities for every state in the Union in the years 1897, 1928, and 1946. According to the table, in 1897 Illinois' Thirteenth district had a voting population of 184,027, and its Twenty-Second, 159,186; in 1928 its Seventh district contained 560,434 voting souls, and its Fifth, 158,092; in 1946 the Seventh included 941,053 voters, and the Fifth 112,116.[54] Appendix II boasted maps of electoral districts in four states (Alabama, California, Illinois, and Pennsylvania), presumably to indicate that districts in other states as well as Illinois had crazy-quilt shapes and radically different sizes.[55]

Justice Rutledge's opinion, as mentioned, was not entitled either concurring or dissenting, but the substance indicates that he concurred with the result and dissented from the reasoning behind it. He agreed that the case was covered by Article I Sections 2, 4, and 5 of the Constitution, but pointed out that the ruling in *Smiley* v. *Holm* was to the contrary (i.e., there the Court had accepted jurisdiction). He concurred also that the Court should avoid deciding constitutional questions except when absolutely unavoidable, "especially when this may bring our function into clash with the political departments of the Government." [56] If precedent was to be followed—and Justice Rutledge assumed that was the purpose of precedent—*Smiley* meant that the Court could accept jurisdiction; *Wood* v. *Broom* meant that the bill should be dismissed for want of equity. This is an interesting interpretation of the precedent set by that case, as the majority had held that it was unnecessary to decide the question of equity, and it was the four concurring justices who thought that the bill should have been dismissed for that reason. In any case, Justice Rutledge adhered to the doctrine that equity relief should not be granted unless the Court can definitely enforce its decree. It was especially true that a want of equity existed in the instant case because "the cause is of so delicate a character." Although the plaintiff's complaint was "strong," "the relief it seeks pitches the Court into delicate relation to the functions of state officials and Congress." [57] The phrase "delicate relation" certainly carries with it an aura of enforcement difficulties.

Justice Rutledge went on to make the same kind of "limited time" argument he was to employ two years later in the *MacDougall* case: [58]

> The shortness of the time remaining makes it doubtful whether action could, or would, be taken in time to secure for petitioners the effective relief they seek. To force them to share in an election at large might bring greater equality of voting right. It would also deprive them and all other Illinois citizens of representation by districts which the prevailing policy of Congress commands.[59]

Further on, stating that the right to voting equality was not "absolute," Justice Rutledge added that ". . . the cure sought may

be worse than the disease." [60] These observations led many commentators to believe that Justice Rutledge was concerned with the
time element only. As indicated above, he was concerned with
the enforcement problem as well. This is evidenced again by his
assertion that it was doubtful whether action could or *would* be
taken. He ended his opinion by declaring that since there could
be, at best, "only a rough approximation" of voting equality, the
legislature obviously possessed "considerable latitude" in the exercise of its judgment. [61] The opinion can be summarized as meaning
that the Court had jurisdiction and the plaintiff's case was "strong,"
but the Court could not exercise its powers where enforcement
would lead to more problems than it would solve.

Justice Black wrote a dissenting opinion on behalf of Justices
Douglas and Murphy and himself. As might have been expected,
he was very much concerned with the glaring inequalities which
constituted the foundation for the case, citing both the pertinent
figures (sizes of districts) and the attempts made within Illinois
to secure legislative or judicial action. [62] He specifically mentioned
the interest of state legislators in perpetuating the inequality [63] and
proceeded to assert, in rapid order, that: the Court had jurisdiction;
the case was justiciable; the appellants had standing; the suit was
properly brought against officials as individuals rather than against
the state; no one had denied that the right to vote and equal
protection of the laws had been infringed; and as no adequate
legal remedy for this deprivation existed equity could and should
grant relief. [64] It was quite apparent that the Fourteenth Amendment
had been violated; under the Illinois statute, one of the appellants,
whose voting district included more than 900,000 citizens, had a
vote of much less consequence than those residents living in the
district with 112,000 voters. Just as the equal protection clause
would not permit the state to decide that certain groups of citizens
could not vote (and Justice Black cited *Nixon* v. *Herndon* and *Nixon*
v. *Condon*), it would "prohibit a law that would expressly give
certain citizens a half-vote and others a full vote," and it would
forbid a law requiring all Congressmen to be elected by one county
or arbitrarily giving twenty-five Congressmen to the smallest county
and one to all the others. The principle here was similar, he argued,
as the Act gave some voters a vote one-ninth as effective as others.
Surely this was the kind of discrimination the equal protection
clause had been framed to prevent. [65] The Constitution did not

specifically state that election districts had to contain approximately equal populations, but this was clearly implied by the "constitutionally guaranteed right to vote and the right to have one's vote counted." The power of the states to legislate in this area was meant to implement these constitutional guarantees. Where the states do not make "real efforts" to implement them, "it is the Court's duty to invalidate the state law." [66]

> It has always been the rule that where a federally protected right has been invaded the federal courts will provide the remedy to rectify the wrong done.[67]

Voting, as part of elections, is political, but this did not mean that courts "have nothing to do with protecting and vindicating the right of a voter to cast an effective ballot." Justice Black cited *Nixon* v. *Herndon, U.S.* v. *Classic, Wood* v. *Broom, Giles* v. *Harris,* and *Lane* v. *Wilson.*[68] As in *Smiley,* the Court could "leave the State free" to conduct elections at large. "It is said that it would be inconvenient for the State to conduct the elections in this manner," but it would have the "virtue" of "not discriminat(ing) against some groups to favor others." [69]

The dissent focused on the problem of the right to vote in elections, and all the ramifications of that right: the right to have one's vote counted; the implied right to be permitted to exercise the right to vote; and, leading into the reapportionment cases, the right to have one's vote given as much weight as that of everyone else. The history of this problem and its treatment by the Court deserves some attention, especially as it later became the basis for the Court's decision in *Gray* v. *Sanders.*

In 1875, the Court held that the right to vote was derived from the state and could not receive federal enforcement.[70] This decision was modified in 1884, when a number of white men were convicted of conspiring to intimidate a black man in the exercise of his right to vote for a member of Congress, by beating him.[71] Questioned as to whether Congress had the power to penalize such acts, the Court replied that it did, for from the Congressional power to regulate elections can be deduced a power to insure free and pure elections.

The right to vote was specifically mentioned in the Fifteenth Amendment, but the breadth of that right was open to judicial determination. It was undeniably a political right, and therefore

bound to become mixed up with the whole category of justice
termed "political." Political rights presumably issue from a political
body, and the Court was understandably reluctant to accept cases
which would have forced it to order political bodies not to infringe
political rights, especially when those bodies were composed of
white Southerners.

In 1903, a black Alabaman brought an action in equity in the
Court, claiming that he and more than 5,000 others in Montgomery
had been kept from registering to vote solely on the basis of color.[72]
He asked that the defendants be required to enroll him and the
others on the voting lists, and that pertinent sections of the Alabama
constitution be declared void. Justice Holmes and four other justices
refused to accept jurisdiction on technical grounds relating to the
Court's right to handle this kind of equity case.[73] Said Holmes:

> . . . equity cannot undertake now . . . to enforce political rights.
> . . . In determining whether a court of equity can take jurisdiction,
> one of the first questions is what it can do to enforce any order
> that it may make. . . . Unless we are prepared to supervise the
> voting in that State by officers of the court, it seems to us that
> all that the plaintiff could get from equity would be an empty form.
> Apart from damages to the individual, relief from a great political
> wrong, if done, as alleged, by the people of a State and the State
> itself, must be given by them or by the legislative and political
> department of the government of the United States.[74]

In spite of his refusal to grant the relief prayed for, Holmes implicitly accepted Giles' story,[75] and added:

> . . . we are not prepared to say that an action at law could not
> be maintained on the facts alleged in the bill.[76]

Justice Brewer either didn't realize or chose to ignore the fact that
Holmes was really addressing himself to the enforcement problem,
and accordingly dissented on the grounds that the deprivation
involved was of legal rights which should be upheld by the Court.

Justice Frankfurter did not mention the equity problem in the
Colegrove case, but, as discussed above, Justice Rutledge did, saying
that the Court had jurisdiction but should dismiss the bill for want
of equity. Justice Black replied that since rights had been abridged
and no adequate legal remedy existed, equity could grant relief.

Justice Holmes' broad hint in the *Giles* case was not taken until
Nixon v. *Herndon*,[77] an action at law which relied upon *Giles* v.

Harris as a precedent. It was used again in 1939 when a black Oklahoman sued state officials for damages because he had been kept from registering by a statute which in effect discriminated against Negroes.[78] The law in question contained a so-called "grandfather clause," and such statutes had been specifically held unconstitutional by the Court in 1915.[79] Writing the majority opinion, Justice Frankfurter distinguished the case from *Giles* v. *Harris* as an action at law rather than a suit in equity, and struck down the statute on the basis of the Fifteenth Amendment.[80]

The Court was willing to act where the question was one of declaring a law invalid, rather than of trying to force local officials to take positive steps, and thus it hid behind the demure skirts of equity. The "white primary" cases,[81] however, led the *Colegrove* dissenters to believe that an unshakeable and enforceable right to vote had been accepted by the Court, and they questioned the Court's decision to protect only the Negroes' right to vote. If the general right to vote had been broadened to include the right to cast a ballot and to have it counted honestly,[82] then why not widen it to include equal weighting of all votes?

Two years after *Colegrove*, the Court heard the case of *Mac-Dougall* v. *Green*.[83] Although in purely formal terms it involved elections rather than reapportionment, *MacDougall* must be considered in the light of *Colegrove*. The Court's decision was handed down *per curiam*, and its sole citations were of *Colegrove* v. *Green* and *Colegrove* v. *Barrett*.[84]

Colegrove and *MacDougall* both challenged the overrepresentation of rural areas, *MacDougall* dealing with the unequal weight given those areas in determining which parties should appear on election ballots. The Illinois Election Code required that in order to be granted recognition (i.e., to be allowed a place on any ballot), a new political party had to present a petition signed by 25,000 qualified voters, including at least 200 from each of 50 of the 102 Illinois counties. As 52 per cent of the state's registered voters lived in Cook County, 87 per cent in the forty-nine most populous counties, including Cook, and only 13 per cent in the fifty-three least populous counties,[85] no new party which did not command widespread support in the rural counties could fulfill the requirements. This was the situation found by the Progressive Party, which could not secure the necessary number of rural signatures, although it had obtained 200,000 signatures, largely from voters in Cook

County. The Party sued to enjoin enforcement of the requirement of at least 200 signatures from each of at least 50 counties, claiming that the law violated due process, equal protection, Article I Sections 2 and 4, Article II Section 1, the privileges and immunities clause of the Fourteenth Amendment, and the Seventeenth Amendment.

This controversy represented the tail-end of a prolonged political attempt to keep the Progressive Party off the Illinois ballot. In 1947, the Party had run its candidates for the office of judge of the Cook County Superior Court, and it assumed that this entitled it to be considered an established rather than a new political party. The Illinois Election Code, however, excluded elections for judges from those in which a party could enter candidates if it wished to be recognized as established. As the Party claimed, this restrictive definition of "general election" had been added to the Code in 1936 as a way of permitting coalition judicial tickets under the Democratic Party label in Democratic Cook County without depriving the Republican Party of its established party status. When it was denied a place on the 1948 ballot in Cook County, the Party filed suit against election officials. The Cook County Circuit Court declared that the Party was not an established one, and although this decision was reversed by the Illinois Supreme Court,[86] the Circuit Court delayed issuing an order requiring officials to print appropriate ballots until compliance was impossible. When the Party asked the State Officers Electoral Board for a place on the state ballot, the Board refused its request, and the Party and its candidates (Henry Wallace for President, Glen Taylor for Vice President, Curtis MacDougall for Senator, Grant Oakes for Governor) filed a complaint against Governor Dwight H. Green in the District Court, asking for a declaratory judgment and injunctive relief. This plea was denied.[87]

The Supreme Court agreed that none of the Party's claims was valid.[88] Then, in what was probably an attempt to keep such cases as *MacDougall* and *Colegrove* from cropping up again, the Court added,

> To assume that political power is a function exclusively of numbers is to disregard the practicalities of government.[89]

Each state was held to have a right

> . . . to assure a proper diffusion of political initiative as between
> its thinly populated counties and those having concentrated masses,
> in view of the fact that the latter have practical opportunities of
> exerting their political weight at the polls not available to the
> former.[90]

The Constitution, "a practical instrument of government," did not
deny this right of each state.[91] If one wishes to invoke practicality,
then this argument appears fallacious. If those counties having
concentrated masses had a practical opportunity to exert their
weight, the *MacDougall* case would never have come into existence.
The doctrine, however, was clear cut. The Court wished to remain
outside the area of equal protection and weighted voting, and it
refused to be shoved in through any side door.

As in *Colegrove*, the figure of Justice Rutledge loomed large
in the case. For, once again, Justice Rutledge felt that "the cure
sought may be worse than the disease," [92] and that his colleagues
had made the right decision for the wrong reasons. In effect, he
told the Party that it had a good case but that it chose to bring
it at the wrong moment. He himself made the analogy with the
Colegrove case,[93] and pointed out that the instant case appeared
"on the eve of the election" scheduled for November 2.[94] If relief
was granted, it would do "more harm than good"; it would be
impossible to print and distribute new ballots in the short time
remaining before the election, and in all the confusion far too many
people would be disenfranchised. Absentee ballots had already been
mailed, and the time was not sufficient to ensure that absentee
voters would not lose their votes. It was for this reason, and this
reason only, that Rutledge agreed with the Court's decision to deny
relief.[95] He made it quite clear that he thought the appellants'
position absolutely justified. As a matter of fact, he said, even the
Attorney General of Illinois conceded the validity of the position
and the error of the District Court.[96] What the justice did not
mention was that the Attorney General, a Republican, was only
following his party line. The Illinois Republican Party, which controlled the state government, hoped the Progressive Party would
win its suit, thinking that its existence would siphon off votes
normally cast for Democratic candidates. Governor Green had
joined the Attorney General in asking that the law be declared
unconstitutional.[97]

Justices Black, Douglas, and Murphy followed the precedent they had set in the *Colegrove* case and dissented; this time the dissent was written by Justice Douglas. It is very similar to the one written by Justice Black in *Colegrove* v. *Green.* As in that opinion, Douglas agreed that the system violated the equal protection clause because it was an arbitrary discrimination against certain voters. There had been no attempt "to make the required signatures proportionate to the population of each county"; [98] the law "offers no basis whatever to justify giving greater weight to the individual votes of one group of citizens than to those of another group," and it thus "has the same inherent infirmity" as the one in question in *Colegrove.*[99] The effect of the law was to make it impossible for 87 per cent of the voters to form a new political party. This was both unconstitutional and unrepublican.

> The notion that one group can be granted greater voting strength than another is hostile to our standards for popular representative government.[100]

> Discrimination against any group or class of citizens in the exercise of these constitutionally protected rights of citizenship deprives the electoral process of integrity.[101]

> Free and honest elections are the very foundation of our republican form of government.[102]

Ignoring precedent, Douglas thus added the criterion of free and honest elections to the partial definition given by the Court of "republican form of government." It seems unlikely that this phrase was used unintentionally; either Douglas himself, or Black or Murphy, reading the opinion, would surely have noticed the wording. Could the three men have been suggesting that another traditional political question be opened for discussion? This is possible, at least for Douglas, in view of his remarks on the entire subject in his opinion in *Baker* v. *Carr.*[103] Be that as it may, they certainly disagreed with their brother Rutledge that an unconstitutional act could be allowed to stand because of practical considerations; again reminiscent of Black in *Colegrove,* Douglas went on to say that the disruption of an election should not be allowed to deter the Court from striking down an unconstitutional statute, especially as the state officials involved did not claim that such disruption would result.[104] And, as Black had, Douglas pointed to the Negro right-to-vote decisions, and declared himself unable to see a substantial difference between those cases and the one in question.[105]

One important point should be noted: *MacDougall* v. *Green* was decided on its merits. The District Court had held that it had no jurisdiction in such matters; the Supreme Court denied not its own jurisdiction but the validity of the plaintiffs' claims. What happened to Justice Frankfurter's axiom that it was "pernicious" for judges to intervene "in an essentially political contest," an area from which the Court had "traditionally held aloof"? [106] The answer may lie in the Court's belief that the control given to Congress over its members by Article I Section 4 precluded judicial action in that area. The election involved in *MacDougall* v. *Green*, however, was a Presidential one; Article II Section 1 Paragraph 2 gives complete power over the appointment of Electors to the states. There would seem to be no federal body other than the Court which could take remedial action in this area; certainly, separation of powers and respect for a coordinate branch were not involved. In *Colegrove*, the Court had been disturbed at the prospect of the Illinois legislature refusing to redistrict, and the elections at large which would be the consequence of such a refusal.[107] No action on the part of the legislature would be required here, however; if the Court should invalidate the contested portion of the statute, the bulk of the machinery for putting new parties on the ballot would remain.[108] The enforcement problem would not exist, for no positive action would be called for. No constitutional or democratic principle would be violated by the remaining sections of the law.

This explains the *MacDougall* decision in terms of the enforcement problem. It does not explain it from the viewpoint of Justice Frankfurter, who would, presumably, refuse to consider a case solely in terms of enforcement. In 1934, the Court had upheld Congress' power to enact legislation dealing with Electors,[109] and Justice Frankfurter might well have agreed that Article II Section I gave Congress the sole federal power over Electors, and therefore the sole power to declare them properly or improperly chosen and to lay down regulations for their nomination. If one assumes that he was not guided by the enforcement problem, the only possible conclusion is that Justice Frankfurter continued to believe this type of case outside of the Court's jurisdiction.

The Court accepted *MacDougall,* however, and one is left with the question of why Justice Frankfurter did not dissent. The answer may be found by counting the votes of the other justices. Chief Justice Vinson, who did not sit in *Colegrove,* was part of the majority in *MacDougall,* which means his view was one of the following: he felt the Court did not have jurisdiction; or, he felt the Court had jurisdiction, but that MacDougall's case was not adequate. The same two choices can be surmised from the inclusion of Justice Jackson, who did not sit in *Colegrove,* in the majority. Justices Reed and Burton may have felt, as they did in *Colegrove,* that the Court did not have jurisdiction, although the other possibility exists. This makes four justices who seemingly might have denied jurisdiction. All four of them could not have wished to deny jurisdiction, however, for if they had, Justice Frankfurter would have joined them and created a majority. At least one of the four must have voted to accept jurisdiction and decide for the defendant, and the others must have been persuaded to go along; or, possibly, all four wanted to accept jurisdiction and decide against Mac-Dougall. Judging from Justice Frankfurter's votes in later cases,[110] it is reasonable to assume that he did not want the Court to accept jurisdiction in the instant case. But why then did he join the majority? There are only two possible answers. Either Justice Frankfurter, along with his brethren, was subject to considerations of enforcement difficulties, and his arguments in *Colegrove* and *Baker* were just so much judicial hyperbole;[111] or he decided that joining his colleagues in a silent *per curiam* was preferable to splitting the Court so thoroughly that a majority opinion would become impossible, as it had been impossible in. *Colegrove.* The prestige of the Court's decisions varies with the size of its majorities, and it cannot be doubted that Justice Frankfurter was fully aware of this. It is entirely possible that a situation along these lines was responsible for *MacDougall* v. *Green's* being decided in a *per curiam* opinion, especially as an examination of Justice Jackson's opinions lead to the conclusion that he might well have agreed that the case was not justiciable.[112] Would Justice Frankfurter maintain silence for such a reason? It does seem possible, although we may never know; it would go far towards explaining why the Court decided a case not much different from *Colegrove per curiam,* on its merits.

Inequalities in representation between rural and urban districts continued to increase as more and more farmers moved to the cities.[113] The farm population diminished and the city population multiplied, but the districts and the number of representatives allotted to each remained the same, and it was the rurally-controlled legislatures which controlled the states. One delegate to the Vermont House of Representatives, which had last been reapportioned in 1793, represented thirty-eight citizens; one of his colleagues spoke for 33,155.[114] The constituency of the largest district having one representative in the Alabama House was 104,767 in 1961; the smallest, 6,731. The number of people in the largest and smallest districts represented in the respective lower houses (and these disparities are only the most glaring) was as follows: [115]

State	Largest District	Smallest District
California	306,191	72,105
Connecticut	81,089	191
Florida	311,682	2,868
Georgia	185,422	1,876
Idaho	15,576	915
Iowa	133,157	7,910
Louisiana	120,205	6,909
Massachusetts	49,478	3,559
New York	190,343	14,974
Pennsylvania	139,293	4,485
Rhode Island	18,997	468
Utah	32,380	1,164
West Virginia	252,925	4,391

Districts within which representatives to the United States House of Representatives were elected were no more equitable; Michigan's largest and smallest were 802,994 and 117,231, respectively.[116] All of the states were guilty, although the purposes served by the inequalities were not precisely the same. In most cases conservative and largely Republican farmers were glad to limit the influence of more liberal and largely Democratic city-dwellers, but in Tennessee it was the western Democratic sections, with an average of 372,769 constituents to a state assembly district, which discriminated against the eastern Republican districts with approximately 487,352 constituents.[117] In the Southern states blacks, who were concentrated in cities (where the blacks most likely to be willing to fight for their rights lived), were effectively ignored. Immigrant groups in various parts of the country were granted the same treatment. Rural legislators enjoyed their power and utilized it to give their districts the bulk of financial aid.

> In the 1957–58 apportionment of the county aid funds, the General Assembly permitted 23 counties to receive 57.9% more state aid than would be the case on a basis of state aid per capita, and it turns out that these counties had 23 more direct representatives than permitted under the state constitution. Ten counties, having 25 less direct representatives than permitted under the Tennessee Constitution, among them Shelby, Knox, Hamilton, and Davidson, received 136.9% less state aid than on a per capita basis. Expressed another way, a voter in Moore County (with a voting population in 1950 of 2,340) has 17 times as much representation in the Lower House as does a voter in Davidson County (1950 voting population 211,930), and Moore County receives 17 times the apportionment per vehicle of state gasoline taxes as does Davidson County.[118]

As of 1960, Alabama had last been reapportioned in 1901, Colorado in 1932, Indiana in 1921, North Dakota in 1931, Delaware in 1894. With minor variations, other states followed suit.[119]

In 1960, the population of Tennessee was 3,567,089. The population of the largest state Senate district was 237,905 and that of the smallest, 39,727; in the House the figures were 79,301 and 3,454. It was possible for 26.9 per cent of the population to elect a majority of the Senate; 28.7 per cent could control the House.[120] West Tennessee, whose political philosophy emphasized the virtues of segregation and prohibition and the vices of evolution, included the rabid segregationist Haywood and Fayette counties. With the single exception of Shelby county (Memphis), West Tennessee was overrepresented in the state legislature. In East Tennessee, which included such liberal integrationist centers as Nashville, even rural areas were considered contaminated, and were grossly underrepresented.[121] Chester and Lake counties, in the western part of the state, had less than 10,000 people each, and each had a direct representative in the House; in the eastern portion, nonmetropolitan Sullivan county (population 114,000) and Washington county (population 64,000) also had one direct representative each.[122] "Direct"

and "floterial" representatives added to the systematized mini-
mization of certain votes. Tennessee did not have a system of
single-member districts. Four metropolitan counties had several
representatives, elected on a county-at-large basis. Floterial representatives were elected from more than one county.

> The seats are rotated among the counties in accordance with party
> agreements which are made with little regard to their respective
> populations, and sometimes with votes cast only in the candidates'
> county. This arrangement has required Davidson County (popula-
> tion 399,000) to allow neighboring Wilson County (population
> 27,000) to nominate this representative periodically and similarly
> requires Knox County (population 250,000) to defer to Loudon
> County (population 24,000).[123]

As of 1962, Tennessee had last been reapportioned in 1901, when
its population stood at 2,020,616 and included 487,380 voters. There
were 2,092,891 voters in Tennessee in 1960. A group of urban
voters,[124] claiming that the debasement of their votes was unconstitutional, and unable to get relief from the rural legislature, decided
to go to the federal courts.[125] They argued that this debasement
constituted a denial of the equal protection of the laws directed
by the Fourteenth Amendment, and sued in behalf of themselves
and others similarly situated. Asking the federal District Court to
declare the existing Reapportionment Act of 1901 unconstitutional,
they also asked that, should the General Assembly refuse to act,
the court decree reapportionment by the mathematical application
of the Tennessee constitutional formulae, based on the latest federal
census figures, or order elections at large. Article II Section 4 of
the Tennessee Constitution requires that a reapportionment be
undertaken every ten years; Sections 5 and 6 state that representatives are to be apportioned "according to the number of
qualified voters" in each county or district. The Act of 1901 provided that the apportionment be made on the basis of the federal
census.

The District Court dismissed the complaint, citing *Colegrove*,
saying that it had no jurisdiction, and that no claim was stated
upon which relief could be granted. Plaintiffs appealed their case
to the Supreme Court, and thus became the immediate cause of
that body's decision in *Baker* v. *Carr.*[126] The Solicitor General of
the United States argued as an *amicus curiae;* similar briefs were

filed by the Governor of Oklahoma, the city of St. Matthews, Kentucky, and the Tennessee cities of Nashville, Chattanooga, and Knoxville.

The opinions handed down by the Court are especially important because the concept of political questions was well thrashed out among them.[127] Justice Brennan's opinion for the Court accepted both the category as legitimate and the popular belief that it derives its existence from the separation of powers theory, but he attempted to distinguish between the Court's jurisdiction and the inherent justiciability of a case. His idea was that the Court has jurisdiction of such cases, but may refuse to handle them where the element of justiciability is lacking; i.e., where the only standard the justices may utilize as a guide is the ambiguous "republican form of government' clause. Justice Douglas, concurring, seemed at first to reject the notion of political questions, specifically criticizing the *Luther* v. *Borden* decision; then he applauded the Court's refusal to become involved in *Kentucky* v. *Dennison,* citing this as a proper usage of the category. He thus came closest to discussing the enforcement problem, adding that previous judicial involvement in reapportionment controversies had been a catalyst for legislative action. Justice Clark ignored the controversy to emphasize his belief that the Court was competent "to fashion an effective decree" and should have decided the case for the plaintiffs. All of the talk by his various brethren disturbed Justice Stewart, who felt compelled to make clear what the Court had done: it had not decided on the merits; it had merely accepted jurisdiction and remanded the case to the District Court for further action. In strictly analytical terms he may have been correct, but the effect of the combined opinions was to indicate to the lower court what its decision should be. Justice Frankfurter, dissenting, returned to the political question problem, reiterating the importance of the doctrine and the necessity to maintain it in order to ensure legal continuity. Justice Harlan, dissenting, similarly deplored the entrance of the justices into the field of political theory, but went on to deal directly with the enforcement problem:

> The majority seems to have accepted the argument . . . that if this Court merely asserts authority in this field, Tennessee and other "malapportioning" States will quickly respond with appropriate political action. . . . At the same time the majority has wholly failed to reckon with what the future may hold in store if this optimistic prediction is not fulfilled.[128]

One of Justice Harlan's worries was that there was no universally accepted standard for reapportionment, and thus no guide for judges; he expounded on this issue in a ten-page appendix showing "The Inadequacy of Arithmetical Formulas as Measures of Rationality of Tennessee's Apportionment." [129]

Nominally, the decision was a 6-2 one, meaning that six of the justices agreed. In reality, the *Baker* case followed what seems to have become the frequently-used twentieth century pattern of a majority opinion which satisfied only a minority, and a handful of individual concurrences. John Marshall's belief that the Court must present a united front has been forgotten; or perhaps it is not appropriate in the transitional twentieth century, when the justices can be expected to reflect the variety of views circulating throughout the community; or perhaps the theories of sociological jurisprudence and legal realism have encouraged the justices to regard dissent as being as important as agreement. In any case, students of the function of concurring opinions can undoubtedly find a great deal of material in *Baker* v. *Carr*. The various pronouncements deserve to be examined in some detail.

Justice Brennan divided his opinion into three sections: jurisdiction, standing, and justiciability. As the claim involved arose under the Constitution (the Fourteenth Amendment) and the District Court had not deemed it unsubstantial, the Supreme Court had jurisdiction.[130] Justice Brennan did not merely state this, however; judicial reversals are invariably accompanied by many citations and much "explanation" of previous cases, and the instant opinion was no exception. The Court had accepted jurisdiction in *Davis* v. *Hildebrant, Smiley* v. *Holm, Koenig* v. *Flynn, Carroll* v. *Becker, Wood* v. *Broom, Cook* v. *Fortson* and *Turman* v. *Duckworth, MacDougall* v. *Green,* and later *per curiams,* all of which Justice Brennan listed.[131] He also discussed *Colegrove,* pointing out that the majority of justices involved had assumed the Court had jurisdiction, and adding,

> Indeed, it is even questionable that the opinion of Mr. Justice Frankfurter . . . doubted jurisdiction of the subject matter.[132]

This novel thesis, contradicting Justice Frankfurter's explicit statement in *Colegrove,* was based on the belief that such a "doubt" would have been inconsistent with Frankfurter's reliance on the holding in *Wood* v. *Broom* (where the Court had accepted jurisdiction). It is undoubtedly a defensive measure for subsequent courts to deny that previous ones could have been guilty of inconsistency. One wonders what Justice Frankfurter thought when he read this interpretation; that it was far from his own was made clear in his dissent.

Discussing the question of standing, Justice Brennan cited earlier decisions [133] in which the Court had recognized state impairment of votes as a violation of a right secured by the Constitution. This, he pointed out, was not the same thing as saying that the plaintiffs were entitled to relief from the Court, but they did have standing to seek it.[134]

Then Justice Brennan came to the central problem of justiciability and the attributes of a political question, which, "in various settings, diverge, combine, appear, and disappear in seeming disorderliness." [135] He would make it his task to impose seeming orderliness, and he started out to do so by asserting that the protection of a political right presents a political question only if it involves the guarantee of a republican form of government. The assumption that reapportionment cases could be argued only on the basis of this clause, however, was not correct.[136] Justice Brennan neglected to say just whose assumption this was or had ever been.[137] Nonetheless, it was wrong; but the reader must wait to find out why. Justice Brennan was more concerned with the nature of a political question, which he defined as one involving "the relationship between the judiciary and the coordinate branches of the Federal Government":

> The nonjusticiability of a political question is primarily a function of the separation of powers.[138]

There is nothing here about encroachment in the area of federal-state relations; political questions would seem to be a matter for purely federal concern. But the decision as to "whether a matter has in any measure been committed by the Constitution to another branch of government, or whether the action of that branch exceeds whatever authority has been committed," constitutes a "delicate exercise" which must be performed by the Court.[139] This left Justice Brennan with the task of indicating the line between these two situations—a herculean task, indeed, whose difficulty the justice himself implied by going on to discuss the various categories of political questions, showing that not all cases in each category had been considered political. He listed cases dealing with foreign relations, the date of duration of hostilities, the validity of enactments, and the status of Indian tribes.[140] And then he came to his definition:

> Prominent on the surface of any case held to involve a political question is found a textually demonstrable constitutional commitment of the issue to a coordinate political department; or a lack of judicially discoverable and manageable standards for resolving it; or the impossibility of deciding without an initial policy determination of a kind clearly for nonjudicial discretion; or the impossibility of a court's undertaking independent resolution without expressing lack of the respect due coordinate branches of the government; or an unusual need for unquestioning adherence to a political decision already made; or the potentiality of embarrassment from multifarious pronouncements by various departments on one question.[141]

Any student of the Court can demolish this list by pointing out cases in which all of these criteria have been present, and that were nonetheless decided by the Court.[142] One can find or not find a "textually demonstrable commitment" or a "judicially manageable standard" wherever and whenever one so desires, if one is at all versed in legal legerdemain. Every Court decision is a "policy determination," but what is "a kind clearly for nonjudicial discretion"? Inter-branch respect has never been a hallmark of the American government, and the only instance in which "unquestioning adherence," may, arguably, be absolutely justified is one involving war and peace. There is something in the last phrase of this paragraph, however. Precisely what is meant by "potentiality of embarrassment"? If all that is implied is that the Court's saying an act is illegitimate and another branch's saying it is constitutional might be embarrassing, then Justice Brennan must have been arguing against judicial review—which is not likely. But if he was referring to a situation in which the Court makes a pronouncement unacceptable to the executive, which is therefore ignored and unaffected, then he was undoubtedly correct in labeling this embarrassing. The remainder of the paragraph lists situations in which the Court might or might not decide to act, and is therefore of very little use.

Rejecting the Frankfurterian notion that aspects of the political process are not meant for judicial intervention, Justice Brennan agreed that the case "does, in one sense, involve the allocation of political power within a State," but so did many cases decided under the equal protection clause.[143] The Court must intervene when the question is "the consistency of state action with the Federal Constitution," and that was the question raised by *Baker* v. *Carr.* It did not come into the untouchable category:

> We have no question decided, or to be decided, by a political branch of government coequal with this Court. Nor do we risk embarrassment of our government abroad, or grave disturbance at home if we take issue with Tennessee as to the constitutionality of her action here challenged. Nor need the appellants, in order to succeed in this action, ask the Court to enter upon policy determinations for which judicially manageable standards are lacking.[144]

Critics of the opinion were quick to take issue with this, and logically so. The question had been decided by a coequal branch; while the instant case involved the Tennessee state legislature, the willingness of Congress to seat representatives from malapportioned districts drawn by a malapportioned legislature cannot be interpreted as anything but such a decision, whether right or wrong or fashioned from nothing more than self-interest. If "grave disturbance at home" were a criterion, the decision in *Brown* v. *Board of Education* should never have been handed down. Perhaps Justice Brennan meant only that he was making a shrewd guess that no disturbance would result from this particular decision—that the legislatures might complain but that the decision would be enforced. What led him to think so?

It is quite apparent that the problem of reapportionment was a child of urbanization, and as one commentator has noted, *"Baker* v. *Carr* is best treated as an episode in the urbanization of the American community." [145] The growth of large cities and chains of cities has led to a feeling among urbanites that their interests are similar to those of other urbanites in other states and sections of the country, and that they have little in common with the rural residents of their own states. Yet it was the rural sections which controlled state governments, and finding their legislatures blind to city problems of all kinds, urban dwellers began to look to the federal government as the only cure for their troubles. More by coincidence than design, their appeal became a concerted one, reflected in their numerical strength in presidential elections. The city voters throughout the country discovered that they constituted the national majority, and it was this majority which captured the presidency. The President now became the spokesman for the urbanites, whose votes could reelect him and his colleagues. He might not be able to ensure Congressional consideration of their problems, but he could utilize whatever discretion he possessed in order to alleviate their difficulties. One form of this discretion is the Executive's power of publicity. His ability to command headlines and media coverage enables the President to stir voters into making demands of Congress and local legislators. This, indeed, may be the most important of the extra-Constitutional presidential "powers", especially when the President is faced with a recalcitrant Congress. Urbanites would certainly respond to an appeal from the President they elected when, as here, doing so could yield them increased representation without financial or any other kind of sacrifice. If the President, then, were to endorse the Court's action, the powers of publicity and self-interest would take care of the enforcement problem. And the Court didn't even have to guess; Solicitor General Archibald Cox's appearance as *amicus* made President Kennedy's concern plain, as did the President's proposal for a cabinet department of urban affairs.

It might also be suggested that sufficient publicity had already been provided by the headlines of the preceding few years. Americans had become aware of the traumas of urbanization and particularly of the interrelated ills of over-crowding, poverty, and crime It was increasingly obvious that the old social solutions could not make the recently-discovered evils disappear, but no easy new panaceas were forthcoming. How heartening it would be to blame the whole bewildering mess on conspiring rural lawmakers and to bask in the assurance that stripping them of their power would quickly eradicate the ugliness. Perhaps there was also a sneaking hope that more equitable representation for cities would somehow alleviate black resentment before it became too immediately demanding.

> Granting . . . the felt necessity of the time to attack the urban problem, and the growing realization that the urban majority was not able to attack the problem because the rural-oriented legislatures were exploiting *Colegrove* to maintain their own positions, the result in *Baker* was almost inevitable.[146]

Enforcement, then, would not be a problem; and if the agreement of a strong national majority is the requirement for a social consensus, the existence of a potential consensus was equally clear.

This is not to imply that a militant majority had been loudly demanding immediate reform. Quite the contrary; repeated rebuffs by the legislatures and courts had convinced the victims of this particular discrimination that their cause was a hopeless one, and their anger gradually became submerged in apathy and a vague feeling of dissatisfaction with the political process. But just as *Brown* v. *Board of Education* revived the hopes of blacks who had begun to believe that their cause was slowly going nowhere, so *Baker* v. *Carr* was to reinvigorate forces which had been forced to remain dormant. On the day after the decision was handed down, the *New York Times* reported that the "political consensus" was that "the court has dramatized a critical situation," and that "once the court has brought the issue to the center of national attention, public opinion will produce the pressure for greater representation from the urban and suburban areas." [147] Such was proved to be the case. The Court's realization that a societal majority and its Presidential representative would be sufficient insurance against enforcement difficulties caused the reapportionment issue to be dusted off and removed from the political question shelf.

Holding that the instant case was not inextricably involved with the guarantee of a republican form of government, and that previous reapportionment cases had not been decided only because of "the controlling view of a want of equity" (a view he did not hold), Justice Brennan announced that the appellants were therefore entitled to a trial and reversed the decision of the District Court, remanding the cause for further proceedings. [148]

Justice Douglas agreed that the case did not involve interrelationships among the federal bodies but rather "the relation of the federal courts to state agencies," and that if the Court had competence to decide similar cases involving racial segregation it was competent here as well. [149] He also agreed that federal courts have equity jurisdiction in cases concerning voting rights. [150] He did not agree with Brennan's delineation of political questions:

> I feel strongly that many of the cases cited by the Court and involving so-called "political" questions were wrongly decided. [151]

Nor did he agree with Brennan's conclusion that Article IV Section 4 is inherently non-justiciable:

> The statement in *Luther* v. *Borden* . . . that this guaranty is enforceable only by Congress or the Chief Executive is not maintainable.
>
> . . . Moreover, the Court's refusal to examine the legality of the regime of martial law which had been laid upon Rhode Island . . . is indefensible.[152]

He quoted copiously from Justice Woodbury's dissent in *Luther*. And reiterating his point, he added,

> The category of the "political" question is in my view narrower than the decided cases indicate.[153]

But this did not mean that he did not accept the validity of the category. Although he did not think *Georgia* v. *Stanton* constituted a political question, he did agree with the Court's decision in *Kentucky* v. *Dennison,* because there "the performance of a 'duty is left to the discretion and good judgment of an executive officer.'" [154] Why he should have singled out this particular case is problematic, unless it reflects the civil libertarian philosophy for which Justice Douglas is well known. The case, of course, involved a runaway slave and a fugitive freed Negro.[155] In addition, Justice Douglas seems to have his doubts about extradition as a legal practice.[156]

Dealing directly with the enforcement problem, Justice Douglas cited the cases in which a judicial decision that reapportionment should take place had stimulated legislative action.[157] Like most of his other significant pronouncements in the case, he placed this statement in a footnote. Apparently he felt that generalizations about the abstract notion of political questions did not quite belong in the opinion proper, but neither could he allow Justice Brennan's conclusions to remain unchallenged. But what was Justice Douglas' feeling about political questions? It would seem to have been an acceptance of the device, coupled with a desire to limit its application when its utilization would prevent maximum enforcement of individual rights. Justice Douglas is an acknowledged exponent of the "preferred freedoms" doctrine; at the same time, he does not wish to close the door too tightly on what is occasionally the Court's only possible exit from a tricky situation.

Justice Clark wrote the kind of opinion one might almost have expected from Justice Douglas: a forthright assertion of the validity of the plaintiffs' claim. And he minced no words. His opening sentence gives the tenor of the whole:

> One emerging from the rash of opinions with the accompanying clashing of views may well find himself suffering a mental blindness.[158]

The law of the case lay with *MacDougall,* not with *Colegrove,* for in the latter case the Court was not only "bobtailed" but could not even muster a majority opinion.[159] The path of right decision in the instant case was equally clear, Tennessee's districts constituting "but a crazy quilt" with no rational design.[16] Even so, he would not have counselled intervention had "any other relief" been available to the plaintiffs.[161] But there was judicial competence, not only to "blackjack" the legislature into reapportionment, but, as Solicitor General Cox had suggested, "to fashion an effective decree." [162] Justice Clark felt the Court should have decided the case on its merits, and in saying so he also contributed to the growing literature on the function of the majority and concurring opinions:

> Nevertheless, not being able to muster a court to dispose of the case on the merits, I concur in the opinion of the majority and acquiesce in the decision to remand. However, in fairness I do think that Tennessee is intitled to have my idea of what it faces on the record before us and the trial court some light as to how it might proceed.[163]

He added that it need not proceed on the basis of absolute "mathematical exactness." [164]

Here, then, are three different views of the political question. Justice Brennan saw it as a necessary concomitant of separation of powers, which is in turn reflected in the republican form of government guarantee; Justice Douglas agreed with the first half of this view, but not with the second, and thought the category should not apply to civil rights where its use would tend to place limitations on them; Justice Clark felt it should be disregarded when a flagrant violation of rights could not be corrected in any other fashion, but did not venture into esoteric definitions. The result is to leave one wondering what a political question is.

If a judicial answer is to be found anywhere, surely one is justified in expecting it to come from Justice Frankfurter, who usually followed his pronouncements to their intellectual conclusions. His dissent in Baker is a powerfully written cry from the heart of a man who sincerely believed that his colleagues were making a tragic error,[165] but it is curiously inconsistent.

A firm believer in judicial tradition and the necessity for stable legal rules, Justice Frankfurter did not approve of the Court's "massive repudiation" of many previous decisions, because its intervention "in the essentially political conflict of forces" might "impair" its position as a detached legal body whose only authority lies in "sustained public confidence." This confidence will exist only as long as the Court stays out of "political entanglements" and abstains "from injecting itself into the clash of political forces in political settlements." [166] Justice Frankfurter knew that courts are necessarily involved in the clash of political forces, but his feeling was that the Court should not intervene where those forces meet directly; i.e., in the electoral process.[167] The Court was justified in intervening in such situations only where it had a direct Constitutional mandate, the Fourteenth and Fifteenth Amendments, to prevent Negro disenfranchisement.[168] The inference is that the mandate is direct there because the framers of the Amendments had the Negro in mind—a return to the historical school of jurisprudence. His concern with public confidence is interesting. Does it reflect an attempt to retain the nineteenth-century mystique of judicial neutrality? Or is it an attempt to be realistic, predicated on the belief that the public would not accept judicial action in the area of reapportionment? That it would accept such activity in the electoral realm was made obvious by the reaction to previous voting decisions. Justice Frankfurter could not have been worried about the reactions of the South, because he made it clear that he thought Negro voting cases deserved the Court's attention. Probably, he misjudged the depth of the public's devotion to the one body for which it has an almost reverential respect, and the readiness of that public to greet reapportionment decisions with favor.

"The claim is hypothetical and the assumptions are abstract," he continued, because the Court did not lay guidelines for the lower courts.[169] It might be noted that the Court laid no such guidelines in *Brown* v. *Board of Education,* in which Justice Frankfurter concurred. He was concerned with the "mathematical quagmire" into which *Baker* would throw the lower courts, although this would seem no more of a bog than the "all deliberate speed" of the *Brown* decision.[170] He repeated his *Colegrove* contention that recent districting inequalities were not "unique." And, finally, he worried about potential judicial impotence should the states refuse to act.[171] All of which might be contrasted with his concurrence in *Niemotko* v. *Maryland*,[172] which involved permit systems for street meetings:

> It is not for this Court to formulate with particularity the terms of a permit system which would satisfy the Fourteenth Amendment . . . many a decision of this Court rests on some inarticulate major premise and is none the worse for it. A standard may be found inadequate without the necessity of explicit delineation of the standards that would be adequate, just as doggerel may be felt not to be poetry, without the need of writing an essay on what poetry is.[173]

Contradicting Justice Brennan, Justice Frankfurter interpreted the various opinions in the *Colegrove* case to mean that a majority had agreed that this kind of case was not to be handled by the courts.[174] But he admitted, as most of the other justices had not, that one could not set up criteria for political questions:

> From its earliest opinions this Court has consistently recognized a class of controversies which do not lend themselves to judicial standards and judicial remedies. To classify the various instances as "political questions" is rather a form of stating this conclusion than revealing of analysis.[175]

He disagreed, too, that the case did not involve the republican guarantee. In this instance, as in all such, governmental action worked to the advantage of certain groups.

> It would be ingenuous not to see, or consciously blind to deny, that the real battle over the initiative and referendum, or over a delegation of power to local rather than state-wide authority, is the battle between forces whose influence is disparate among the various organs of government to whom power may be given. No shift of power but works a corresponding shift in political influence among the groups composing a society.[176]

In other words, where a Court decision will effect a shift in power, that decision, by definition a political "policy," should not be made. The argument is hardly logical; what Court decision has not effected a shift in power? The Court was being asked to decide that one theory of representation—based solely on numbers—was better than another—based on geographic areas etc. This, said Frankfurter, meant that the Court was "ultimately" choosing "among competing theories of political philosophy." [177]

> . . . a court could not determine the equal-protection issue without in fact first determining the Republican-Form issue, simply because what is reasonable for equal-protection purposes will depend upon what frame of government, basically, is allowed.[178]

One might ask what the Court was doing when it chose to renounce the laissez-faire philosophy for that of the welfare state. But Justice Frankfurter's argument went further; he in effect tried to show that a reasonable man might believe that the particular philosophy adopted by the Court was wrong, and for this purpose he launched into a detailed discussion of representation practiced in Great Britain, the colonies and early Union, the states at the time of the addition of the Fourteenth Amendment, and the states in contemporary times.[179] He did not seem to consider the argument that while the justices were undeniably adopting a political philosophy, it was one that was included in both federal and state constitutions, one which was assumed to be the backbone of American government, and one which had been considered sufficiently important to receive lip service for many years. Still, the implications disturbed him; the "practical significance of apportionment is that the next election results may differ because of it," and that meant that the case belonged to the "class of political controversy which, by the nature of its subject, is unfit for federal judicial action." [180] It is difficult to tell whether the subject of the claim or the possible consequences of judicial decision is the controlling factor, or if Justice Frankfurter thought them to be identical. In sixty-four pages of dissent, he made it evident that he thought the Court should stay out of non-Negro election cases and should utilize the political question category to do so, but the basis for that conclusion was not made as clear. Presumably, it lay in Justice Frankfurter's doctrine of legislative supremacy—of the judiciary's acceptance of legislative policies because legislatures represent the majority will. What he apparently chose to ignore was that it is possible for the legislature to reflect anything but the majority will, and that this possibility had become the fact in Tennessee.

The most immediate and most practical problem involved in equality of voting strength is of course the exact meaning of "equality." Recognizing that, despite its disavowals, the Court's decision in *Baker* v. *Carr* placed the judicial imprimatur on such equality, Justice Harlan chose to devote himself to the definition the Court avoided. He attached to his opinion an appendix, purporting to indicate the impossibility of establishing an adequate arithmetical formula.[181] Apparently proceeding on the assumption that if a definition of equality was sufficiently elusive, no right to that equality could exist,[182] Harlan, with the concurrence of Frankfurter, declared that there was no right of equal voting weight, and that the case therefore involved no federal question. The Tennessee distribution was not "capricious"; on the contrary, the protection of the agricultural interests from "the sheer weight of numbers" of urbanites was completely rational.[183]

Going beyond this, Harlan objected to the real basis of the majority's decision. He recognized that the Court had acted because the plaintiffs could not get relief elsewhere, and because it gratuitously (as he saw it) assumed that state action would follow judicial. Harlan, however, challenged this assumption:

> At the same time the majority has wholly failed to reckon with what the future may hold in store if this optimistic prediction is not fulfilled. Thus, what the Court is doing reflects more an adventure in judicial experimentation than a solid piece of constitutional adjudication.[184]

What Harlan offered in place of "adventurism" was a blindness as to the nature of judicial activity combined with mathematical computation.

The Georgia County Unit System

Closely related to the reapportionment cases are a number of decisions dealing with Georgia's county unit vote system. Here, again, the Court dramatically reversed itself within a few years, but in this instance it more firmly declined to acknowledge its reversal.

The Neill Primary Act, which was passed in 1917, provided for the nomination of Georgia's senators in the national Senate, her governor, and other state officials. Each of her 159 counties (under the Georgia constitution, the number could not be increased) was given a number of unit votes equal to two times the number of representatives it had in the state House of Representatives. Thus, if a county had one representative in the state House, it was entitled to two unit votes. A maximum of six voters per county was ordered, so that no matter how huge the population of one county might have been, that county could not possibly have more than six votes. The candidate who received the highest popular vote in each county during the Democratic primary was given all of that county's unit votes. As of 1950, eight counties had six votes each, thirty counties had four votes each, and 121 counties had two votes each.[185] At that time, the unit system gave counties votes as follows: [186]

County	Voters	Unit Votes
Quitman	739	2
Cherokee	3,560	2
Dodge	5,113	2
Tattnall	7,396	2
Chattooga	10,378	2
Troup	5,929	6
Burke	1,789	4
Bulloch	10,160	4
Cobb	11,144	4

Counties varied in area from 114 to 965 square miles.[187]

The system had begun in the days when the franchise was based on the ownership of land. There was more land in the rural counties, and it was argued that those counties should therefore have the majority of votes. The Democratic Party continued to utilize the system long after it outlived its legitimate usefulness, and it became an issue in the intra-party fights between urban and rural factions. In 1906, urbanites maneuvered the state Democratic Convention into eliminating the system and scheduling the primaries for the time of year when farmers could not leave their crops to vote, but this decision was reversed by the Convention of 1908. Rural legislators in 1917 prevented a recurrence by seeing that the system was formally codified as the Neill Act. Under this law, candidates for governor and United States Senator had to receive a majority of unit votes; all other office-seekers needed only a plurality.[188] It seems quite obvious that the unit system was designed to preserve rural domination over the growing urban areas. There is no evidence that black disenfranchisement was among the aims of the legislation,[189] but as Georgia's black population gradually migrated to the cities, it came to have that effect.[190] One commentator, writing in 1950, called the system "the mainspring in promoting and maintaining the suppression of Negro voters." [191] Certainly the legislation achieved its primary objective. It led to the "virtual disenfranchisement in primary elections of voters in the urban areas," [192] and the Democratic nomination in Georgia was equivalent to election. It was estimated that the system permitted 5.2 per cent of the people to elect a majority of the State Senate.[193] Appeals to the state legislature, controlled by the very rural representatives and segregationists who benefited from the system, were of course futile, and while the Georgia Constitution provides for referenda in the case of constitutional change, it has no provision for an initative. It is clear that in this case, as with the reapportionment problem, the only relief could come through the courts. Interestingly enough, much the same system was instituted in Tennessee in 1937; the Tennessee Supreme Court, however, invalidated it as an unconstitutional violation of the state constitution's equal protection clause.[194]

The first two cases to reach the Court arrived in tandem, and over both loomed the controversial figure of Eugene Talmadge and the still-smothered problem of segregation. It was the politics of Talmadge and his forebears which, more than any other one factor, divided Georgia into rural and urban entities.[195] He was quoted after the 1946 election as saying that he had been elected by the people "where the street cars don't run," [196] and he was all too accurate. In their reliance on the white rural vote, the Talmadges were heavily aided by the county unit system, which in the two decades prior to 1949 had been responsible for the election of a governor, a state treasurer, a public service commissioner, and a judge of the court of appeals, all of whom had lost the popular vote but had won unit-vote majorities.[197] They and the Talmadges were helped additionally by the high proportion of disenfranchised Negroes in rural areas, which increased the voting power of rural whites even more disproportionately.[198] If a "moderate" segregationist, much less an integrationist, and/or an urban-minded government were ever to be elected in Georgia, the county unit system would have to be nullified.

In 1946, when he was running for governor, Talmadge campaigned on a straightforward platform of strict white supremacy, and loudly warned Georgia blacks to stay away from the polls. His principal opponent was James V. Carmichael, who, although a segregationist, was sufficiently moderate to receive the support of outgoing "liberal" Governor Ellis Arnall. The results of the election were not a new experience for Georgia: although Carmichael received more popular votes than Talmadge,[199] the latter won 242 unit votes to Carmichael's 146. Blacks played a very small part in the election, as those who dared to vote were concentrated in the underrepresented urban centers. A few days after the election, a group of voters, including Mrs. Robert Lee Turman, a former president of the Atlanta League of Women Voters, and Dr. Cullen B. Gosnell, a professor of political science at Emory University, filed a suit asking for an injunction to restrain party and state officials from certifying any candidate in the gubernatorial primary who had received a majority of the county unit votes but not a plurality of the popular vote.[200] At the same time Earl P. Cook, a student at Georgia Tech, filed to have the contest in the Fifth Congressional District nullified.[201] There, incumbent Mrs. Helen Douglas Mankin had received more popular votes than had Judge James C. Davis, who had won on the basis of county units. It was Judge Davis who would appear on the ballot. The district court, finding for the defendants, expressed its disapproval that the actions were brought immediately after the primary election, rather than before,[202] and unanimously upheld the system. Pointing to the example of the Electoral College, it said that equality of voting power was not contemplated by the American form of government, and that as the system was not "irrational," no deprivation of equal protection had occurred. The court agreed that glaring inequalities existed, but, relying on *Colegrove* v. *Green,* suggested that the remedy was "to be sought through changes in the law rather than by appeal to courts of equity to upset the law as unconstitutional because of a hardship that had arisen." [203]

   The Supreme Court dismissed the two cases *per curiam.* Its only citation was *United States* v. *Anchor Coal Co.,*[204] in which a District

Court had been ordered to dismiss the bill of complaint because the controversy had become moot. In the instant case, the District Court had held itself unable to grant an interlocutory injunction, citing *Colegrove* as precluding equitable relief, but it had also stated that the Fourteenth Amendment had not been violated. The Supreme Court did not make clear which argument it supported, and Justice Rutledge objected to this. After summarizing the background of the cases and the lower court's decisions, Rutledge turned to *Colegrove* v. *Green.* The majority opinion there had not indicated whether the jurisdictional question or the merits of the case had been decisive, and for that reason Rutledge felt that the county unit cases should have been given a full hearing. In order to clear up the problem, *Colegrove* should have been reheard.[205]

Colegrove, however, was not reheard, and there the situation rested until 1950. In that year, the Court handed down a *per curiam* decision in the case of *South* v. *Peters.*[206] Two voters residing in Fulton County (City of Atlanta), Georgia's most populous county, felt that a system which made their votes worth only one-tenth of votes cast in other counties was both unreasonable and illegal, and brought suit to restrain adherence to the system in the forthcoming Democratic Party primary. The District Court, acting under the aegis of *Cook* and *Turman,* dismissed the complaint.[207] The Supreme Court decision said only, "Federal courts consistently refuse to exercise their equity powers in cases posing political issues arising from a state's geographical distribution of electoral strength among its political subdivisions."[208] *MacDougall, Colegrove,* and *Wood* v. *Broom* were cited. One was left with the picture of the 1950 Court blithely relying on *stare decisis.* Justices Douglas and Black disagreed with their brethren, and, in an opinion written by Justice Douglas, took this opportunity to make clear the basis of their disagreement. Justice Douglas began his opinion by saying, "I suppose that if a State reduced the vote of Negroes, Catholics, or Jews so that each got only one-tenth of a vote, we would strike the law down."[209] Here the discrimination is "equally invidious"; a vote in one of Georgia's counties is worth 120 times one cast in the plaintiff's county.[210] But this is not the only form of discrimination implicit in the system; since the Negro population is heaviest in the large cities, the system "heavily disenfranchises" them, giving the system its name as "the 'last loophole' around our decisions holding that there must be no discrimination because of race in primary as well as in general elections." [211] Douglas went on to discuss the "right" which had been acknowledged by the Court in *U.S.* v. *Classic, Ex parte Yarbrough, U.S.* v. *Saylor, Nixon* v. *Herndon,* and *Smith* v. *Allwright:*

> There is more to the right to vote than the right to mark a piece of paper and drop it in a box or the right to pull a lever in a voting booth. . . . It also includes the right to have the vote counted at full value without dilution or discount.[212]

Because this right was flagrantly violated by the system, the plaintiff's prayer should have been granted. There would have been no disturbance of the coming election, nor would Georgia have needed to be redistricted:

> The impact of the decree would be on the tallying of votes and the determination of what names go on the general election ballot.[213]

There was ample time to act. No "overhauling of the State's electoral process" would be involved. And urging courage upon his colleagues, Douglas added, "No conflict with any policy of Congress is possible." [214] As a coda he pointed out that the system as allowed to stand undermined the Court's own decisions in the *Nixon, Classic,* and *Allwright* cases.[215]

Two points in the Court's decision should be noted. In accepting the case, the Court apparently assumed that it had equitable jurisdiction, but denied the plea solely as a policy matter. And yet the one-sentence paragraph did not make clear whether the Court was relying on Frankfurter's view in *Colegrove* (lack of jurisdiction because this was not a valid case in equity) or on the Court's opinion in *MacDougall,* which assumed jurisdiction but denied the plea on its merits. The second point, later to be debated in *Gray* v. *Sanders,* was the Court's assumption, disputed by Douglas and Black, that the case involved geographical distribution of electoral strength rather than the right to vote.[216] Perhaps enheartened by *South* v. *Peters,* Governor Herman Talmadge asked the voters in the November, 1950 election to ratify a proposed constitutional amendment which would have applied the system to Georgia's general elections. Because urbanites possessed a majority of the popular votes, the proposal was defeated at the polls, with some

rural counties voting 10-1 in favor of the amendment.[217] And perhaps encouraged in their turn by the defeat, Georgia city dwellers
continued to ask the courts for relief. In 1952, W.M. Cox, a voter
in Cherokee County, brought suit against the Chairman of the
Georgia State Democratic Executive Committee, but his plea was
turned down by the courts.[218] The Court handed down a *per curiam*
opinion rejecting the suit "for the want of a substantial federal
question," with Justices Black and Douglas stating that probable
jurisdiction should have been noted. When Cox requested a rehearing, the Solicitor General of the United States filed as *amicus*
in his behalf, but the Court was not ready to enter this particular
arena, and the case was not reheard.[219]

By 1958, the Mayor of Atlanta, William B. Hartsfield, decided
to see what he could do. Hartsfield was a political moderate, serving
his sixth term as mayor, who argued that the Civil Rights Act
of 1957 gave the Justice Department and the courts a new power
to protect the right to vote. He also claimed that no bar in equity
existed to prevent the courts from handling the case, and therefore
asked for a declaratory judgment against the use of the system
in the forthcoming election of September, 1958. His suit was supported by the Conference of Mayors, which was composed of
mayors of approximately 300 United States cities with populations
of 50,000 and up. District Court Judge Sloan, who was in charge
of the case, refused to call the three-judge panel required whenever
a suit seeks to enjoin a statute as unconstitutional, on the grounds
that the constitutional question involved was "unsubstantial."
Hartsfield thereupon asked the Supreme Court for leave to file
a petition for the writ of mandamus, and this motion was denied
per curiam, over the dissent of Chief Justice Warren and Justices
Black, Douglas, and Brennan.[220] Opponents of the system seemed
to be defeated.

Baker v. *Carr* was decided by the Court on March 26, 1962.
On that day, James O'Hear Sanders, a voter in Fulton County
and the chairman of an Atlanta organization called Active Voters,
sued in a federal District Court to restrain Georgia from utilizing
the system "as a basis for counting votes in a Democratic primary
for the nomination of a United States Senator and statewide officers,
and for declaratory relief." [221] Sanders claimed that the system
violated the equal protection and due process clauses of the Four-

teenth Amendment, and the Seventeenth Amendment. To support his claim, he indicated that although 14.11 per cent of Georgia's population resided in Fulton, that County had only 1.46 per cent of the state's total unit votes; whereas Echols County, with .05 per cent of the population, possessed .48 per cent of the unit votes. One unit vote in Echols was equal to 938 residents, but 92,721 inhabitants of Fulton had among them only one unit vote. A popular vote in Echols was therefore worth 99 times that of one cast in Fulton. The defendants claimed that this system was rationally designed "to achieve a reasonable balance as between urban and rural electoral power." [222]

It had been obvious in Georgia that if the decision in *Baker* v. *Carr* immediately or ultimately supported the urban plaintiffs, a new case challenging the county unit system would reach the courts. Responding to the initiation of *Sanders* v. *Gray*, Governor Ernest Vandiver called a special session of the legislature in mid-April. It revised the system, increasing Fulton County's unit vote weight twenty times, and making other changes: instead of winning a primary with a plurality of unit votes, a candidate now had to receive a majority of both unit and popular votes. Should this necessitate a run-off, that contest would be between the candidates with the highest unit vote and the one who had garnered the most popular votes, and would be decided on the basis of unit votes won in the run-off.[223] According to Justice Harlan, the law as amended resulted in the following figures: [224]

County	Population	Unit Vote	Population per Unit Vote	Ratio to Fulton County
Fulton	556,326	40	13,908	
DeKalb	256,782	20	12,839	
Chatham	188,299	16	11,760	
Muscogee	156,623	14	11,330	
Webster	3,247	2	1,623	8 to 1
Glascock	2,672	2	1,336	10 to 1
Quitman	2,432	2	1,216	11 to 1
Echols	1,876	2	938	14 to 1

The changes were made while the case was in the District Court, which eventually decided it on the basis of the revised law. In spite of the innovations, the District Court held that the system was unconstitutional, and issued the requested injunction. Casting about for an objective standard, the three-judge court said that the system would be valid when the disparity between counties was no greater than that existing among States in the Electoral College.[225] With the choice of a popular election or further amendment of the system before them, the members of the Democratic Executive Committee agreed to hold the 1962 primary on a popular vote basis, and that primary thus became the first popular primary held in Georgia in the twentieth century. Its results were of clear political importance: Carl Sanders, whom the *Times* labelled "a moderate-minded urban resident" [226] was elected governor. In the Fifth Congressional District, Representative James C. Davis, described as "an implacable foe of all forms of racial desegregation and as an implacable conservative on most other political and economic issues," lost his bid for renomination to Charles L. Weltner, "a 'moderate' on the racial issue." Davis, who would have been reelected under the county unit system, had been known as "the Mayor of Washington," since he had utilized his membership in the House Committee on the District of Columbia to "heavily influence(d) the operation of the municipal courts and school system in the capital for many years." And it was Fulton County—more specifically, Atlanta—which, finally allowed the voting weight commensurate with its population, beat him.[227]

Justice Douglas, who wrote the opinion for the Court, agreed with the lower court that the system violated the equal protection clause, but rejected the analogy with the Electoral College because that system was not meant to apply to statewide elections as regulated by the state, and was the outgrowth of a political view (Presidential elections should not be left to the people) rejected by the Fifteenth, Seventeenth, and Nineteenth Amendments.[228] But instead of following the reasoning in *Baker* v. *Carr,* as might have been expected, Douglas based his entire opinion on the well-established right to vote, and his citations were of cases involving that right: [229] *Nixon* v. *Herndon, Nixon* v. *Condon, U.S.* v. *Classic, Ex parte Yarbrough, Wiley* v. *Sinkler,*[230] *Swafford* v. *Templeton, U.S.* v. *Mosley, Ex parte Siebold,*[231] *U.S.* v. *Saylor, Smith* v. *Allwright* and *Terry* v. *Adams.*[232] He specifically rejected the reapportionment cases as controlling:

The present case is only a voting case.[233]

> If a State in a statewide election weighted the male vote more heavily than the female vote or the white vote more heavily than the Negro vote, none could successfully contend that that discrimination was allowable. How then can one person be given twice or ten times the voting power of another person in a statewide election merely because he lives in a rural area or because he lives in the smallest rural county? [234]

> . . . once the class of voters is chosen and their qualifications specified, we see no constitutional way by which equality of voting power may be evaded.[235]

The case was therefore remanded to the District Court.

Justice Harlan dissented. In an angry opinion, he insisted that the case was very much related to *Baker* v. *Carr,* which should not have been decided in the first place.[236] That case had led to a great deal of litigation,[237] and in addition to rejecting a perfectly acceptable philosophy of sectional representation, had neglected to establish a rational arithmetical substitute:

> I do not understand how, on the basis of these mere numbers, unilluminated as they are by any of the complex and subtle political factors involved, a court of law can say, except by judicial fiat, that these disparities are in themselves constitutionally invidious.[238]

Surely, said Harlan, there is nothing unconstitutional or irrational in a state's deciding to ensure itself against a predominance of urban interests.[239] Rejecting Douglas' assertion that government has been or must be based on a rule of "one person, one vote," Harlan cited Frankfurter in *Baker* v. *Carr* to the effect that such had not been the historical case, pointed to the Electoral College as an example of what he meant, and agreed with *Macdougall* v. *Green* that political power is not a function of numbers only.[240] And refusing to agree that previous election cases were controlling, Harlan pointed out that Douglas had not even mentioned the previous four cases which had challenged the system and which the Court had decided quite differently.[241] But if Harlan was annoyed at the majority, Justices Stewart and Clark were just as peeved with him. In a terse concurring opinion of one paragraph, Stewart, joined by Clark, reiterated what they concluded Harlan had maliciously misunderstood: the instant case did not involve "the validity of a State's apportionment of geographic constituencies from which representatives to the State's legislative assembly are chosen," nor was it connected to or concerned with *Baker* v. *Carr*.[242]

The idea that *Gray* v. *Sanders* had nothing to do with *Baker* v. *Carr* is hardly credible. In purely formal terms, it can be said that the issue in one case was a voter's right to have his or her vote counted on the same basis as all the other voters' ballots, and that the problem in the second was that of equality of legislative districts. But such legalistic interpretation of cases rarely does anything except camouflage the true nature of the point in question. In both cases, the Court was asked to decide whether deliberate and increased discrimination by rural officials against urban dwellers was to be permitted to continue. It was requested to do so by private citizens, but their cause was championed by the executive,[243] who, for political purposes, had become their representative. Or, to rephrase the problem slightly, urbanites demanded to know whether a diminishing minority was to be allowed to negate the principle of majority rule.

The Court phrased its answers in terms of "equal protection" and "right to vote." Both of these phrases, however, are derived from a conception of absolute, numerical legal equality, and can have no meaning if they are divorced from that idea. In the Georgia case, the court said, this meant "one person, one vote"; in the Tennessee case, it refused to define the boundaries of the idea. The reason for the disparity explains the Court's reliance upon "the right to vote" in *Gray* v. *Sanders*. In a purely physical sense, there is nothing difficult about counting ballots equally, and in the ideological sphere the slogan of one-man-one vote had a firm ancestry. But it is physically difficult, if not impossible, to draw lines on a map so as to make each section encompass the same number of people. In a highly mobile society, such lines, assuming that they could be drawn one day, would have to be changed with each succeeding day; and people in the same massive apartment building could find themselves in different voting districts. This practical problem was probably responsible, in part, for the lack of definitive ideology concerning the extent to which equality must be an invariable arithmetical entity. Beyond this consideration, the idea that sectional interests should be guaranteed representation in the halls of government, although occasionally antithetical to the philosophy of numerical equality, remained a strong current in American thought. So in this area, there seemed as yet to be no social consensus, even among the underrepresented majority, upon which the Court could draw. And just as a legislator might examine his or her mail in order to discover his or her constituents' thinking, the Court returned the reapportionment case to the lower courts to see what kind of solution might be hammered out and how the electorate would react. Like *Brown* v. *Board of Education*, *Baker* v. *Carr* was "bad law" in that it prepared the way for a flood of litigation that could have been halted by the establishment of an absolute standard. It was good social politics, however, and to the extent that both decisions were to arouse hostility and the enthusiasms which would eventually vanquish opposition, it was clever politics as well.

There may have been a further reason for the Court's caution in *Gray*. Following the *Baker* decision, various states began ratifying one or more of a group of three proposed constitutional amendments. They would have kept the Court out of the reapportionment field, set up a superior court composed of the chief justices of every state, and eliminated the requirement that Congress participate in the constitutional amendment procedure. The Court has weathered innumerable proposed disciplinary amendments in its time, and so it cannot become too alarmed every time a new one appears. Nevertheless, in the weeks immediately following *Baker* v. *Carr*, a number of state legislatures quietly approved the changes.[244] This may have figured in the Court's determined effort to keep echoes of reapportionment out of its decision in *Gray* v. *Sanders*. In addition, the Court may have felt that its mystique had been slightly injured by its about-face in *Baker* v. *Carr*, and therefore chose not to be quite so explicit about its reversal in this instance.

The proposed Constitutional amendments, however, disappeared as soon as their behind-the-scenes existence was made known, and the over-all legislative reaction to *Baker* and *Gray* proved to be relatively mild.[245] Even state legislators found it impossible to deny that malapportionment had reached scandalous proportions, and so instead of lambasting *Baker* they accepted it as given and turned their attention to finding ways of mitigating its sting. It was inevitable that the Court would venture further to overrule *Colegrove* v. *Green.*

The Court was given its opportunity to do so when it heard a suit brought by citizens in Georgia's Fifth Congressional District. The district, composed of three counties, including Fulton County (Atlanta), had a population of 823,680 in 1960, whereas the average population of the ten Georgia districts was 394,312. Such disparity, plaintiffs claimed, constituted a deprivation of the right to vote, in violation of Article I Section 2 of the Federal Constitution; the Due Process, Equal Protection, and Privileges and Immunities Clauses of the Fourteenth Amendment; and Section 2 of the Fourteenth Amendment.[246] The three-judge District Court which heard the case agreed that disparity existed, but utilized Justice Frankfurter's *Colegrove* opinion as the basis for dismissal.[247]

Justice Black, speaking for the majority of six, rejected the reliance on what he pointedly referred to as "Mr. Justice Frankfurter's minority opinion" and stated that the reasoning which led to the *Baker* decision was applicable to the instant case.[248] He quoted the Court's holding in *Baker* that *"Smiley, Koenig* and *Carroll* settled the issue in favor of justiciability of questions of congressional redistricting." [249] The problem than became Frankfurter's contention that Article I Section 4 [250] put final disposition of apportionment questions in the hands of Congress. "The right to vote", said Black, "is too important in our free society to be stripped of judicial protection by such an interpretation . . . "[251]

> . . . nothing in the language of that article gives support to a construction that would immunize state congressional apportionment laws which debase a citizen's right to vote from the power of courts to protect the constitutional rights of individuals from legislative destruction, a power recognized at least since our decision in *Marbury* v. *Madison* . . .[252]

If Black's citation of *Marbury* v. *Madison* in a reapportionment case is startling, it nevertheless serves as a clue to his approach. He apparently saw the problem as a conflict between a state legislature and a citizen's federally-protected rights (a reversal of the interposition doctrine), rather than between Congress and the Court.[253] Where civil rights are involved, of course, Justice Black was on the side of the individual. He chose to base his decision on Article I Section 2 [254] rather than on Equal Protection, presumably as an answer both to Justice Frankfurter and to Justice Harlan's dissent, but the libertarian rationale is apparent nonetheless.

Holding that Article I Section 2 "means that as nearly as is practicable one man's vote in a congressional election is to be worth as much as another's",[255] Black attempted to support his interpretation by sketching the political situation which resulted in the Constitutional Convention's adoption of the "Great Compromise".[256] The assumption at the Convention and during the ratification controversy, Black maintained, was that equal numbers of people would have equal representation in the House.[257] Citing earlier cases involving voting,[258] Black concluded in a paragraph seemingly aimed at Justice Harlan's dissent in *Baker* v. *Carr*:

> While it may not be possible to draw congressional districts with mathematical precision, that is no excuse for ignoring our Constitution's plain objective of making equal representation for equal numbers of people the fundamental goal of the House of Representatives.[259]

The lower court decision was reversed and the case remanded.[260]

Justice Clark, concurring in part and dissenting in part, agreed that courts could scrutinize congressional districting but disagreed with Justice Black's historical survey insofar as it found that "one person, one vote" was written into the Constitution.[261] He would have decided the case on the basis of the Equal Protection Clause, remanding it for a hearing on the merits. The lower court, added Clark, "should apply the standards laid down in *Baker* v. *Carr.*"[262] He did not explain what "standards" he was discussing. The only thing approaching a standard that *Baker* yields is the requirement of rationality, which in this context means that sharp differences among the populations of various districts will not be accepted if those differences are not logically and constitutionally justifiable. The problem of defining "logically" and "constitutionally" remains in spite of the partial definition of constitutionality as not involving "invidious discrimination" or "crazy quilts".[263]

Justice Harlan's dissent is a much better put-together piece of work than his earlier opinions in *Baker* v. *Carr* and *Gray* v. *Sanders*. Deploring a decision that "cast grave doubt on the constitutionality of the composition of the House of Representatives", Harlan pointed out that

> The Court's "as nearly as is practicable" formula sweeps a host
> of questions under the rug.[264]

As discussed above, the Court's sweeping was deliberately designed
to enable lower courts to feel their way through to an acceptable
solution which would then be adopted by the Court. But, although
Harlan criticized the lack of a numerical standard, he did not
approve of the Court's "focusing exclusively on numbers" as a
criterion, disregarding "area and shape" of a district, "as well as
party affiliations" within it. Numerical "abstractions" bore "little
relevance to the realities of political life." [265]

The right to vote was not at issue, said Harlan; "All of the
appellants do vote." [266] The real problem was "the Court's confusion
of two issues: direct election of Representatives within the States
and the apportionment of Representatives among the States." [267]
Although many, "perhaps most", of the delegates to the Convention
believed in representation on the basis of population within each
state, "they did not surreptitiously slip their belief into the Constitution . . . to be discovered 175 years later like a Shakespearian
anagram." [268] Indeed, they twice rejected that belief: by creating
the three-fifths rule, which indicated that the Convention thought
of Representatives as representing a whole state, including nonvot-
ing groups; and by guaranteeing each state one Representative
no matter how small its population.[269]

Even were such a belief written into the Constitution, Article
I Section 4 made it clear to Harlan that "the supervisory power"
was given to Congress.[270] And if that was not enough for the Court,
statements at the Convention and immediately thereafter indicated
that the "one person, one vote" principle had far from universal
acceptance, and that districting was considered to be a matter for
resolution by state legislatures under the eye of Congress.[271]

And, he continued, Congress had been watchful. In spite of the
"unstated premise of the Court's conclusion . . . that the Congress
has not dealt, and . . . will not deal, with the problem of congressional apportionment in accordance with what the Court believes
to be sound political principles", Congress had acted.[272] The legislative history of Section 3 of the 1911 Act and similar sections of
other acts meant that "the Court is not simply undertaking to
exercise a power which the Constitution reserves to the Congress;
it is also overruling congressional judgment." [273]

Voting cases, Harlan added, were irrelevant. The Court should have dealt with the views expressed by Justice Frankfurter in *Colegrove* v. *Green,* especially as *Baker* v. *Carr* did not discuss the meaning of Article I Sections 2 and 4 and therefore could not be relied upon here.[274]

Asserting that the court's decision "strikes at one of the fundamental doctrines of our system of government, the separation of powers", Harlan took issue with the majority's conception of its role: the Court's stability, said Harlan, was dependent upon its recognition of its limitations, for the Constitution "does not confer on the Court blanket authority to step into every situation where the political branch may be thought to have fallen short." [275]

> What is done today saps the political process. The promise of judicial intervention in matters of this sort cannot but encourage popular inertia in efforts for political reform through the political process, with the inevitable result that the process is itself weakened.[276]

Harlan may have been right—but to which corner of the political process was Sanders to turn? Perhaps the sapping was done by Congress and the state legislatures rather than the Court.[277]

There was nothing hidden about the significance of *Wesberry* v. *Sanders.* It would have an impact on the make-up of future Congresses, it sharply limited the scope of the political question, and it reiterated a far-reaching conception of the judicial function. The serene reaction to *Wesberry* was therefore almost extraordinary. As Anthony Lewis noted,

> Most Congressmen who spoke out had no quarrel with the idea that grossly unequal districts are intolerable. The Texas delegation in the House, which fears possible at-large election if the legislature does not redistrict, sought some way to delay the judicial day of reckoning, but even it did not criticize the substance of the decision.
> The fact is that inequality among Congressional districts is so notorious and of such long standing that even the beneficiaries of the discrimination do not defend it in principle. The proposition that people in a rural area should have two or three Representatives while the same number in a city have one is not easy to argue.[278]

The response to *Baker* and *Wesberry* enhanced the strength and prestige of the Court in particular and courts in general even where the reaction to the decisions was negative. No state legislature refused to reapportion; a number acted relatively quickly.[279] The mass of litigation generated by the two cases indicated that opponents of reapportionment would expend the major portion of their energies in a judicial rather than a legislative setting. Thus, presumably emboldened by the reception of *Baker* and *Wesberry*, the Court could push further into the thicket.

Still unresolved was the question of what constituted a legitimately apportioned state legislature. Blatant discrimination was now illegal, but the Court had not told legislatures how much they could diverge from a numerical standard. What considerations could be given to the representation of minorities? Was numerical representation to be considered more important than the representation of groups with similar interests? The answers to these questions lay in the realm of political theory, and it was an indication of how far the Court had gone since *Colegrove* that it marched right in. *Reynolds* v. *Sims* [280] followed *Wesberry* v. *Sanders* by a short five months.

The fact situation leading to the *Reynolds* case could have been duplicated almost anywhere in the nation. As of 1961, when the case was begun, Alabama's most recent reapportionment had been based on the 1900 federal census figures. 25.1% of the people controlled the majority in the state Senate; 25.7% lived in districts which elected that of the Assembly.[281] The smallest assembly district included 6,731 people; the largest, 104,767. Similar figures for the Senate were 15,417 and 634,864.[282] A group of voters in the largest district therefore filed a complaint challenging the constitutionality of the apportionment and asking that a three-judge District Court be convened to enjoin further elections unless reapportionment took place. On March 29, 1962, three days after *Baker* was handed down, the plaintiffs asked the court to issue an injunction requiring the 1962 legislative primaries and elections to be held at large. The court responded by setting the case for hearing on July 16 and suggesting strongly that if the legislature did not act before that date the court would probably revamp the districts itself and assign more legislators to underrepresented areas. Alabama's Legislature thereupon went into Extraordinary Session and on July 12 announced that it had adopted two plans, one of which would go into effect in time for the 1966 elections. The first plan consisted of a proposed constitutional amendment which would allow the

Senate to be controlled by 19.4% of the electorate and the House by 43%. The second plan would be utilized if the proposed amendment was rejected by the voters or negated by the federal courts. It took the form of a legislative enactment permitting 27.6% of the people to control a majority in the Senate and 37% to control a majority in the House.[283] Four days before the deadline, then, Alabama belatedly took action by suggesting plans which would not go into effect for four years and which would then render apportionment even more unequal.

On July 21, the District Court found the old apportionment and both proposed plans to be in violation of the Equal Protection clause of the Constitution.[284] It ordered a temporary amalgam of the two rejected plans to be utilized for the 1962 election, with the House to be chosen according to the formula established by the proposed amendment and the Senate to be elected on the basis of the new statute.[285] The legislature thus elected in 1962 adhered faithfully to the pattern of its predecessors by adjourning in 1963 without taking action on the apportionment problem. It was not scheduled to meet again until 1965.[286] This was the situation when the Supreme Court heard and decided the case.

Asked by Solicitor General Cox, among others, to affirm the decision of the lower court, and seemingly confident of the country's support, the Court no longer needed to camouflage what it was doing. Chief Justice Warren, writing for a majority of six,[287] could openly connect voting and reapportionment cases and announce that, taken as a whole, they established the axiom that "the fundamental principle of representative government in this country is one of equal representation for equal numbers of people." [288] Justice Douglas' careful differentiation of the two categories of cases in *Gray* v. *Sanders* was abandoned. Although *Reynolds* would take the Court farther into the political thicket than it had yet dared to go, it could no longer be doubted that the nation would follow. "One man-one vote" had become the accepted criterion for apportionment schemes, and the only question remaining was "whether there are any constitutionally cognizable principles which would justify departures" from this "basic standard." [289] The answer was no.

> Legislators represent people, not trees or acres. Legislators are elected by voters, not farms or cities or economic interests. As long

as ours is a representative form of government, and our legislatures are those instruments of government elected directly by and directly representative of the people, the right to elect legislators in a free and unimpaired fashion is a bedrock of our political system . . . if a State should provide that the votes of citizens in one part of the State should be given two times, or five times, or 10 times the weight of votes of citizens in another part of the State, it could hardly be contended that the right to vote of those residing in the disfavored areas had not been effectively diluted . . . the effect of state legislative districting schemes which give the same number of representatives to unequal numbers of constituents is identical.[290]

An apportionment law which deviates from the standard therefore creates an impermissible and invidious discrimination, for

Population is, of necessity, the starting point for consideration and the controlling criterion for judgment in legislative apportionment controversies.[291]

Discrimination on the basis of place of residence is a denial of constitutionally protected rights. When such discrimination occurs, it is the duty of the Court to intervene.[292]

The legal importance of *Reynolds* is that it follows this chain of reasoning to conclude that "both houses of a . . . state legislature must be apportioned on a population basis." [293] Any other system would endanger individual and majority rights.[294] The Court's position is clear: *Colegrove's* doctrine of judicial non-involvement has been obliterated.

It must not be thought that *Reynolds* came into existence as a landmark decision only because the Court tentatively ventured into the realm of apportionment and reacted to electoral acceptance.[295] by gradually expanding its rulings. *Reynolds* was not produced by a simple snowball effect. Passages in the Court's opinion make it clear that Warren and the majority of his colleagues were concerned about a particular political problem: the possibility of effective political action by the individual in twentieth century America. The word "effective" is prominent in a key paragraph:

State legislatures are, historically, the fountainhead of representative government in this country . . . representative government is in essence self-government through the medium of elected representatives of the people, and each and every citizen has an inalienable right to full and effective participation in the political processes of his State's legislative bodies. Most citizens can achieve this participation only as qualified voters through the election of legislators to represent them. Full and effective participation by all citizens in state government requires, therefore, that each citizen have an equally effective voice in the election of members of his state legislature. Modern and viable state government needs, and the Constitution demands, no less.[296]

There is no use pretending that the above passage does not define "a republican form of government", partial though the definition may be. "Representative" is substituted for "republican" but the meaning is clear. The Court, doing no more than it has always done, has proclaimed its answer to a political problem. In *Reynolds* the Court responded to the most political of problems in a republic: that of who shall wield ultimate power. It involved itself in the politics of the people and emerged unscathed, still clothed in the garb of constitutionalism. This is surely no more and no less than the legitimate function of the Court. It is highlighted by the last sentence quoted above. Warren does not claim to be doing anything more than interpreting the Constitution, and yet he is admittedly influenced by the needs of viable government. The two seemingly contradictory functions—interpreting a fixed piece of paper and enabling a government to change itself as the circumstances of its electorate change—are reconciled by the underlying assumption that the Constitution was written precisely so that it could undergo constant transformation. Warren and his Court obviously believed that although neither the original framers of the Constitution nor the writers of the Equal Protection clause could foresee a nation of fifty states and over 200,000,000 people, they meant those people to live under a representative government—whatever "representative" might have to mean at any given historical moment. Only the goal remains constant; the means must vary if the goal is to be kept alive, and the guardians of the written goal must verify the legitimacy of each procedure as its appropriateness becomes apparent. It is thus no exercise in sophistry for Warren to say that the Constitution demands whatever the government needs as long as that government retains the outlines established by the Constitution. The real argument of the Court's critics is that the government does not need what the Court gives it (or, conversely, that it needs more). The existence of a need, however, is a value judgment that can be made only by the majority of the people in a democratic society. The Court will not proclaim the presence of a need without a reasonable expectation that the people will validate the proclamation by ensuring its enforcement, and that they will do so because the judgment is one that, however inarticulately, they have already made. Certainly the Court can misread the temper of the people, but it requires evidence that its reading is correct before it will continue to hand down a series of decisions in the service of a particular idea.* The idea here is one man-one vote, and the people clearly accepted both it and the legitimacy of its expression by the Court.

Recognizing this, Warren could go on to deal with the practical problems that arise once a theory is accepted as given. Of what value is bicameralism if the population standard is required? [297] What factors other than population, if any, may be considered in reapportioning? [298] How frequent must reapportionment be? [299] What kinds of action should lower courts take if legislatures do not properly apportion themselves? [300] The remainder of his opinion attempts to suggest solutions. Whether or not his solutions are wise, they indicate the Court's realization that enforcement of the answers can be taken for granted and does not present a "political question".

---

* The idea of the Court responding to "the people" should be amplified. The majority of the people have the power thru the electoral process, to confer ultimate political legitimacy on a decision made by one or more of the branches of government. General dissatisfaction with the record of a President or a Congress—or non-specific dissatisfaction with the state of things in general—can lead to a defeat at the polls for the incumbents. Dissatisfaction with the actions of the Court can be manifested by the President, who can refuse to enforce a decision; by the Congress, through the threat or actuality of limitation of appellate jurisdiction; or by candidates for office, as in Nixon's 1968 campaign. All of this is after the fact. The "people" who are instrumental in the formulation of policy constitute an elite. Depending on which theory of elitist rule one accepts, "elite" can mean a relatively static and coherent entity or a fluctuating coalition of groups and interests. In either case, the Court responds to the consensus of outside forces (elites) which matter to it: the legal profession, particularly the decisions of lower court judges and that portion of the intelligentsia which filters the intellectual trends of the day through its law review articles; the President and Congress, etc. Presumably all of these forces make demands predicated in good part upon their assessment of a combination of the needs of the people and the potential for popular acceptance of a policy. (The legal elite may be slightly more concerned with needs, the members of government more concerned with acceptance; the ratio obviously varies, as does the proportion of self-interest.) "The temper of the people" which is read by the Court is actually the elite's assessment of what it ought to and can do. Popular rule legitimizes or negates the assessment. Cf. Thomas R. Dye and L. Harmon Zeigler: *The Irony of Democracy: An Uncommon Introduction to American Politics* (Belmont, California: Wadsworth Publishing Co., Inc., 1971).

Dissenting from this view, Justice Harlan argued against both the Court's political role and its definition of representation. He charged that *Wesberry, Gray,* and *Reynolds* placed "basic aspects of state political systems under the pervasive overlordship of the federal judiciary." [301] The Court was involving itself and lower courts too actively in the affairs of the state legislatures.[302] The consequences of *Wesberry* and *Reynolds* would be the same:

> . . . I believe that the vitality of our political system, on which in the last analysis all else depends, is weakened by reliance on the judiciary for political reform; in time a complacent body politic may result.[303]

As in *Wesberry,* he may or may not have been correct, but the overriding point for the majority of the Court was that individual rights were being violated. Harlan also took issue with his brethren by contending that although it is true that legislators represent people,

> . . . it is surely equally obvious, and, in the context of election, more meaningful to note that people are not ciphers and that legislators can represent their electors only by speaking for their interests—economic, social, political—many of which do not reflect the place where the electors live.[304]

Again, either view may be correct. The importance of the debate about possible definitions of representation is precisely that it occurred—that the Court's decision necessarily involved acceptance of a particular political ideology, as do all Court decisions, and that the choice was made unhesitatingly because a societal consensus guaranteed enforcement.

On the same day it announced the *Reynolds* rule, and as if to show how far it could safely go, the Court handed down five decisions invalidating as many apportionment schemes.[305] One of the approaches overturned had been incorporated in a constitutional amendment ratified by the voters. The Court disposed of this by declaring that

> A citizen's constitutional rights can hardly be infringed simply because a majority of the people choose that it be.[306]

A week later, the Court used the same principles to decide ten more reapportionment cases in memorandum decisions.[307] Thus, in a few days, it had struck down apportionment enactments in fifteen states [308] and had issued a rule which meant that

> at least one house of the legislature in virtually every state, and in most instances both houses, are punatively unconstitutional, whether or not formally so declared.[309]

It had raised enormous questions, both of theory and of implementation.[310] It had publicly engaged in an ideological debate about the nature of republicanism, with Justice Warren insisting on a rigid interpretation of one man-one vote, Justices Stewart and Clark advocating the more flexible test of rationality, and Justice Harlan demanding that the Court leave all the defining to someone else. It had enmeshed itself in the politics of the people as thoroughly as was humanly and institutionally possible. And no thunderbolts crashed from on high; no citizens took to the barricades; Earl Warren was not impeached. Even the persistent fog-horn of Everett Dirksen failed to rouse the Congress or the electorate to punitive action.[311] In the midst of Senator Dirksen's short-lived attempt to stir Congress to righteous legislative fury, Senator Douglas could cite a Gallup poll showing the nation behind the Court's ruling by 3 to 2.

The lack of public outcry is more surprising still when it is remembered that the Court had refused even to discuss the problems of reapportionment less than twenty years earlier. During those years, a good many societal changes (particularly in urban areas) had gradually led to public willingness to deal with the problems the changes brought with them. The same years brought the Court's reevaluation of itself and public acceptance of a Court which donned a new political face.

That the "new look" of the Court was radical is beyond question, for its essential component was a claim that the judiciary exists—at least in part—to remedy all wrongs suffered by the citizenry, when no other instrument of reform is available. Captained by Justices Black and Warren, the Court announced its intention of implementing a myth; of replacing illusion with reality. The vision of the judiciary as policeman, standing between a liberty-loving populace and a many-tenacled government, its proudly muscled arm raised in an indomitable "No further!", became the glowing idea of a possibly astigmatic Court. But there is more: above the unbowed head of the Guardian of the Law waves a banner proclaiming "Fairness". And in the name of that euphemism for Justice, the Court marched on.

What the Court did was no less than to effect the substitution of an active for a relatively passive conception of the judicial function. In the years immediately preceding the reapportionment cases, the Court was viewed as a champion of civil liberties and the filter through which emerging revisions of the idea of government and society flowed in order to become part of the law of the land. Now the Court declared that it would seek out wrongs and correct them, even when to do so required an invasion of hitherto inviolate Congressional territory. Where no other governmental organ chose to heed a societal consensus, the Court would not hesitate to do so.

Whether or not Congress became somewhat emasculated in the process, and whatever the swing back to judicial restraint found in the Burger Court, a new chapter in the history of the interaction between Congress and the Court was written. In 1954 the Court acted; in 1964 Congress belatedly followed. While this is not to suggest that the Court's action in *Brown* v. *Board of Education* was the sole or most important motivation for the passage of the Civil Rights bills, or even that the Court was an absolutely necessary catalyst for the events which were the important factors behind the legislation, the chronology is suggestive.

Brown v. *Board* and the reapportionment cases are closely connected when viewed as a response by the Court to the problem of an unrepresentative Congress. Justice Black's form of libertarian activism was given a boost by the necessity for the Court to deal with segregation and with reapportionment. To what extent might the segregation decisions have been rendered superfluous by representatives from equal, compact, and continguous districts? The question is as intriguing as it is impossible of solution. The answer would probably not be "entirely", but might not it be "somewhat"?

The nature of the political question did not change in 1962. What did happen is that societal consensus in the area of reapportionment, coupled with legislative reluctance to act, opened the way for a libertarian Court to proclaim the ascendancy of a particular judicial philosophy. The Court followed its fiat in *Wesberry* with a series of decisions striking down various apportionments

of state legislative and Congressional districts and extending the
one man-one vote doctrine to various kinds of local governmental
entities.[312] There can be no doubt that the reapportionment decisions
as a whole represented a triumph, desirable or not, for judicial
activism. Like most judicial triumphs, however, this one has been
shown to have its limitations. The justices have found it wiser not
to penetrate all the way into the political thicket. In 1972, the
Court denied certiorari to an appeal from a decision by the Court
of Appeals for the District of Columbia that delegates to the 1972
Democratic National Convention need not be divided among the
states on a strict basis of one-Democrat, one vote.[313] There are
aspects of apportionment that may yet constitute a political question.

CHAPTER 4

LAWS AND ELECTIONS

During the history of the Court, a number of cases have arisen in which various laws have been challenged on procedural grounds; e.g., they were not passed properly, they were not signed properly, etc. Logically, there is no reason for the Court to place these cases in a special category; a bill which has been promulgated within a state by a governor without having received the legislature's consent would certainly be declared void as an unconstitutional usurpation of power.[1] There can be no question that it would be just as illegal as a properly passed bill which contained unconstitutional provisions. The Court has nevertheless chosen to give these cases a career which bears a checkered look, and has enunciated three different and conflicting doctrines: the Court will decide such cases; the Court will not decide such cases; the Court will claim not to decide such cases but will actually do so in *obiter dicta*. The reasons for this disparity must be examined. Before the various instances are dissected, however, one observation should be made. It has become apparent that the Court will not strike down a functioning government, when to do so would be to negate a chain of actions performed by that government and its citizens during its existence. Besides creating chaos in a particular case, it would undermine the confidence of the people in any government to establish the doctrine that a government and its acts could at any time be declared retroactively illegal. The problem necessarily exists side-by-side with judicial review, and its possible consequences are undoubtedly among the reasons for the Court's self-limiting policy in the constitutional area. Laws would not be obeyed if the mathematical probability of their being struck down was high. The situation is similar in the procedural area. The Court wishes to avoid both immediate chaos and a chaotic precedent, and so it is likely that it will skirt the issue wherever possible.

And here, again, the difficulty of enforcement appears. Can the justices give life to a man who was executed under a law which is now being challenged on the grounds that it was improperly passed? Surely if the substance of the act is constitutional, the Court will be strongly inclined to let it stand. But with its prestige as a wise and honest institution constantly in the balance, the Court cannot simply say, "This act wasn't passed properly, but we're going to let it stand anyway." It doesn't have to; the exit is clearly marked; it can label this a political question and defer with all constitutional propriety to the other branches of government. And of course this is what happens when the Court dislikes a bill but dislikes even more the prospect of striking it down. However, there are occasions on which the Court believes a bill has been properly passed. It can't come out and say so, because to do this would be to set the precedent of deciding such issues instead of dropping them into the lap of the "political branches." Nevertheless, the Court wishes to make it clear that it is not advocating remedial action on the part of the legislature or executive, and so it adds to its opinion an *obiter dictum* stating the reasons for which it would uphold the mechanical proceedings behind the act, if it could. Eating one's cake and having it is rumored to be impossible. Perhaps the Court's maneuvers in these cases will enhearten optimists.

The first such case to reach the Court was *Gardner* v. *The Collector,* in 1867.[2] Congress had passed a bill which set certain duties on tea, and the act had been signed by President Lincoln. Gardner, a merchant, refused to comply with the terms of the act, claiming that the bill was illegal because Lincoln had neglected to indicate the year in which he signed it. All registered bills must include the date on which the executive signed them, said Gardner, so that *ex post facto* laws can be prevented. Justice Miller and the entire Court apparently did not see the possible implications of deciding the case; they did see that Gardner's claim had no merit. Agreeing with the government's argument that the Constitution does not require the President to indicate the date when signing a bill into law, Miller said that Congressional statutes implied that the date could be ascertained by examining the Secretary of State's files. It was his duty to receive all bills and indicate the date of Presidential approval, which date is the day the law went into effect.[3] Far from treating this as a political question, Justice Miller attempted to lay down guidelines for future litigation in this area. The Court, in deciding such questions, could take judicial notice of the Secretary's files, the Congressional journals, the President's messages, and any other facts which it considered "circumstantial" or "capable of conveying to the judicial mind a clear and satisfactory answer." [4] To Justice Miller and eight other justices, questions of procedure were not appreciably different from those involving substance.

The *Gardner* case was relatively uncomplicated. As Miller pointed out, it was not necessary for the President to indicate a date, and so the claim was unfounded. In 1871, the Court was handed a more complicated and much more potentially explosive issue. It was in effect asked to decide whether Congress had coerced Georgia into accepting the constitution she had adopted during the Reconstruction period. [5] The Court found this to be a political question; the rather obvious conclusion is that it had no desire to enter the politically charged thicket surrounding Reconstruction—especially as a good case could be made that coercion *had* been employed. Justice Swayne said that as Congress had recognized the constitution as legitimate, that action "cannot be inquired into. The case is clearly one in which the judicial is bound to follow the action of the political department of the government, and is concluded by it." [6]

Having called such questions justiciable in 1867 and political in 1871, the Court relabeled them justiciable in 1875 and political in 1891. The 1875 case was *Phillips* v. *Payne.* [7] Virginia had ceded a piece of territory to the United States to become part of the District of Columbia. Congress decided not to use the gift, and under the referendum it thereupon authorized, the territory's residents opted to rejoin Virginia. Virginia promptly resumed rule of the land, now titled Alexandria County. In 1875, Virginia's right to the territory was challenged by a resident and taxpayer who asked the Court to nullify a government which had been exercising power since 1847 with the explicit approval of Congress. Both Virginia and the Congress wanted the state to control the territory. Neither was prepared to face the question of how Virginia's actions in the county between 1847 and 1875 were to be justified if its rule during those years was now labeled illegitimate. With Congress and Virginia in agreement and with the residents' referendum as further encouragement, the Court could ignore the plaintiff's contention that procedural irregularities voided the law authorizing the referendum. A unanimous Court held that as Virginia was the

government *de facto* of the land, under United States law it was
the government *de jure* as well. Justice Swayne for the Court
discussed previous political question cases and specifically rejected
them as controlling here. His reasons were plain: Congress had
passed the referendum act, Virginia had been running the territory
since 1847, the United States had not objected to that rule, and
Congress had recognized its validity in subsequent acts.[8] Here again,
the Court would not strike down a functioning government.

A more difficult problem reached the Court in 1891.[9] The Congress of 1890 had passed a tariff bill, one section of which was
omitted by error when the bill was signed by the Vice President,
the Speaker, and the President. Marshall Field & Co., which had
paid duties under other sections of the act, sued to recover these
monies on the grounds that the omission voided the Act.[10] This
claim could not be dismissed as lightly as Gardner's had been;
here the President had signed a bill different from that which had
been passed. Justice Harlan's opinion for the majority clearly indicated that he was aware of the possible implications of the case.
He mentioned that it was the first occasion on which the Court
had had to decide what evidence it could consider when a claim
was made that a bill had not been passed by Congress, and went
on to examine the consequences of that decision:

> . . . we cannot be unmindful of the consequences that must result
> if this court should feel obliged, in fidelity to the Constitution, to
> declare that an enrolled bill, on which depend public and private
> interests of vast magnitude, and which has been authenticated by
> the signature of the presiding officers of the two houses of Congress,
> and by the approval of the President, and been deposited in the
> public archives, *as an act of Congress,* was not in fact passed by
> the House of Representatives and the Senate, and therefore did
> not become a law.[11]

Field had claimed that the Court was bound by the Congressional
journals, because otherwise a conspiracy of President and presiding
officers could sign into law bills that had not been approved by
Congress.[12] Harlan rejected the idea, both because it violated "the
respect due to a coordinate branch of the government" and because
he felt it would be foolhardy for the validity of a law to depend
upon the efficiency of the "subordinate officers" who kept the
journals. Surely it was wiser to accept the signatures of the two

presiding officers and of the President and the receipt by the Secretary of State as conclusive evidence of legal passage.[13] The signing of the bill by all three and the placing of it in the Secretary's custody was a "solemn assurance" that it had been passed by the legislature.

> The respect due to coequal and independent departments requires the judicial department to act upon that assurance, and to accept, as having passed Congress, all bills authenticated in the manner stated: leaving the courts to determine, when the question properly arises, whether the act, so authenticated, is in conformity with the Constitution.[14]

The Court thus agreed to be bound by the word of three members of the executive branch (President, Vice president, Secretary of State) and one of the legislative (Speaker), and in effect removed itself from this sphere.[15] Perhaps Justice Harlan was wise enough to understand the enforcement problems which were latent in every problem of certification. When the executive signs a bill and his Secretary of State receives it, the bill has become a law—and it is the executive who carries out laws of the land. The spectacle of a Court declaring that a bill had not become a law while the President went about executing it would not be welcome, least of all to the Court. In areas which involve executive discretion, the Court cannot afford to be less than excessively cautious.

During the year in which the Field case was decided, a state case reached the Court.[16] Dick Duncan, who had been convicted of murder, questioned the validity of the "Penal Code and Code of Criminal Procedure" under which he had been tried, claiming that it had not been properly enacted by the Texas legislature and therefore constituted a violation of due process and equal protection. Duncan asserted that the bill had not followed the required constitutional procedure: it had not been referred to committee or read in each house of the legislature on three days; the versions of the two houses did not agree, and neither house had kept a journal; the copy filed with the Secretary of State differed from that codified in the Revised Statutes; etc.[17] In addition, Duncan claimed that the judges of the Texas Court of Appeals, where his appeal was pending, had an interest in the case, because the statutes involved bore a relationship to their jobs and salaries.[18] Chief Justice Fuller, in a rather circular opinion, agreed that all legislative acts had to conform to the constitution, but held that the decision as to the existence of that conformity had to be made by the state courts.[19] He denied the allegation that the Texas court was not qualified to sit, and pointed out that courts in that state had earlier upheld the validity of the law in question.[20] Part of the reasoning behind his decision was explicit:

> For eleven years prior to the conviction of Duncan, these codes had been recognized and observed by the people of Texas; had been amended by the legislature and republished under its authority; and their provisions had been repeatedly construed and enforced by the courts as the law of the land.[21]

Once again, legal relief was denied for political reasons—and, perhaps, because the Court declined to question the legitimacy of judicial motivation. Justice Fuller's rhetoric about a republican form of government requiring that the laws be consistent with the constitution seems no more than an attempt to camouflage his Court's refusal to alleviate an unethical situation.

All of these cases were brought by citizens questioning the legitimacy of certain acts performed by the officials they had elected, and who were presumably responsible to them. Ignoring the political question for a moment, the legal doctrine involved is clear: under a philosophy of popular sovereignty, an elected official cannot legitimately undertake any kinds of action other than those contemplated by his electors when they chose him. The categories available to him are stated in the fundamental law, or list of categories, under which the government was established by the people, and in all subsequent elucidation of those categories, or legislation (and judicial opinions). Thus if an official is accused of violating his trust, of attempting to negate the categories by executing a deed not included in them (e.g., the President's allegedly causing a bill which had not been passed by the legislature to be promulgated, thus himself legislating and overstepping the boundaries of the executive category, as in *Field* v. *Clark*), the Court recognizes the dominant philosophy by pleading powerlessness to validate an act which had not received the permission of the citizenry.

The problem is somewhat different when the legitimacy of a constitutional amendment is questioned, for then one of the people challenges a decree to which the majority of the people has given its explicit approval (usually through its elected representatives). The existence of judicial review can be defended only if the judiciary is envisioned as a watchdog, guaranteeing that the provisions of the contract between the people and their government are maintained intact. What, however, can be the justification for a court, which is supposedly the instrument of the people, preventing the majority from changing the categories which they originated? If the concomitant of popular sovereignty is assumed to be majority sovereignty, the only situation in which such a step would be acceptable is one in which the announced will of the people is not their true will—votes were deliberately miscounted, the amendment was promulgated before the requisite number of states had ratified it, etc. Concerned with self-preservation as well as with legitimacy, a court which chose to intrude upon the mystique surrounding the "will of the people" would have to be absolutely certain that either deliberate fraud or glaring error was involved. Such a situation may be possible, but it has not yet arisen in American constitutional history. The chances are good that it never will, or at least that it will never be judicially recognized if it does, because the judiciary-cuminterest group understandably prefers to leave self-destruction to other bodies. It would take either a very brave or a very foolhardy court to invalidate a constitutional amendment.

This explains the Court's decisions in the five relevant cases, all of which were implicitly or explicitly treated as political questions. Of course the fact situation varied with each case, but the Court's motivation did not: this particular hot potato was too likely to burn.

The first announcement of this doctrine appeared as a relatively innocuous aside in the *National Prohibition Cases*.[22] Justice Van Devanter assumed that the Eighteenth Amendment had been properly enacted, implying that the Secretary of State's 1919 proclamation of the Amendment as ratified was proof enough for him.[23] He later had occasion to deal again with the legitimacy of this Amendment, when it was challenged on the grounds that Congress had acted unconstitutionally in setting a limit on the time period during which the proposed amendment had to be ratified.[24] The timespan in question was seven years. Speaking for a unanimous Court, Van Devanter held that it was within Congress' power to arrange the details incident to ratification, and that the definition of a reasonable period of time was one of these details.[25] In effect, then, he said that the Court would be bound by Congress' decision, whatever that decision might be; procedural details concerning amendment are Congress' business, and the Court would not intrude. This was his decision, and this was all he had to say. But then he apparently felt constrained to indicate the justices' agreement with Congress. The Constitution implied that ratification should be "sufficiently contemporaneous" in three quarters of the States "to reflect the will of the people in all sections at relatively the same period, which of course ratification scattered through a long series of years would not do," and the periods of time necessary for ratification of previous amendments indicated that seven years could not be considered unreasonable.[26] After refusing to interfere with Congress' absolute power in this sphere, Van Devanter interfered sufficiently to pat Congress on the back for being so reasonable. In effect, he decided the case on its merits but managed not to set a precedent for doing so again.

The next case was handled somewhat differently. A group of male voters in Maryland sued to have the names of women voters stricken from the register, claiming that the Nineteenth Amendment had not been adopted.[27] Five of the states (Missouri, Texas, West Virginia, Tennessee, Rhode Island) whose votes for the Amendment had been necessary for ratification included in their own constitutions provisions which forbade the state legislatures to adopt amendments changing the character of the electorate, and Leser therefore argued that those legislatures had acted unconstitutionally in voting to ratify the Amendment. He added that changing the character of a state's electorate without the consent of the state destroyed the original state. Justice Brandeis and the entire Court quickly picked up this thread in the argument, pointing out that if Leser's assertion was correct the Fifteenth Amendment was invalid, in spite of its having been "recognized and acted on for half a century."[28] This prospect obviously upset the justices considerably. However, this was not a sufficient answer for a legal system which demanded that attention be paid to legal logic rather than to social consequences, and Brandeis went on to call the Secretary of State's proclamation of ratification "conclusive upon the courts." He cited *Field* v. *Clark* and *Harwood* v. *Wentworth*.[29] Here the

Court did not decide the case on its merits, even in an *obiter dictum,* but it made quite clear what its decision would have been had it done so. Political theory aside, the Court of 1922 knew quite well that it could not reopen the Civil War. The choice of rejecting Leser's political theory was always present, of course, but with the possibility of another case like *Field* v. *Clark* appearing in the future, the justices had no intention of entering this potentially dangerous thicket. The same kind of decision was made for the same kind of reason in 1931, when *United States* v. *Sprague* [30] once again trotted the Eighteenth Amendment before the bench. This time the claim was that the Amendment had not been legally ratified because it had been voted on by legislatures rather than conventions.[31] The Court was unanimous in continuing its policy of self-denial. Justice Roberts said that the Court had "repeatedly and consistently de-clared that the choice of mode rests solely in the discretion of Congress," [32] which was all he needed to say. This was not, however, all he did say. Indulging in a bit of historical interpretation, Roberts announced that the framers of the Constitution had accepted ratifi-cation by legislatures as legitimate.[33] Whether or not the interpreta-tion was correct, it was certainly not necessary to the decision. Justice Roberts, the advocate of logical analysis, went on to indicate the role of possible consequences in the justices' thoughts by point-ing out that all the Amendments to the Constitution had been ratified by legislatures. He particularly mentioned Amendments Thirteen through Sixteen and Amendment Nineteen, which in-volved the important subject of individual rights, thus refuting Sprague's contention that all previous amendments dealt with governmental machinery rather than with individual rights. Once more, a decision and a non-decision were wedged into the same legal space.

To date, the most thorough examination of the Court's position appeared as its various opinions in *Coleman* v. *Miller.*[34] Up to 1939, constitutional amendment cases had been decided unanimously. This precedent was broken when Justices Butler and McReynolds dissented in the instant case. Their reason seems clear; it will be remembered that McReynolds voted with the majority when an earlier Court struck down the Child Labor Law,[35] and Butler's record on the bench is sufficient evidence that he shared McReynolds' political and economic beliefs. The lonely dissent of two old men from another era did not impair the safety of the Court's decision.

The issue, if not the question, was a political one. In 1925, the Kansas legislature rejected the proposed Child Labor Amendment, which rejection was duly registered with the United States Secretary of State. A ·new legislature reargued ratification in 1937. Twenty out of forty Senators voted for passage, twenty against, and the Lieutenant Governor of the state, presiding over the Senate, broke the tie by voting for the amendment. The lower house adopted the ratification resolution. Hoping to negate final passage, a group of senators and representatives brought suit in the Kansas Supreme Court, asking for a writ of *mandamus* to compel the Kansas Secretary of State to declare that the resolution had not been passed and to restrain him from delivering it to the federal government. Grounds for the suit were that the Lieutenant Governor had no right to cast the deciding ballot and that the proposed amendment had lost its validity because it had not been ratified within a reasonable time. The plaintiffs claimed that between June, 1924, and March, 1927, twenty-six states had rejected the proposed amendment whereas only five had ratified it, and that those dates constituted a reasonable time limitation. The Kansas Supreme Court rejected the plaintiffs' contentions.[36]

The Roosevelt administration apparently had hopes that the amendment would eventually be ratified, for its Solicitor General appeared in Court as *amicus curiae*. He was joined by the Attorney General of Wisconsin. The amendment's prospects were not good. As of 1937, when the case was decided in Kansas, twenty-seven states had ratified.[37] At least ten of them had previously rejected the amendment, however, so that the possibility of a legislative reversal was potentially important if the amendment was ever to be ratified. The Kentucky Court of Appeals had held that the amendment was no longer open to ratification for three reasons: it had been rejected by more than one-fourth of the states; rejection and subsequent ratification by a state was impermissible, at least when more than one-fourth of the states had recorded their rejection; more than a reasonable time had elapsed since original submission of the amendment in 1924.[38]

After presenting the background material, Chief Justice Hughes set out to prove that the Court acted properly in accepting jurisdiction. The case raised federal questions under Article V of the

Constitution, and the Senators involved had a real interest in it.[39] Hughes' extended discussion of "real interest" cases [40] is surprising until one gets to Justice Frankfurter's concurring opinion, stating that the petitioners had no standing and no real interest.[41]

Hughes noted that the Court was divided as to whether the question of the Lieutenant Governor's being part of the legislature for purposes of ratification was or was not political, and therefore the Court offered no opinion on that point.[42] The other problem was more easily resolved. Drawing on previous instances of states changing their minds about proposed amendments, Hughes held that there were clear precedents for the Court to follow. When Ohio and New Jersey attempted to withdraw their ratification of the Fourteenth Amendment, their withdrawal was specifically rejected by both the Secretary of State and Congress; and when North and South Carolina chose to ratify that amendment after having previously rejected it, Congress and the Secretary of State included these two in their lists of states which had accepted the amendment:

> Thus the political departments of the Government dealt with the effect both of previous rejection and of attempted withdrawal and determined that both were ineffectual in the presence of an actual ratification.[43]

This, however, was not the Court's decision. Although Congress and the Secretary had decided that a ratification could not be withdrawn but a rejection could, it was the political departments which had set this precedent, and therefore it was the political departments which would have to go on settling such disputes. Congressional control over the adoption process rendered this a political question, and so where Congress had not seen fit to set a time limitation the Court could not substitute its own.[44] Hughes went on to present a classic example of refusing to hand down a decision while making it extremely clear what that decision would have been had it existed:

> It is true that in Dillon v. Gloss the Court said that nothing was found in Article V which suggested that an amendment once proposed was to be open for ratification for all time, or that ratification in some States might be separated from that in others by many years and yet be effective; that there was a strong suggestion to the contrary in that proposal and ratification were but succeeding steps in a single endeavor; that as amendments were deemed to

be prompted by necessity, they should be considered and disposed of presently; and there is a fair implication that ratification must be sufficiently contemporaneous in the required number of States to reflect the will of the people in all sections at relatively the same period; and hence that ratification must be within some reasonable time after the proposal. These considerations were cogent reasons for the decision in Dillon v. Gloss that the Congress had the power to fix a reasonable time for ratification. But it does not follow that, whenever Congress has not exercised that power, the Court should take upon itself the responsibility of deciding what constitutes a reasonable time and determine accordingly the validity of ratifications.[45]

A determination of an appropriate timespan would involve the Court in appraising relevant political, social, and economic conditions, all of which are suited for political and not judicial decision.[46] The considerations which make such appraisals political are "the appropriateness under our system of government of attributing finality to the action of the political departments and also the lack of satisfactory criteria for a judicial determination. . . ."[47] Taking Hughes' hint, Congress decided that seven years was a reasonable time for ratification, and all subsequent amendments have included a provision rendering them inoperative unless ratified within that time.

This hint, however, was what led to the writing of the two concurrences. Speaking for himself and Justices Roberts, Frankfurter, and Douglas, Justice Black rejected the Court's opinion to the extent that it "even impliedly assumes a power to make judicial interpretation of the exclusive constitutional authority of Congress over submission and ratification of amendments. . . ."[48] He chided Hughes for not overruling Dillon v. Gloss' implication that the Court possessed the power to decide what a reasonable time might be.[49] Concluding a strong opinion which repeatedly scolded Hughes for going too far, Black asserted that "any judicial expression amounting to more than mere acknowledgement of exclusive Congressional power over the political process of amendment is a mere admonition to the Congress in the nature of an advisory opinion, given wholly without constitutional authority."[50]

Writing for the same group of four, Justice Frankfurter addressed himself to the question of jurisdiction. The Kansas legislators, having no grievance not possessed by every Kansan, had no standing.[51] His words were portents of his subsequent opinions in *Colegrove* v. *Green* and *Baker* v. *Carr.* What bothered the legislators was "a political concern which belongs to all," not a "specialized interest"; they were not claimants with "a special, individualized stake," but merely "self-constituted" spokesmen "of a constitutional point of view." The question of whether the amendment was dead applied equally not only to all Kansans, but to all United States citizens as well.[52] Referring to Justice Holmes' famous distinction, in *Nixon* v. *Herndon,* between political questions and private damage caused by political actions,[53] Frankfurter accepted the conception that "a voter's franchise is a personal right, assessable in money damages," but added:

> The procedures for voting in legislative assemblies—who are members, how and when they should vote, what is the requisite number of votes for different phases of legislative activity, what votes were cast and how they were counted—surely are matters that not merely concern political action but are of the very essence of political action, if "political" has any connotation at all. . . . In no sense are they matters of "private damage." They pertain to legislators not as individuals but as political representatives executing the legislative process. To open the law courts to such controversies is to have courts sit in judgment on the manifold disputes engendered by procedures for voting in legislative assemblies.[54]

Does this mean that Frankfurter would have accepted a suit by individual Illinois or Tennessee voters, for money damages, against individual Illinois or Tennessee legislators, on the grounds that their personal franchise right had been debased and therefore violated? [55]

The two concurring opinions—Black's and Frankfurter's—are interesting as an indication that the two frequent opponents possessed at least one ideology in common. Black's opinion is perhaps the more impassioned of the two. In it, Black urged the Court to mind its own business and not Congress', and indicated that he believed in the necessity for the political question label as strongly as did Frankfurter. The difference between the two men involved the determination of what Congress' business was. Black's insistence on the absolute nature of the Bill of Rights, and especially the First Amendment, was no more than a statement that this was not Congress' business. Black dissented from Frankfurter's opinion in *Colegrove* v. *Green* on the grounds that a clear violation of individual rights had occurred, and—although this was not stated—in such a case Black was not going to pause at the arbitrary boundary between "law" and "equity." According to Frankfurter, a political question can crop up in any realm of the litigation brought before the Court, whereas Black held that the delineation of a question as political was not possible in the area of civil rights. It should be remembered that it was Douglas, not Black, who spoke in *Baker* v. *Carr* about the error of the Court's ways in labeling so many cases "political." [56] The agreement and the difference between Black's and Frankfurter's viewpoint was expressed by Frankfurter in the instant case:

> [As] . . . considerations governing the exercise of judicial power are not mechanical criteria but derive from conceptions regarding the distribution of governmental powers in their manifold, changing guises, differences in the application of canons of jurisdiction have arisen from the beginning of the Court's history. Conscious or unconscious leanings toward the serviceability of the judicial process in the adjustment of public controversies clothed in the form of private litigation inevitably affect decisions. For they influence awareness in recognizing the relevance of conceded doctrines of judicial self-limitation and rigor in enforcing them. [57]

Although this may have been meant as a slap at Hughes, it nevertheless defines the position of the two men. They were agreed as to the necessity for judicial self-limitation, but not as to the way in which governmental powers were or should have been distributed or as to the particular "serviceability of the judicial process in the adjustment of public controversies." Like most of their predecessors and subsequent brethren, however, they were both aware of the existence of certain areas in which it was wiser for cautious courts not to tread.

There is a small category of political question cases which can be loosely lumped together under the heading of "elections." The few important cases are not similar, but they all deal with problems revolving around election procedure or results. So, of course, do the reapportionment cases and some of the republican form of government cases; the election cases spill over into both those areas. Almost any constitutional case is so complex that its consequences are bound to affect more than one discrete field within the amorphous entity called constitutional law, but this complexity is perhaps seen most clearly in the field of political questions. If it is at all true that the common denominator for these questions is an enforcement problem, then it stands to reason that fear of the direction in which one case might lead will be enough to keep the Court from deciding it, even though the case itself seems innocuous. As indicated above, the outstanding example of the interrelationship of cases in somewhat different areas is *MacDougall* v. *Green.*[58] Another is the way in which *South* v. *Peters* followed *Colegrove* v. *Green,* as *Gray* v. *Sanders* inevitably crowded the heels of *Baker* v. *Carr.*[59] As will be demonstrated below, there was also a correlation between *Baker* and *Powell* v. *McCormack.*[60]

The election cases as a whole have been tricky; this was certainly true of *Boyd* v. *Nebraska ex rel. Thayer,*[61] the first such case. Boyd, elected governor of Nebraska in 1890, had been born in Ireland. His father brought his family to the United States and began naturalization proceedings in the state of Ohio. The question of whether he had ever completed these proceedings, and whether Boyd was therefore a citizen eligible to hold office, was raised by Thayer, Boyd's predecessor as governor. Thayer sued to have Boyd ousted and himself reinstalled until a legitimate successor could be elected. Boyd's father had exercised the privileges of citizenship and had held office in Ohio for forty-two years. Boyd, who had moved to Nebraska in 1856, had voted; held various offices, including that of mayor of Omaha; served in the Army, and helped write the Nebraska constitution. Learning of Thayer's intentions, Boyd had gone to the District Court of Nebraska in 1890, and that Court had held he was a citizen. The Nebraska Attorney General refused to prosecute the case.

Speaking for the Court, Chief Justice Fuller held that Boyd was a citizen, both under the Enabling Act by which Nebraska became a state and because minors acquired "inchoate status" by a parental declaration of intention. Justice Field objected to the Court's acceptance of jurisdiction:

> My objection to the decision is not diminished by the fact that there is no power in this court to enforce its decision upon the State of Nebraska should resistance be made to it. Should the incumbent declared by this court not to be entitled to the office, refuse to surrender it and the state authorities should stand by him in such a refusal, what could be done about it? . . . How could this court in such case enforce its order? The presence of the marshal

with a posse to attempt it would be a painful exhibition of weakness. Would the court call upon the general government to send an army into the State to force upon it a governor who has been declared by its duly constituted authorities not to be entitled to the office and to oust the one who has been declared by them to be entitled to it?

I doubt whether any such proceedings would be successfully carried out or that the attempt to do so would be sustained by the Executive or by Congress or by the people anywhere. . . .[62]

Here is the essence of the enforcement problem; here too is the essential reason for the Court's lack of willingness to interfere in certain categories of state cases, and for the sometime philosophy that the state electoral process cannot be touched by a federal organ. A President who is also a politician can hardly be expected to force a state government to install officers it does not want, no matter how proper the claim of those officers. The "states rights" banner can still marshal many men with many motives, as it certainly could in 1892. The difference between Justice Field's opinion and that of the Court can be explained by their different readings of the political situation as it existed in Nebraska in 1892, as well as by Justice Field's more abstract recognition that this could have been a dangerous precedent for the Court. Similar elements were present in 1962, when the two opinions were cited by differing members of the Court in *Baker* v. *Carr*.[63]

The enforcement problem does not appear in the Court's opinion, written by Chief Justice Fuller, deciding the case of *McPherson* v. *Blacker*.[64] A Michigan law, passed in 1891, which provided for the election of Presidential Electors by districts, was challenged as not conforming to Article II Section 2 of the United States Constitution.[65] McPherson interpreted that section to mean that all Electors had to be elected by the "State"; i.e., at large. Considering the second clause of the sentence, this interpretation would not seem to have much merit, but the problem reached the Court nevertheless. The key to Blacker's response was not that McPherson's interpretation was faulty, but rather that the whole question was not a matter for judicial cognizance because the courts did not have final power to dispose of it. Whatever decision the Court reached was reviewable by four different "political" officers or agencies: the state board of canvassers, which decides who is elected; the state legislature, which handles any contested board decisions; the governor, who must certify the action of the board, and may have to decide between boards; and both houses of Congress.[66] Blacker thus hinted rather broadly that the Court could turn this into a political question. The Court declined to take the hint, and decided the case on its merits. The Chief Justice found the Michigan statute constitutional, holding that "State" could mean "State by legislature," and listing all the states which utilized a similar system.[67] There was no danger in deciding this case, as long as the Court upheld the statute; Michigan was certainly willing to uphold the decision, as the President must have been, for he had of course been elected by Electors chosen under this system. And the Court was probably influenced by the illogicality of Mc-Pherson's argument. In addition, the cases summarized under "Laws," above, indicate that the Court tends to uphold statutes under which irreparable actions have already been repeatedly performed. This is not only a necessary legal doctrine; it is also quite safe, as so many political entities will have accumulated vested interests under the statute that a decision validating the status quo will not be seriously challenged by those in power. In the instant case, a refusal by the Court to handle the question would have carried with it the implication that Presidents of the United States had been improperly elected.

In 1900, the Court suddenly found itself presented with a problem which could not have been regarded with equanimity by any judicial body. It involved a contested gubernatorial election in Kentucky, and the background of that election illustrates the complexity of the case.[68] In 1895, and for the first time since 1859, Republicans won the Kentucky gubernatorial election. Its still-Democratic legislature functioned under the guidance of William Goebel, Senate Majority Leader and a foe of corporation interests, especially the railroads and their Republican spokesmen. In 1898, Goebel helped push through a revised election law which centralized the machinery for election supervision, putting it into the hands of the Democrats in the legislature. The 1898 election found the Democrats retaining their majority in the legislature but once again losing the governorship. Taylor and Marshall were declared governor and lieutenant-governor, respectively, by the General Assembly. When Goebel and Beckham, the defeated Democratic candidates,

contested the election, the General Assembly set up Boards of
Contest to review it. Goebel and Beckham charged that secrecy
of balloting had been violated; Democratic voters had been intimi-
dated by the state military, which had been unlawfully called out
the day before elections, and by illegal observers at the polls, and
by "desperate armed men," and by employers working in collusion
with Taylor and Marshall; large-scale bribery and illegal balloting
had taken place, etc. The Boards of Contest, without bothering
to recount the ballots, decided for Goebel and Beckham, and the
General Assembly accepted their report. On January 30 Goebel
was shot and wounded by a would-be assassin; on January 31
Taylor issued a proclamation of insurrection and adjourned the
General Assembly, ordering it to reassemble in another city on
February 6; on February 2 the General Assembly, prevented by
the military from meeting in the State House, met at a hotel in
the capital city and inducted Goebel and Beckham into office;
on February 3 Goebel died and Beckham assumed the duties of
governor. Taylor and Marshall had refused to surrender their offices
and the records and archives connected with them, claiming that
the action of the Boards and the General Assembly was the result
of a conspiracy on the part of some members of those bodies,
that the Boards were fraudulently selected, that the entries on the
journals of the General Assembly were fraudulent, that the General
Assembly which had adopted the Boards' report lacked a quorum,
etc. By the beginning of February, the breaking point was near
at hand:

> With both parties claiming legal possession of the state executive,
> the situation bordered on civil war. On February 1 Lieutenant
> Governor Beckham, sworn in as acting governor, issued an order
> removing the Republican adjutant general from the command of
> the National Guard and appointing in his stead John B. Castleman,
> a Democrat. An armed clash seemed inevitable.[69]

Fearing the consequences of such a clash, party leaders managed
to agree to abide by the vote of the General Assembly, pending
a judicial decision. Beckham brought a *quo warranto* proceeding
in the Circuit Court against Taylor and Marshall, charging usurpation of office. Taylor and Marshall replied that Beckham's installa-
tion would both deprive them of property without due process
and deprive them and the electorate of liberty without due process

and of a republican form of government. The Circuit Court and the Kentucky Court of Appeals both found for Beckham. On February 19, the General Assembly, reinstalled in its State House, adopted a resolution redeclaring the election of Goebel and Beckham. Charges, however, continued to fly back and forth. In this atmosphere, which had apparently been generated by a good deal of corruption and illegal practices on both sides, the Supreme Court met to declare its lack of jurisdiction, citing precedents for not accepting cases of contested state elections in which state courts had found for one or the other of the contestants.[70] Chief Justice Fuller also cited cases to the effect that public office is not property,[71] and cited *Luther* v. *Borden* as indicating that the enforcement of a republican form of government belonged to the political departments.[72] The Chief Justice said that as far as the federal government was concerned, there had been no violation of the Constitution; the state bodies were operating peacefully, and there was no reason for the Supreme Court to intervene.[73] Although they agreed with the decision of the Court of Appeals, Justices Brewer and Brown thought the Court had jurisdiction; Justice Harlan felt the Court should have accepted jurisdiction and decided for Taylor and Marshall.[74] The motivation for the Courts' refusal of this case is clear; here indeed was one of Justice Frankfurter's "political thickets," with the Court's majority only too happy to leave the whole problem in the lap of the state courts.[75]

Election cases have had the dubious honor of falling victim to one of the rules of equity. Specifically, the doctrine that equity protects only property rights has been extended to include the corollary that there is no property right in a public office. The leading case is *In re Sawyer*,[76] which in its won way was quite as messy as *Taylor & Marshall* v. *Beckham*. A police judge and a city council were jockeying back and forth for power, with the council getting the upper hand by beginning proceedings designed to remove the judge from office. Figures of gamblers and professional political managers hovered dimly in the background. Evading a potential trap, the Court held that equity had no jurisdiction to restrain the removal of a public officer, since there is no property right in an office. This ruling was confirmed in *Taylor & Marshall* v. *Beckham*,[77] and in 1924, a unanimous Court held that a court of equity did not have jurisdiction in a case brought by a state officer to enjoin impeachment proceedings against him.[78]

Bond and Powell

There would seem to be two recent exceptions to the Court's refusal to involve itself in election cases. Upon closer examination, the first results from the Court's definition of a political question in *Baker* v. *Carr*; the second appears to be a temporary departure from a rule which will remain the norm.

In 1965, Julian Bond was elected to the Georgia House of Representatives. Prior to the convening of the House, Bond, a black activist and Communications Director of the Student Nonviolent Coordinating Committee, endorsed a Committee statement expressing support for Americans who refused to be drafted to fight in Vietnam. Seventy-five members of the House reacted by claiming that Bond's endorsement of civil disobedience indicated his inability to take the Georgia oath of office declaring fealty to the Georgia and United States constitutions, and by filing a petition challenging his right to be seated. The clerk of the House refused to administer the oath to him at the swearing-in ceremony. Bond then asked the federal courts for injunctive relief and a declaratory judgment that the House's action violated his First Amendment rights. After the District Court refused to grant relief,[79] and while his appeal to the Supreme Court was pending, a special election was called to fill Bond's seat. He won the election overwhelmingly; was again denied the right to take his seat; ran in the regular election in 1966, and repeated his earlier victories. A month later, the Court unanimously held that it had jurisdiction and that the House's refusal to seat Bond had indeed violated his First Amendment rights.[80]

In *Baker* v. *Carr*, the Court emphasized its definition of a political question as involving the separation of powers. Clearly, the Court was not dealing here with a coequal branch of the federal government, but with a Southern state legislature which had refused to seat a duly-elected black man on the sole basis of his public utterances. The case arose at the height of the civil rights movement and after the passage of the Voting Rights Act of 1965. To acquiesce in Bond's exclusion would have been to deny the effectiveness of legislation and of the political process as a means of bringing black Americans into the political mainstream. Once the Court accepted jurisdiction, it could scarcely do otherwise than uphold Bond's claim; and the limits the Court placed on the political question doctrine in *Baker* left it little grounds for declining jurisdiction. *Bond* was a matter of the right case at the right moment in history, and thus became the first time in the legal history of the United States that a federal court "ruled against a legislative action pertaining to membership." [81]

Within three months of the *Bond* decision, the federal House of Representatives declined to seat Adam Clayton Powell, and thus began the process that resulted in *Powell* v. *McCormack.*

Powell, the black representative from Harlem, had accumulated sufficient seniority to become Chairman of the House Committee on Education and Labor. He also accumulated a great deal of publicity, largely because of his flamboyant private life. His excursions within and without the country with a series of attractive women and his expensive living habits were duly recorded by the press. When questioned about the appropriateness of his life style for a representative of the people, Powell replied that he was merely doing openly what other congressmen did secretively, and added,

> As a member of Congress, I have done nothing more than any other member and, by the grace of God, I intend to do not one bit less.[82]

This, clearly, was not calculated to endear him to his colleagues. Neither were his constant threats to bolt the Democratic Party, his support of Eisenhower over Stevenson during the 1956 Presidential race, his appalling Congressional attendance record, and his reputation in the House for general unreliability.[83] Powell was far from a favorite with both the rank-and-file of the House and its leadership by the time he began to involve himself with some of the more explosive ideas of the civil rights movement. This included his admonition to black Americans that "You need not obey laws enacted in political forums wherein you are not represented." [84]

Powell was a high-handed committee chairman who, not unlike other chairmen of Congressional committees, ran his committee as his personal fiefdom. This ultimately led to a revolt within his committee in 1966, based in part on what most of its members claimed was misuse of committee funds. The spokesman for the revolt, which resulted in procedural changes designed to curtail Powell's abuses, was Representative Sam Gibbons. Powell publicly charged Gibbons with being a racist, and this so infuriated Gibbons that he asked the House Administration Committee to investigate Powell's accounts. This became one of the factors in the establishment of a Special Subcommittee on Contracts of the Committee on House Administration.[85] whose sole function was to investigate the expenditures of Powell's committee--which meant, in reality, to investigate Powell's use of committee funds. The subcommittee reported to the House that Powell and certain of his staff members had lied about their travel expenses and that he had probably made illegal salary payments to his wife.[86] The 89th Congress was drawing to a close; Powell's actions, although reprehensible, were hardly unique within Congress; and the House took no formal action. The report of the Subcommittee, however, began to find its way into the nation's press, and generated a substantial amount of pressure for some kind of punishment. During this period, Powell ran for re-election, and in November, 1966, he was elected to the 90th Congress.

Behind the establishment of the Special Subcommittee lay not only Powell's misbehavior in Congress but also the drama that would ultimately result in his exclusion from the House. It began in 1950, when, both on the floor of the House and in a subsequent television program, he charged one Mrs. Esther James as being a "bag woman" for the New York City Police Department. Mrs. James promptly brought a suit for libel against him, winning a judgment for $211,739 (later reduced by an appellate court to $46,500.) in a jury trial. A rash of litigation followed, resulting from Powell's refusals to pay the judgment, his non-appearances at court hearings, and his fraudulent transfers of his and his wife's assets to avoid payment. The net result was the issuance of four contempt citations (three civil and one criminal) and of four arrest orders, so that Powell was forced to avoid his Congressional district for fear of arrest.[87] All of the suits, the non-appearances, the charges and counter-charges, the judgments, and the court decrees were reported in great detail by the press. The spectacle of a Congressman openly, defiantly, and cheerfully evading the law, along with Powell's continued very public and rather high style of living, finally became too much for his colleagues. The result was the Special Subcommittee investigation.

The demise of the 89th Congress was not accompanied by the end of publicity about Powell. Reaction to the Subcommittee report remained intense, and a good many Congressmen apparently became uncomfortable under it and under the concomitant speculation about general Congressional ethics. Before the 90th Congress was organized, its Democratic members caucused and voted to remove him as chairman of his Committee. At the formal swearing-in ceremony, he was asked to step aside while the other successful candidates took the oath. The first action of the House subsequent to the oath-taking was a vote authorizing the Speaker to appoint a Select Committee to determine Powell's eligibility to sit in the House, and the simultaneous passage of a resolution barring him from his seat until the Select Committee reported back. He was, however, granted his pay and allowances during the interim.[88]

Powell appeared at the first hearing of the Select Committee, chaired by Emanuel Celler, with a battery of legal talent which included, among others, Jean Camper Cahn, Arthur Kinoy, William Kunstler, and Herbert O. Reid.[89] On advice of counsel, he refused to answer questions unrelated to his age, citizenship, and inhabitancy. Article I Section 2 of the United States Constitution says that "No Person shall be a Representative who shall not have attained to the Age of twenty-five Years, and been seven Years a Citizen of the United States, and who shall not, when elected, be an Inhabitant of that State in which he shall be chosen." Powell's counsel therefore argued that those were the only factors that could legitimately be considered by the House in deciding whether to seat him.[90] The House, and the Select Committee, relied on Article I Section 5 paragraphs i and ii, which read, in part, "Each House shall be the Judge of the Elections, Returns and Qualifications of its own Members . . . Each House may . . . punish its Members for disorderly Behavior . . ." Powell did not appear at subsequent hearings of the Select Committee, although counsel for him continued to attend. The *James* v. *Powell* cases were discussed in great detail;[91] testimony and records of airline officials were introduced, showing travel charged to the Committee on Education and Labor but enjoyed by non-personnel;[92] and Powell's estranged wife, who was on the Committee payroll, testified that her work for the Committee had become nominal and that she had received only two of the salary checks made out to her—and those were sent to her only after the investigation of Powell had begun. Additionally, she admitted to doing the limited work completed for the Committee while residing in Puerto Rico, although law required that a Congressman's employees work in his district or in the District of Columbia.[93] The Select Committee reported to the House that although Powell met the standing qualifications of Article I Section 2, he "had asserted an unwarranted privilege and immunity from the process of the courts of New York; that he had wrongfully diverted House funds for the use of others and himself; and that he had made false reports on expenditures of foreign currency to the Committee on House Administration."[94] The report recommended that he be sworn but that he ought also to be censured, fined $40,000 (to compensate for wrongfully-diverted funds), and deprived of seniority.

Upon discussion of the Select Committee's report, the House decided that its recommendations did not go far enough. By a majority vote of 248-176, the House adopted an amendment to the report, excluding Powell from the 90th Congress and declaring his seat vacant, and then voted 307-116 to adopt the resolution as amended.[95] Powell and thirteen of his constituents brought suit against the Speaker, Clerk, Sergeant at Arms, and Doorkeeper of the House, and against several Congressmen, asking for what amounted to an injunction against the denial of Powell's seat and a declaratory judgment that his exclusion was unconstitutional. Powell and his constituents argued, among other things, that the House had no right to consider qualifications other than the three listed in Article I, Section 2; that the action violated the right of the constituents to choose their own representative; that the disparity between the treatment of Powell and that of other representatives in similar situations demonstrated discrimination; and that the entire procedure was a violation of due process.[96] The respondents argued, in part, that the matter was a political question, and that the courts therefore lacked jurisdiction and the matter was non-justiciable; and that Article I Section 6[97] made the Representatives immune from judicial review.[98] The District Court agreed that it lacked jurisdiction;[99] the Court of Appeals, while finding that the federal courts had jurisdiction, ruled that the case was not justiciable.[100] Powell then appealed to the Supreme Court.

While the case was wending its way through the courts, a special election had been held in April 1967 to fill Powell's seat. Repeating the Bond action, he entered the race and won. He won again in the regular election in November, 1968. This was pointed out by Congressman Celler during the debate about seating Powell that ensued at the opening of the 91st Congress. Celler reminded his colleagues that since Powell's exclusion, he "has twice been overwhelmingly reelected . . . If we again deny him his seat . . . he would again be reelected overwhelmingly." [101] Celler also noted that Powell had already been amply punished: he had lost his seniority, the chairmanship of his committee, and two years' salary (approximately $55,000, more than the $40,000 which Powell had extracted from his committee's funds for non-committee purposes); and he had satisfied the judgments of the courts of New York.[102] There seems to have been a general feeling among the Representatives that Powell's district had gone unrepresented long enough,[103] and it voted to fine him $25,000 but to seat him.[104] This enabled the respondents to his suit to add the claim of mootness to their argument. By the time the Court decided the suit, then, Powell had been seated as a member of the 91st Congress.

With only one dissent, the Court upheld Powell's claim that his exclusion was unconstitutional.[105] The importance of the Court's decision was underlined by Chief Justice Warren's decision to write the 61-page majority opinion himself. He disposed of the mootness argument by noting that although Powell was currently seated in Congress and the 90th Congress was no longer in existence, his claim for back salary remained.[106] Tracing the history of the doctrine of legislative immunity, he indicated the Court's belief that there was no reason to apply the immunity of the speech and debate clause to legislative employees. Suits against legislative employees, he reasoned, would not put any burden of defense on the legislators and therefore would not interfere with their ability to perform their duties.[107] Examining the question of whether the House's action constituted exclusion or expulsion, Warren concluded that it must have been exclusion. Article I Section 5 clearly requires a two-thirds vote for expulsion, but at the time of the vote the Speaker of the House ruled that a simple majority vote was all that was needed, thus indicating that he believed the House to be voting on exclusion rather than expulsion.[108] One of the members of the House later wrote an article expressing doubt that a two-thirds vote for expulsion could have been achieved.[109] Additionally, the rules and history of the House show that the House will not expel a member for misconduct during a prior Congress.[110] Thus, the action must have been exclusion rather than expulsion, and the Court was left to test the action taken against Powell "by whatever standards may govern an expulsion." [111] Agreeing with the Court of Appeals that the District Court had jurisdiction over the case,[112] Warren had next to tackle the problem of justiciability.

He saw two aspects to the justiciability question.

> First, we must decide whether the claim presented and the relief sought are of the type which admit of judicial resolution. Second, we must determine whether the structure of the Federal Government renders the issue presented a "political question"— that is, a question which is not justiciable in federal court because of the separation of powers provided by the Constitution.[113]

The first question was quickly answered. The claim presented (that the House had a duty to seat Powell) could be judicially identified, and judicial resolution was provided for in the authority of the federal courts to issue the kind of declaratory judgment sought here.[114] The problem of the political question doctrine remained.

Quoting Brennan's six-part definition of a political question in *Baker*, Warren noted that the claim of respondents here was that Article I Section 5 constituted a "textually demonstrable constitutional commitment of the issue to a coordinate political department." [115] In seeking to determine whether the claim was correct, the Court had to decide exactly what Article I Section 5 meant; and in order to do that, the Court had to examine the historical evidence. It concluded that while the phrase granted Congress the power to expel a member, it did not confer upon it the right to exclude any duly elected Representative who satisfied the requirements specified in the Constitution.[116] Warren interpreted the English and colonial precedents to mean that a member could be excluded only after he had first been expelled,[117] and even this right of post-expulsion exclusion was eventually repudiated by the House of Commons in the case of a man who had become a hero in the colonies.[118] Congress seemingly accepted the notion that its only right was expulsion, not exclusion, through the Civil War period.[119] After that, the precedents became mixed, and the Court disposed of the instances in which Congress had excluded potential members in the following fashion:

Particularly in view of the Congress' own doubts in those few cases where it did exclude members-elect, we are not inclined to give its precedents controlling weight. The relevancy of prior exclusion cases is limited largely to the insight they afford in correctly ascertaining the draftsmen's intent. Obviously, therefore, the precedential value of these cases tends to increase in proportion to their proximity to the Convention in 1787.[120]

This is strange language from a Court devoted to giving Congress the benefit of the doubt when it chooses to exercise power and equally devoted to the proposition (cf. *Brown* v. *Board*) that what was meant at the time of the writing of various parts of the Constitution was less important than the spirit of the Constitution reinterpreted in light of the perceived current social necessities. Warren appeared to answer the latter charge by arguing that the reason the Constitutional Convention limited Congress' expulsion power was to safeguard the "fundamental principle of our representative democracy" that the people have the right to choose whomever they want to represent them.[121] The spirit of the Constitution, then, required the Court to interpret the power to judge qualifications narrowly and to insist on adherence to the two-thirds expulsion rule. Any residual concern about Congress' ability to maintain its "institutional integrity" by disciplining members is amply satisfied by the other methods of punishment available to it and by the expulsion power.[122]

In response to the claim that Court action would produce a "potentially embarrassing confrontation between coordinate branches," Warren asserted that all the Court was doing was interpreting the Constitution:

> Our system of government requires that federal courts on occasion interpret the Constitution in a manner at variance with the construction given the document by another branch. The alleged conflict that such an adjudication may cause cannot justify the courts' avoiding their constitutional responsibility.[123]

True adherence to this dictum, of course, would negate the existence of the political question doctrine in domestic cases—but Warren did not choose to take note of that.

The other elements of the Brennan definition were dismissed in a paragraph as irrelevant here,[124] and the Court ordered the

District Court to enter a declaratory judgment for Powell and to consider his plea for a *mandamus* for his back pay.[125]

Justice Douglas, concurring, cited the need to maintain "the basic integrity of the electoral process" and lashed out at "the racist overtones" of the *Powell* case.[126] He discussed in great detail an earlier Senate debate leading to that body's decision that it had no right to exclude a member who was actually under indictment for conspiring to solicit political contributions from federal employees.[127] Justice Stewart, in dissent, argued, in part, that the case was moot, and that the proper place for Powell to go to adjudicate his claim for back salary was the Court of Claims.[128]

It has been argued [129] that the Court's definition in *Baker* effectively limited the use of the political question category to conflicts among the branches of the federal government and that as a result there was nothing extraordinary about the Court's willingness to decide the *Bond* case. It has been argued further that the Court's decision in *Powell* telescoped the six *Baker* criteria into the one question of whether the Constitution confers authority over a matter to a coordinate branch [130] or at least that it put the other five criteria into a subordinate position.[131] It is true that the one realistic factor in the *Baker* definition is its recognition that the political question doctrine is a function of the separation of powers, although neither *Baker* nor *Powell* makes explicit the role that the enforcement problem plays in the determination of whether authority over a matter has been granted to a coordinate branch. This would seem on the surface to make the Court's decision in *Powell* all the more confusing, since a separation-of-powers conflict was present and since the Court could have relied on its own precedents declining involvement in election cases. Adding to the initial confusion is the highly questionable accuracy of the Court's excursion into historical analysis. A slew of commentators, reviewing the events and precedents cited by the Court, have at least raised serious doubt about the validity of the Court's interpretations.[132]

It is the thesis of this volume that the Court takes refuge in the political question when it is faced on the one hand with a basic tenet of the American democratic ethos and on the other with the clear probability of non-enforcement. Although the basic tenet was present in the *Powell* case, the threat of non-enforcement was not.

The *Powell* case arose in large measure because of Powell's color. It is perfectly true that the brazenness of his life style, of his flouting of the courts of New York, and of his misappropriation of public monies could only have frightened many of his esteemed colleagues into wondering whether the public would demand a general investigation into the behavior of Congressmen, or, worse, legislation with some teeth in it designed to reform Congressional ethics. There may have been Congressmen who were genuinely concerned about the disrespect into which they felt Powell was bringing the Congress—although the ability to generate public disrespect and cynicism is not limited to black Congressmen. It must be remembered, however, that Senator Joseph McCarthy, who used his committee to violate the civil liberties of scores of Americans, conducting public "trials" which featured guilt by association and unproven charges and which resulted in "public stigma, scorn and obloquy" [133] as well as economic loss for those caught in the McCarthy dragnet but proven guilty of no misdoing—and surely the widespread deprivation of civil liberties and the effective ruining of lives is a more serious offense than the misappropriation of some forty thousand dollars—and Senator Thomas Dodd, who misused and misappropriated far more money than did Powell, and who was also charged with improper use of influence, were merely censured by the Senate. The inconsistency in the treatment doled out to white as against black did not go unperceived by black Americans. A Louis Harris poll taken in April, 1967, showed that eighty per cent of the black citizens interviewed believed that their respective colors would result in Powell's being treated more harshly than would Dodd.[134] As in the *Bond* case, the Court was faced with an instance in which a decision against the elected representative could only be interpreted by black Americans as proof that the American political process could not work for them. Shortly after Powell's exclusion, Representative Celler charged that the exclusionary resolution was passed in an atmosphere of racism and hysteria.[135] During the debate leading to exclusion, Representative Elmer Holland had stated:

> I find it impossible to shake the conviction that a large part of the intense public campaign against Mr. Powell stems from the fact of his race . . . Adam Powell is being judged, not for his sins alone. He is being punished for the statements of Stokely Carmichael and

the bad poetry of Cassius Clay and the sins of every other Negro in the country, just exactly as every law-abiding decent Negro finds the pattern of discrimination against him "justified" by the argument that some Negroes break the law, . . . No, Mr. Speaker, I cannot accept the notion that Adam Powell is being punished by colorblind justice.[136]

The notion that Powell was being punished in part for the temerity of black Americans in asserting their rights was echoed by Representative John Conyers:

> Certainly Negro Americans cannot forget that Powell is disliked by many white Americans not only because of allegations regarding his personal conduct, but because it was Powell who desegregated congressional facilities for his staff and himself when he first came to Congress in 1945; because it was Powell who attached the "Powell amendment," a desegregation rider to school, housing, and labor bills which Congress was considering passing and which did not outlaw discrimination. It was Powell who forced congressional recognition of discrimination in the Daughters of the American Revolution. It was Powell who brought to a vote the question of segregation in the Nation's Capitol. It was Powell who demanded that Negro journalists also be seated in the Senate and House Press Galleries. It was Powell who introduced a bill prohibiting segregation in the Armed Forces.[137]

Commentators have argued that "The House was forced to take action in the Powell case by the unusual publicity the representative's actions received." [138] and that "press coverage and public outrage were probably the most important reasons why Powell was singled out by his colleagues." [139] While this is undoubtedly true, Powell's race was clearly of major importance in the first instance for the press coverage, and the majority of letters received by Congressmen reflected the racial element in public reaction. Senator Dodd was censured by the Senate after Powell had been excluded from the House and while his suit was pending. It might well be asked whether a white Congressman who received as much publicity as did Powell would have been excluded (and ultimately seated but fined and stripped of seniority and chairmanship) by his colleagues.

In a sense then, the *Powell* case represented the conjunction of two basic tenets of American democracy: the right of the people to choose their own representatives and the right of all Americans to be treated equally by their government. The Warren Court had gone further than any other Court in asserting both of these rights—the first in the reapportionment cases and the second in the series of equal protection cases following *Brown* v. *Board*. As in the *Bond* case, the Court was confronted here with a situation in which there was every reason to believe that a black American was being treated unfairly solely because of his color.

If the Court had denied Powell's claim, then, it would have violated one and possibly two basic elements of American political theory. Given the absolutely basic nature of the axioms as well as the make-up and history of the Warren Court, such a solution was impossible. However, if the Court had felt that upholding his claim would have resulted in enforcement difficulties, it probably would have utilized the political question device. That it did not is an indication that there was no real enforcement problem.

If Powell had been excluded from the 91st Congress, and if the Court had ordered him seated, a Constitutional crisis might well have arisen—the Congress might have refused to seat him. As seen above, however, at the time the Court handed down its opinion, Powell had been seated by the 91st Congress. The timing was clearly important. The Court could have decided the case while the 90th Congress was still in session, since Powell had petitioned for *certiorari* immediately after the adverse decision of the District Court. The Court denied *certiorari*, preferring to wait until the Court of Appeals had rendered its judgment.[140] This also enabled it to wait until the 90th Congress was no longer in existence.

All the Court did—or, to be formally correct, all it ordered the District Court to do—was declare that the House had acted unconstitutionally in excluding Powell. It did not involve itself in the issues of seniority, back pay, and the $25,000 fine. Thus, on the basis of the Court decision alone, there was nothing to enforce—and hence no enforcement problem. The enforcement problem was raised later, when Powell returned to the District Court and asked it to order the House to restore his seniority and pay him both his back pay and his $25,000 fine. The District Court indicated its willingness to issue the declaratory judgment as instructed by the Supreme Court, but asked both sides for further briefs on the matter of relief.[141] Counsel for the defendants replied with a letter to the judge raising the possibility that the House would refuse to comply with an order for any further relief.[142] The District Court again indicated that it would, eventually, issue the declaratory judgment that the exclusion was unconstitutional and that Powell was entitled to court costs, and that it would hold further proceedings but doubted its ability to issue an order requiring back pay and return of the $25,000 fine. Powell then asked the Supreme Court for permission to file a petition for a writ of mandamus, ordering the judge to grant relief; quietly, without an opinion, and after the furor had died down and Powell was safely ensconced on the island of Bimini, the Court denied him leave to file the petition.[143] A few months later, Powell lost the Democratic primary and his chance to run for re-election, retreated once again into quiet seclusion in Bimini, and died shortly thereafter. Thus ended the *Powell* case.

It is enviable to be able to strike a blow for liberty, justice, and democracy, without taking any risks upon oneself. This is precisely what the Court did in the *Powell* case. To say so is not to denigrate the Court's action, for it did in fact set the precedent that duly elected representatives cannot be excluded without first being seated (after which, apparently, legislators are more reluctant to act against a colleague; and after which a two-thirds majority is required), and it did imply that racially discriminatory action on the part of a governmental agency is both unconstitutional and wrong. Nevertheless, it must be understood that the Court was able to act as it did because of the lack of the threat of non-enforcement. As Peter Dionisopoulos has suggested,

> The most we can say is that *Powell* v. *McCormack* focused national attention on the arbitrariness with which a chamber can exercise its power over its members and members-elect.[144]

Power to exclude still lies in the hands of Congress, for it is extraordinarily doubtful that the Court would follow the *Powell* precedent should a putative legislator come to it at a time when Congress was still determined to exclude him or her. The *Powell* case must be understood as an aberration, made possible by fortuitous circumstances and made desirable by the pro-civil rights stance of the Warren Court, which does not alter the Court's general rule of refusing to handle election cases. If a claim is raised by one candidate that he or she was the winner of an election and should have been seated by Congress, and if the claim reaches the Court after Congress has seated another candidate, the Court will not hear the case.[145] It should be remembered that there was no vying contender in the *Powell* case; the fact of his victories in the elections of 1966, 1967, and 1968 was uncontested. And, of course, Congress had seated him before the Court took action.

The situation regarding state legislative elections is less clear. Where, as in *Bond,* exclusion bears a racist tinge or is connected to First Amendment rights, it is probable that the Court will order the excluded member seated—assuming that a special election resulting in the seating of a different person has not occurred in the interim. In spite of *Baker's* seeming limitation of the political question doctrine to federal separation-of-powers cases, it is most unlikely that the Court will order the expulsion of an already-seated state legislator and his or her replacement by someone who has carried his or her case to the Court.[146] The enforcement problem is too serious. Where, as in *Taylor & Marshall* v. *Beckham,*[147] there is a messy local situation with no clear infringement of an individual candidate's rights but with a continuing squabble over who has beaten whom, the Court is likely to refuse the case and leave it in the hands of the state courts. In such a situation, enforcement power will be in the hands of the winner. As long as his or her face is hidden, the Court cannot take the chance of backing the loser. It is an instance in which the validating function of the Court must be held in abeyance, simply because, when the case reaches the Court, there is as yet no one to validate.

CHAPTER 5

THE EXECUTIVE

From *Marbury* v. *Madison* to our own day, the Court has been aware of its dependence on the Executive branch for the enforcement of its doctrines. As Marshall realized, the Executive can have an even more profound effect on the Court, for the refusal by an Executive to carry out a Court order could easily demolish the prestige of the Court; and so the Executive is not to be tangled with. Marshall solemnly disclaimed "all pretensions" to jurisdiction over the "prerogatives of the executive":

> It is scarcely necessary for the court to disclaim all pretensions to such jurisdiction. An extravagance, so absurd and excessive, could not have been entertained for a moment. The province of the court is, solely, to decide on the rights of individuals, not to inquire how the executive, or executive officers, perform duties in which they have a discretion. Questions in their nature political, or which are, by the constitution and laws, submitted to the executive, can never be made in this court.[1]

The relationship of the Court and the Executive is unlike that between Court and Congress. When the Court invalidates a legislative enactment, no consequent positive action is required. Officials are merely ordered not to enforce a law because the "law" as such no longer exists. The officials in question are members of the executive bureaucracy rather than the people who passed the bill. Presumably they do not have the same kind of stake in the bill that legislators do; it is not their creation; the only thing required of them is inaction. Enforcement should not present a problem.

It is easier for people to adhere to a Court decision they dislike if it requires them to take no action than it is for them to obey a decision which demands that they act in a way repugnant to them. Thus, the Court can usually direct an executive official *not* to do something and feel certain that it will be obeyed. What happens, however, when the required act is positive?

If the requirement is aimed at state executive officials, there is always the possibility that the President will give the Court the support it may need. This is what happened dramatically in Little Rock and at the University of Mississippi, when the President ordered the use of arms to ensure the working of the will of the Supreme Court and lower courts, in spite of recalcitrant governors. Executive aid can come in less spectacular but equally effective ways. Such devices as strategic use or threatened non-use of allocated Federal funds, behind-the-scenes conferences and pressures, and appeals to the media all figure importantly. At the same time that the existence of the federal Executive partially ensures enforcement of state-directed commands, however, it also illuminates the dependence of the Court on the President. It is to him that the Court must finally turn when its directives are ignored. The relationship between the two branches is therefore delicate. The Court cannot afford to antagonize the President to the point where he will ignore it. The probably apocryphal story of President Jackson's "Marshall has made his decision; now let him enforce it" is one recognition of this dependency. When asked to issue orders to the Executive branch, the Court must tread lightly for two reasons: the order to take a positive action may be ignored, with consequent loss of vital Court prestige; and it may exacerbate the relationship between the two branches and make the Executive an unreliable ally in the future.

The justices do not follow a total "hands-off" policy toward the Executive. Such cases as *Youngstown* [2] make this clear. The Court, after all, is not always dealing with a recalcitrant President, and given the ordinary day-to-day workings of the political process, a President will not have all his eggs in any basket that the Court is likely to overturn. He will not be dangerously angered by Court negation of any one act. There are bound to be occasions, however, when, although the Court's only option appears to be promulgation of a well-established rule, the requirements of Presidential politics might well necessitate Presidential non-compliance with such a rule. The Court withdraws from such situations by discovering the existence of a political question. Cases involving the Executive branch have their own version of Article IV Section 4; here it is the distinction between ministerial and discretionary acts.

The first important case in this category [3] seemingly concerned the executive of a state rather than of the federal government, but it indicates how the Court must act when a state-directed command will clearly be ignored and there is no possibility of Executive action. Governor Dennison of Ohio had refused to return to Kentucky one Willis Lago, a free Negro accused in Kentucky of having aided Charlotte, a slave, to escape. Dennison was required to extradite Lago under Article IV Section 2 Paragraph 2 of the Constitution [4] and under the Act of 1793 which made this section of the Constitution directly applicable to the Governor, whose responsibility such proceedings became.[5] Kentucky sued for a writ of mandamus, compelling Dennison to return the Negro.

Ohio argued that the issue constituted a political question, involving "the execution of a compact between States—independent as to each other . . . the performance of national engagements addressed itself to the department wielding the political power, and able to weigh political considerations." [6] The "political considerations" referred to were of course the ramifications of the entire slavery controversy. Kentucky made the issue even more overtly political by charging that Ohio had claimed that the act for which the freed Negro had been convicted was a crime neither in Ohio nor under the meaning of the term "crime" in the Constitution.[7]

Chief Justice Taney and his Court did not choose to repeat the loss of discretion which had resulted in the *Dred Scott* decision.[8] This was undoubtedly due in part to the rage provoked by that ruling; but it must also have reflected their realization that Governor Dennison would not hand over the "criminal," no matter what the Court might choose to say. Taney went as far as he could, however, in upholding Kentucky's claim; he agreed that the act involved was a crime under the meaning of the Constitution.[9] Like Marshall in the *Marbury* case, he had thus shown where his sympathies lay; now he had to present a good reason for not indulging those emotions. There was nothing even remotely unconstitutional about the Act of 1793, which left only the alternative of the kind of semantic hair-splitting so dear to justices in an awkward position. Perhaps remembering the "necessary, very necessary, absolutely or indispensably necessary" of *McCulloch* v. *Maryland*,[10] Taney proved himself a worthy follower of Marshall. Taney agreed that the executive of a state had an "absolute right" to "demand" the return of a fugitive, and that the executive of the second state had a "correlative obligation" to deliver him up.[11] There was no choice about this duty; it was "merely ministerial" [12] and involved no "discretionary power." [13] However, the word "duty" had suddenly become problematic. Taney asserted that the Congress of 1793 had not meant it to be "mandatory and compulsory," but merely "declaratory of the moral duty" created by the compact which was the Constitution.[14] In approving the Act, Congress and the President had not meant to "exercise a coercive power over State officers not warranted by the Constitution"; [15] the lack of coercion was implicit in the omission of any mode of compulsion: [16]

> . . . we think it clear, that the Federal Government under the Constitution, has no power to impose on a State officer, as such, any duty whatsoever, and compel him to perform it; for if it possessed this power, it might overload the officer with duties which would fill up all his time, and disable him from performing his obligations to the State, and might impose on him duties of a character incompatible with the rank and dignity to which he was elevated by the State.[17]

At the appropriate judicial call, out trotted the obedient shibboleth of federalism. One sovereign body could not compel another, no matter how minor the second "sovereign" might be, and so the performance of the duty involved was left to depend entirely upon the "fidelity" of the governor to the Constitution.[18] Should he refuse to discharge the duty, the federal government possessed no means of compulsion.[19] The Court did not deal with the question of why a duty which was meant to be merely moral had been translated into a law, for reasons which are quite apparent. It was involved in a situation in which its validation function could not be employed, simply because there was no clear governmental policy to validate. The South was both concerned for its slaves and outraged at the flagrant refusal of the North to obey the law; the North was equally concerned for the slaves and just as determined to coin its own definition of "law." Torn between these two groups, the federal government became more than ever a whole which was only the combination of its warring parts, unable to yield to one and retain the loyalty of the other. The Court had to uphold the sanctity of law while finding a persuasive reason for refusing to enforce one; it had to refuse to return a Southern criminal while making it clear that the South had a right to him. As Taney's biographer has commented,

The decision saved the court from much embarrassment. It put the abolitionist governor of Ohio in the wrong, yet avoided the necessity of issuing a mandamus which probably would not have been obeyed.[20]

The Court had next to deal with the federal Executive. *Mississippi v. Johnson* [21] followed both the Civil War and the Court's loss of prestige after the *Dred Scott* case, and was directly connected with the passions which had caused these events. The North viewed the case as a rebel attempt to undo the Civil War.[22] It involved the Reconstruction Acts, one of which divided the Confederate states into five military districts until they should be permitted to regain representation in Congress, and the second of which limited voter registration in those states to citizens who could swear they had taken no part in the rebellion. Mississippi moved for leave to file a bill asking the Court to enjoin President Johnson from executing the Acts. Mississippi had joined the Union, and she used the position of her conquerors that the act of union could never be nullified to argue that any act which in effect did nullify it must be unconstitutional.[23] Claiming that Johnson would be performing a "mere ministerial duty" under the Act, Mississippi pointed out that the Court had accepted jurisdiction in cases which had involved ministerial duties of executive officials.[24] In arguing for the President, Attorney General Stanbery employed a mixture of rhetoric about separation of powers and not-so-subtle reminders of the Court's vulnerability. He denounced the premise which would have to precede the Court's acceptance of jurisdiction: did the Court consider itself a better judge of his duty to execute the laws than the President himself? If the President is derelict in the performance of his duty he can legally be impeached by Congress, but not until he has been found guilty can he be subjected to the jurisdiction of the Court.[25] Stanbery reminded the Court of its attempt to subpoena Jefferson during its consideration of Aaron Burr's case:

> When the subpoena was received by the President, Mr. Jefferson, did not give it any notice. He did not even make any return to the court, nor any excuse to the court.[26]

He wrote to the district attorney, telling him "that he *would* [27] not go," upon which Burr moved for "compulsory process to compel him."

> At that point, however, the Court hesitated, and not a step further was taken toward enforcing the doctrine laid down by the Chief

Justice. It then became quite too apparent that a very great error had been committed.[28]

Was this a hint that Johnson would not dare to obey the Court's decree? Mr. Stanbery went on to depict the possible consequences of the Court's subpoena. What would happen if the President refused to obey it? The next logical step would be to move for an attachment against him, and this would be highly problematic. If the court issued an injunction order to restrain him and he executed the laws anyway, "the court must now sustain its own dignity."[29] That meant that a motion would be made for a rule to show cause why an attachment should not issue against the President for contempt, by which time a "quasi criminal" process would have begun. And should the President not purge himself of contempt, "this court is bound to put him in jail or to fine him; ordinarily to put him in jail" and keep him there, no other court being able to release him. A jail "or a dungeon" was hardly the proper surroundings in which to perform the duties of the President of the United States. What, then, would become of the country, when "a co-ordinate branch of the government, bound to respect the other branches of the government, not to interfere with their duties or their privileges or their rights . . . has in effect taken, destroyed, annihilated the President who is put there by the people?"[30] No laws could be executed; a state of insurrection could not be proclaimed, should that be necessary:

Is this the way to treat the head of the government?[31]

The Court did not think so, and for good reason: one Northern paper predicted that the Court, "already suspecting that, as now constituted, it is regarded as a diseased member of the body politic, will not run the risk of amputation by touching the edged tools of Sharkey and Walker," those gentlemen being lawyers for Mississippi.[32]

The Attorney General's impassioned plea took eleven pages to record. His rhetoric and the picture of doom he painted must have cowed Chief Justice Chase, whose words required only four pages. The Chief Justice immediately rejected Mississippi's argument by declaring the duties required under the Acts to be "executive and political" rather than ministerial. This meant that they involved "the exercise of Executive discretion," with which the judiciary could not interfere. Chase made it clear that the Court would not exercise prior restraint over the acts of either Congress or the President.[33] Then he painted his own, more famous picture of chaos:

> Suppose the bill filed and the injunction prayed for allowed. If the President refuse obedience, it is needless to observe that the court is without power to enforce its process. If, on the other hand, the President complies with the order of the court and refuses to execute the acts of Congress, is it not clear that a collision may occur between the executive and legislative departments of the government? May not the House of Representatives impeach the President for such refusal? And in that case could this court interfere, in behalf of the President, thus endangered by compliance with its mandate, and restrain by injunction the Senate of the United States from sitting as a court of impeachment? Would the strange spectacle be offered to the public world of an attempt by this court to arrest proceedings in that court? [34]

Two things should be noted concerning the Court's unanimous decision. The first is that the Chief Justice himself chose not to rely merely on the theory of separation of powers; he made it quite clear that the *consequences* of accepting jurisdiction were foremost in his mind. The second point, of significance now as well as then, concerns the rather arbitrary manner in which the Court has distinguished between ministerial and discretionary actions. A ministerial act supposedly involves the exercise of no discretion, but it could certainly be argued that every presidential act involves a degree of discretion. The wording of an executive order, the particular time at which the order is issued—discretion is involved in both. Picayune examples, yes; but the point is that it becomes a matter of quantity rather than quality; the difference is one of degree, not of kind. Where is the line to be drawn? How does one go about measuring an amount of discretion? It should be remembered that the guideline is so inexact as to be nonexistent, and that the Court can therefore choose to place any action in the discretionary category. Today, there is not only the enforcement problem to be considered; the Court has apparently concerned itself with the demands upon both its own time and the administrative process which would result if all acts which could conceivably be labelled "ministerial" were brought before the bench.

The non-interference doctrine may be a wise one, but it is certainly not inevitable. In any case, it is useful, and so it persists. It made its debut in 1838. In *Kendall* v. *U.S. ex rel. Stokes*,[35] the Court was asked to issue a writ of mandamus directing Postmaster-

General Amos Kendall to pay Stokes and three others the monies which they claimed were rightfully theirs. They had contracted with Kendall's predecessor to deliver mail, in return for which they were to receive money, credits, and allowances. Upon assuming office, Kendall ordered the credits and allowances withdrawn. Stokes promptly petitioned Congress, which passed a law directing the Solicitor of the Treasury to adjust the claims. When the Solicitor submitted recommendations for payment to Kendall, the latter challenged the validity of his findings and paid only a fraction of the suggested award. Although Stokes persuaded the Senate Judiciary Committee to issue a statement declaring that under the law Kendall had to abide by the Solicitor's report, Kendall refused to do so. It was rumored that President Jackson had dictated Kendall's action.[36] Stokes thereupon sued for the writ, and the Circuit Court of the District of Columbia decided in his favor.

By the time the case reached the Supreme Court, a great deal of political feeling had been generated. The case was regarded as embodying a struggle between the Executive and the Judiciary, with the courts stoutly maintaining their right to mandamus Executive officials.[37] Kendall argued that he was subject only to the control of the President.

Writing for the majority, Justice Thompson denied that the case involved intra-governmental conflict, since the duty under discussion was ministerial.

> The mandamus does not seek to direct or control the postmaster general in the discharge of any official duty, partaking in any respect of an executive character; but to enforce the performance of a mere ministerial act, which neither he nor the President had any authority to deny or control.[38]

He also rejected the claim that Executive officers were "under the exclusive direction of the President"; within the limits of the Constitution, Congress could "impose upon any executive officer any duty they may think proper,' such duty being "subject to the control of the law, and not to the direction of the President." This was especially true in ministerial cases. The instant case involved a ministerial case, the mandamus could issue, and Kendall had to pay the Solicitor's figure.

Chief Justice Taney dissented on the grounds that the Circuit Court had no power to issue the writ. Justices Barbour and Catron dissented on the same grounds.[39]

Both opinions were violently attacked by partisans. In an unusual move, President Van Buren criticized the Court's decree in his Annual Message to Congress, deploring "the judgment of money out of the National Treasury, for the first time since the establishment of the Government, by judicial compulsion. . . . " [40] In 1839, a bill repealing the District of Columbia's Circuit Court power to issue writs of mandamus passed the Senate, but not the House. The passage of such a law was apparently not necessary, for in the case of *Decatur* v. *Paulding*, the Court indicated its willingness to place stringent limitations on the category "ministerial." *Decatur* v. *Paulding* [41] involved a naval officer's widow's suit for mandamus to compel the Secretary of the Navy to pay her certain pensions and arrears. Counsel for Paulding pointed out that by deciding such questions the Court would transfer to itself the duties involved in granting pensions, etc., "and subject all applicants for pensions to the delay, expense, and embarrassments of legal controversies as to their rights, and to a suspension of the provisions to which they might be entitled under the laws, till these controversies were judicially decided." [42] Taney and his unanimous Court agreed that jurisdiction would result in more problems than it would solve:

> The interference of the Courts with the performance of the ordinary duties of the executive departments of the government, would be productive of nothing but mischief; and we are quite satisfied that such a power was never intended to be given to them.[43]

Notice the reasoning: Taney did not say that the consequences would be undesirable and that the Court could therefore not accept jurisdiction; his argument had to be that the consequences would be undesirable and the founding fathers must have foreseen this and meant the Court to stay out of the area, and therefore the Court could not accept jurisdiction.

The Court's ability to interpret any action it preferred not to touch as discretionary was amply displayed in the case of *Brashear* v. *Mason*.[44] Brashear, who had been the commander-in-chief of Texas' four-vessel navy, claimed that under the Act annexing Texas he was an official of the United States Navy, and entitled to back pay. He asked for a writ of mandamus, compelling Secretary of the Navy Mason to give him his money.

Justice Nelson and his colleagues agreed that officers were not included in the Act.[45] But just to show how far he was willing to go to negate the practical effects of *Kendall*, Nelson added, unnecessarily, that the duty involved here was discretionary: it involved the Secretary's determining what the going rate of compensation was, whether Congress had appropriated money, whether the appropriation was sufficient, and if not, how to apportion it.[46] With all of these issues to decide, it is remarkable that Mason had the courage to continue in office.

The cases above represent only a few instances in which the Court determinedly found a distinction between ministerial and discretionary actions. It has been hoist by its own petard and has continued to make the distinction even in cases which do not clearly threaten a political question—i.e. cases in which a decision for the Executive would not run counter to accepted ideology—simply to preserve the distinction's pseudo-reality.[47] It might be argued that the Court believes the existence of the distinction to be necessary to its own.

The Court can make decisions concerning the Executive branch of the government which the Executive will not like; such cases are merely indications that the mystique of judicial independence will occasionally bite the hand that feeds it. There are times, however, when the Court is called upon to direct the President to perform certain actions which, for reasons of sheer political self-preservation, he cannot do. Then the Court must choose either to make itself look silly, or to risk its prestige by flouting a societally accepted doctrine, or to gather its robes in hand and exit through the door marked "political question." Its choice is obvious. "Non-ministerial" cases are excluded from the judicial purview on the grounds that a proliferation could swamp the courts and turn the administrative process into a stagnant bog. The motivation here is logical and probably quite necessary. It would be neither practical nor ideologically acceptable for the Court to function as a permanent overseer of the Executive branch. The Court, however, has proclaimed itself champion of the individual and his rights. Even where a plea for such rights is raised in such a manner that it is almost indisputable, though, the Court may fall back on the distinction between ministerial and discretionary acts simply because to do otherwise would be to risk the embarrassment of non-enforcement. As an administrative device, judicial non-involvement in the affairs of high Executive officials is realistic. It nevertheless deserves to be understood for the escape clause it is, because both ministerial and discretionary categories are judge-made and can always be expanded or contracted at will.

CHAPTER 6

THE UTILITY OF THE POLITICAL QUESTION

It seems clear that the settled doctrine of judicial avoidance of deciding political questions has its basis in judicial caution rather than in legal or philosophical analysis.[1]

The Supreme Court is a political body, albeit different in nature from the political Executive and the political Congress. As the guardian of the Constitution, the Court's primary function is to expand the verities of that document to encompass needed solutions to new social problems—the "felt necessities" of any era. It does so by declaring that the new answers can be worked into a Constitution which is utilized more as a broad statement of objectives than as a detailed list of limitations on methodology. Each declaration is, in reality, a validation of a particular distribution of political power, for inherent in each societal solution is a new distribution. The power involved may lie along the spectrum of black-white or of urban-rural or industry-labor or state-federal or any one of innumerable others. Sometimes, the division of power tacitly accepted by society runs counter to its own ideology and to the Constitutional commandments. This may be because the society is still unsure of what the best division of power would be and so temporarily accepts the existing one, or because the society has vacated its decision-making function and special-interest groups have stepped in to fill the vacuum. In either case, the Court can neither validate a clearly unconstitutional distribution, and thereby subject its role as guardian to claims of fraud, nor invalidate a functioning system with an order which would be ignored. To do either would be to sacrifice the popular prestige which is the Court's primary source of power. Consequently, it temporarily relinquishes its task of validation by declaring that the entire matter involves a "political question."

This is not meant as a suggestion that legal guidelines and procedures never function as the determining factor in Court decisions. While the adjudication of constitutional questions necessarily reflects the political climate of the country, the judicial process is employed precisely because reliance on legal techniques ensures a certain degree of stability and continuity. When the Court refuses to follow its own precedents and substantive regulations, therefore, it is legitimate to assume that this is an unusual occurrence, and to look for the explanation outside the formal legal machinery. The Court's sometimes acceptance and sometimes refusal of similar cases—particularly those involving Article IV Section 4—is a prime example of refusal to heed precedent.

Why, logically, should Article IV Section 4—or any other portion of the Constitution—be out of bounds for the federal judiciary? It is very true that the section does not specify judicial interpretation of the open-ended phrase, "a republican form of government," but which section does so specify? It is not clear who is to undertake the guarantee. Does "The United States" mean one governmental branch, or any two, or all three? Article I Section 8 Clause iii makes it very plain that it is Congress that has the power "to regulate commerce . . . among the several States," and yet the Court has not hesitated to reject Congressional definitions of interstate commerce or to substitute its own. The claim that the meaning of "republican" is so basic to this country that it should be determined only by the elected representatives of the people appears to be camouflage when it is remembered that the Court's interpretations of the commerce, taxing, and due process clauses were instrumental in transforming a nation predicated on a jealous individualism into a welfare state. These definitions were and are basic to the political structure. If, under a system of the supremacy of law, one accepts the ideology and practice of judicial review, by what criteria is one to differentiate, for judicial purposes, between sections of the Constitution? There are no criteria. The argument that Article IV Section 4 is somehow different from the rest of the Constitution is merely a tactical ploy.

The question next to be considered is whether the political question device, understood to be a political maneuver, is a legitimate one. Any reply is in reality an answer to the question, of what use is the Court itself? If its existence is a necessity, then almost any method within reason which ensures its continuation, and which is not itself unconstitutional or in some way immoral, is valid. And certainly, in a nation which prides itself on the rule of a neutral law, an independent supreme court of some kind is indispensable. The political question device is justifiable because it preserves the Court by enabling it to withdraw from unequal contests, and thus permits it to eliminate the inevitably harmful effects of such combat.

> If the public should ever become convinced that the Court is merely another legislature, that judicial review is only a euphemism for an additional layer in the legislative process, the Court's future as a constitutional tribunal would be cast in grave doubt.[2]

When it declares the presence of a political question, the Court tacitly admits that it cannot find, and therefore cannot ratify, a social consensus which does not violate basic American beliefs. Its language is camouflaged for the same reason that it declines to act; both tactics help preserve its image of neutrality. This, however, does not lessen the validity of its refusal to act. Where a political decision would be sufficiently premature to constitute an open admission of unwarranted partisanship, the Court does not possess the right and should not have the folly to make it. All Court decisions are political in their effects, and yet not all of them are labelled political questions. They all affect the distribution of power—political, economic, social—but in most cases popular opinion is already agreed or is willing to agree that a particular power configuration is beneficial to society. The political question appears before that agreement has had a chance to come into existence; and until such a consensus is either achieved or foreseeable, it would be insufferable for the judiciary to force one. Here, then, is the justification par excellence of the political question: its use can frequently enable the Court to restrain itself from precipitating impossible situations which might tear the always delicate social fabric. Thus, no rules are forced upon a country not yet ready for them; on the contrary, the country at large is permitted to work out its own rules, which can then be translated into constitutionality through judicial fiat. The self-restraint exercised by the Court is more than a self-saving mechanism; it is also the affirmation of a government which finds the source of its actions in popular desires. It prevents the judiciary from usurping the duties of the ballot box.

When the Court heard *Luther* v. *Borden,* American ideology proclaimed all the people as sovereign, but popular pressure would not have been strong enough to oust the Rhode Island government established and participated in by a favored few. Americans did believe that the people were sovereign, but they were not sure exactly who "the people" were. Did or should that term necessarily include urban laborers? Did it include whole classes of people unthought of in 1787? A definitive answer had not been worked out. The Court could not proclaim the final right of state govern-ments to establish categories of voters, for this would have meant the sovereignty of legislatures rather than of the citizenry. Con-versely, a proclamation that the people could ignore their own governmental creations would have been too radical to be heeded. Unable to ignore the basic axiom on the one hand or successfully to demand its ultimate enforcement on the other, the Court had to eliminate itself from the controversy by discovering the presence of a political question. Similarly, in 1946, the Court could not disavow theoretical equality of representation; at the same time, had it issued a command for true equal representation, the agrarian mystique might well have prevented it from being obeyed. The mystique had lost its relevancy by 1962 and the political question consequently disappeared. If the Court admitted such consid-erations openly, however, it would destroy its image as a neutral, objective, eternal body. The civilization able to function without a mythology has not yet evolved; this is a necessary part of ours.

When the court invokes separation of powers, it is merely playing its role in a socially useful drama. There is nothing in the idea of separation of powers which prevents the Court from making any decision it wants to, but there *is* something in the theory which gives the justices an excuse for not deciding an issue they do not wish to touch. What should be remembered is that the reason for this disinclination is the enforcement difficulty; if no social con-sensus has been reached, enforcement may become impossible, and judicial prestige would thereby be sacrificed. Paradoxically, the self-restraining political question technique adds to the Court's ultimate strength by preserving the myth of neutrality; at the same time, it is a partial guarantee to the electorate that the political configurations the Court upholds will be those the people have chosen.

The political question can be misused, however. As John Frank has suggested, it is "useful when it operates to put responsibility at the best place, and is harmful when it puts the decision no place."[3] Professor Frank was particularly concerned with the reapportionment problem, which, when he wrote, had received neither a legislative nor a judicial solution. The evil in that instance may have been a matter of misjudgment, with the Court simply misreading the signs of the times. Unfortunately, bad guesses are sometimes misused by the legislatures, which interpret Court inaction as an indication that they too need do nothing about a situation. Passivity is really the only way in which a Court can express its neutrality, but the effect of a non-decision is to preserve the existing distribution of power, and there is always the danger that it will be regarded as approval of the status quo. Usually, however, the Court's prophetic powers are accurate, and it knows when the rendering of a judicial fiat would do more harm than good. Political questions do not exist as abstractions; they are judge-made, but only when the judges deem them necessary.

What have *Baker* v. *Carr* and *Powell* v. *McCormack* done to the concept of the political question? Not terribly much. The Court has never admitted its willingness to interpret the Guaranty clause; presumably, it will be discovered that future cases which the Court wishes to avoid rest on a definition of "republican form of government" and cannot be decided by a judicial body. This, however, is not the only section of the Constitution which can be declared off-limits. When lower federal and state courts were faced with suits challenging the constitutionality of American involvement in the Vietnamese War, many of them relied upon the Court-endorsed doctrine of political questions for their decisions that only Congress has the right to decide whether Presidentially-decreed military action is in violation of Article I Section 8 paragraph xi.[4] The Court resolutely refused to hear appeals from the lower court rulings.[5] That it did not simply declare the problem to be a political question probably indicates its unwillingness to establish the rule that a President could not be stopped from involving the country in a war absent the two-thirds Congressional vote necessary to override an executive veto.[6] Were the matter to be deemed non-justiciable, future Presidents could count on the re-election-conscious legislators not to risk the accusation of having denied weapons to American soldiers in the field, and could simply deploy troops unilaterally and then demand the necessary appropriations.[7] The Court could have followed the example of some lower courts in citing appropriations as a *de facto* Congressional declaration of war.[8] Its decision not to do so must be perceived as reflecting the justices' desire not to negate the Constitutional requirement of a specific declaration *de jure*. The remaining possible decree—that the war was unconstitutional—would have resulted in a confrontation between the judiciary and the executive which the judiciary might well have felt it could only lose. What should be noted, however, is that the Court *could* have found the issue to be non-justiciable, and that the unwillingness of one group of nine men to do so does not limit the power of future Courts to extend the political question beyond the Guaranty clause. [9]

Because the powers listed in the Constitution are almost all assigned to Congress or to the President or both, the Court can claim that those bodies define their own boundaries. This interpretation was espoused by Thomas Jefferson and is not entirely indefensible. The history of the twentieth century Court in general and the protection extended by that Court to civil liberties in particular render the theory an anachronism. It can, however, be dusted off whenever the Court finds it necessary. While it is impossible now to predict which problems future Courts will be asked to solve before the country is ready to accept a solution that does not violate a basic American axiom, it is certain that the country has not yet seen the end of the political question.

NOTES—CHAPTER 1

¹ John P. Roche, "Judicial Self-Restraint," 49 *American Political Science Review* 762, 768 (1955).

² *Sevilla* v. *Elizalde*, 112 F.2d 29, 32 (1940).

³ *Z. & F. Assets Realization Corporation* v. *Hull,* 114 F.2d 464, 468·(D.C Cir. 1940). Both cases cited by John P. Frank, "Political Questions," *Supreme Court and Supreme Law,* ed. Edmond Cahn (Bloomington: Indiana University Press, 1954), p. 36.

⁴ Cf., for example, Maurice Finkelstein, "Judicial Self-Limitation," 37 *Harvard Law Review* 338 (1924).

⁵ Note, "Political Questions as Distinguished from Judicial Questions," 24 *Notre Dame Lawyer* 231 (1949).

⁶ The political process is the somewhat institutionalized manifestation of the struggle for power. This, however, is not meant to imply that power is sought as an end in itself. It is desirable because it is a necessary prerequisite to the implementation of various ideas and ideologies. In the case of the political question, the justices concern themselves with the power problem in order to retain their freedom to implement their versions of the "good life."

⁷ Cf. *Muskrat* v. *U.S.,* 219 U.S. 346, 356 (1911); *Osborn* v. *Bank of the United States,* 9 Wheat. 738, 819 (1924); In re *Pacific Railway Commission,* 32 F.241, 244 (1887) and *Smith* v. *Adams,* 130 U.S. 167, 173-4 (1889); *Lampasas* v. *Bell,* 180 U.S. 276, 284 (1901); *Massachusetts* v. *Mellon,* 262 U.S. 447, 487 (1923).

⁸ The popular belief in the Court as non-political was exploited in candidate Nixon's 1968 attacks on the Court. Nixon did not accuse the Court of moving from a correct to an incorrect political stance in its decisions expanding the rights of accused criminals; rather, he accused it of moving from a non-political to a political posture. One of his campaign promises was the appointment of a Chief Justice "who would 'interpret the law . . . and not make it.' " Quoted in Garry Wills: *Nixon Agonistes* (New York: New American Library), p. 244. In 1971, announcing his nomination of Lewis Powell and William Rehnquist to the Court, President Nixon distinguished between "judicial" and "political" philosophy and indicated that the good judge would be he who did not "twist or bend the Constitution in order to perpetuate his personal, political and social views." (Quoted in the *New York Times,* October 22, 1971, p. 24 c. 3.) Thus the periodic American dissatisfaction with the Court can be seen as dissatisfaction with individual judges, rather than the institution, on the grounds that they have abused their office by eschewing neutrality for politics.

⁹ This is assuming, of course, that the law in question has been challenged on the grounds of urban underrepresentation.

¹⁰ One of the many background elements in *Brown* v. *Board* was the series of Court decisions requiring the availability of separate but equal higher education facilities in states where it was clear that no such facilities would be made available. In a sense, then, the decisions compelled integration of the existing schools. Cf. *Missouri ex rel Gaines* v. *Canada,* 305 U.S. 337 (1938); *Sipuel* v. *Oklahoma,* 332 U.S. 631 (1948); *McLaurin* v. *Oklahoma State Regents,* 339 U.S. 637 (1950). In *Sweatt* v. *Painter,* the Court held that the separate law school established by Texas

for black students was unequal and, although it refused to review *Plessy* v. *Ferguson*, came close to implying that a separate law school had to be inferior. 339 U.S. 629,632,634,636 (1950).

[11] In the light of the upheaval which followed it, the assertion that the Court's 1954 guess was correct may require amplification. It was many years before meaningful compliance with the decision began; indeed, it can be argued that it would have remained minimal had President Johnson not utilized the 1964 Civil Rights Act to threaten recalcitrant school districts with the loss of federal funds. The slowness of compliance, however, does not negate the fact that as far as the Court's prestige was concerned, the decision was the proper one. One of the many intriguing aspects of the "black revolution" is the way in which its early days quickly became imbued with the respectable patina of long-past history. Much of Lyndon Johnson's appeal to the electorate was based on a straightforward espousal of civil rights—which meant that the President would not only enforce *Brown* v. *Board* and subsequent decisions, but would go beyond them. Even before Johnson took office, the majority of Americans undoubtedly admired both the Court's pronouncement and the courage with which it was uttered. Outside of the South, it was rare to hear the "integration mess" blamed on the Court; on the contrary, the Court was praised, and responsibility was easily attributed to "those Southerners." When pushed into it, the Executive then in office accorded the decision and its offshoots at least token respect by sending troops into Little Rock. As of this writing (1972), *Brown* v. *Board* has become an accepted part of what might be called American patriotic history.

[12] Alexander M. Bickel, "The Passive Virtues," 75 *Harvard Law Review* 40, 50 (1961).

[13] U.S. 549 (1946). See pp. 43ff.

[14] How. 1 (1849). See pp. 12ff.

[15] 307 U.S. 433, 453 (1939). See pp. 105ff.

[16] 307 U.S. 457, 458-460.

[17] 328 U.S. 549, 566 (1946). For the sake of brevity and style, cases are occasionally referred to in an abbreviated fashion; for example, *Colegrove* or the *Colegrove* case for *Colegrove* v. *Green*.

[18] 329 U.S. 675 (1946). This is assuming, as seems likely, that the *per curiam* opinion reflects the majority's desire to label these as political question cases. Cf. Justice Rutledge's call for a rehearing of *Colegrove*, 329 U.S. 678-9. See p. 76.

[19] *Ibid.*

[20] 339 U.S. 276, 277 (1950). See p. 76.

[21] While his opinion is not labeled either concurring or dissenting, its gist suggests that he agreed with the Court's decision but wanted it to clarify the grounds on which it reached its conclusion.

[22] This is equally true of his concurrence in *MacDougall* v. *Green*, 335 U.S. 281, 284-7 (1948), in spite of the fact that there the Court decided the case on its merits. See p. 53.

[23] This motive is even more apparent in *MacDougall* v. *Green*.

[24] Leon Grant Godley, *Outline of Equity* (2d ed., Brooklyn: n.p., 1931), p. 1. Cf. Zechariah Chafee, Jr. and Edward D. Re, *Cases and Materials on Equity* (4th ed.; Brooklyn: The Foundation Press, Inc., 1958), for a further account of the history and nature of equity.

[25] John Norton Pomeroy, *A Treatise on Equity Jurisprudence* (3 vols; 2nd ed.; San Francisco: Bancroft-Whitney Co., 1899), I, 70.

[26] *Ashby* v. *White*, 1 Smith L.C., 90 E.R. 1188, 1189 (1702).

[27] Cf. *In re Sawyer* 124 U.S. 200 (1888) and *Taylor & Marshall* v. *Beckham*, 178 U.S. 548 (1900).

[28] *Gee* v. *Pritchard*, 2 Swanst. 402, 36 Eng. Rep. 670 (1818).

[29] According to Roscoe Pound, the first political question case occurred in 1460, and went by the name of *The Duke of York's Claim to the Crown*, 5 Rot. Part. 375, 376. Just as *Mississippi* v. *Johnson* was to invite the Supreme Court to undo the Civil War (4 Wall. 475 1866), so in 1460 the judges of England were asked to involve themselves in the War of Roses by deciding whether the House of Lancaster or the House of York might validly claim the honor of being Richard II's successor. No fools they, the judges refused to decide, declaring that "they durst not enter into . . . [any] consideration thereof." Roscoe Pound, "Judicial Review: Its Role in Intergovernmental Relations: Foreword," 50 *Georgetown Law Journal* 653, 659 (1962).

[30] *Dalton* v. *Vanderveer*, 8 Misc. 484, 486, 29 N.Y.S. 342.

[31] Quoted in Godley, *op. cit.,* p. 5.

[32] 369 U.S. 186 (1962). *Baker* is the case in which the Court reversed itself to declare that reapportionment cases do not involve a political question and can therefore be heard by the Court. See pp. 59ff.

[33] Fred Rodell, "For Every Justice, Judicial Deference is a Sometime Thing," 50 *Georgetown Law Journal* 700, 707, 708 (1962).

NOTES—CHAPTER 2

[1] *Martin* v. *Mott*, 12 Wheat. 19 (1827).

[2] 12 Wheat. 30-31.

[3] *Luther* v. *Borden*, 7 How. 1 (1849).

[4] Chilton Williamson, *American Suffrage* (Princeton University Press, 1960), p. 245. This work has been drawn upon freely, as have *Social Conditions in Industrial Rhode Island, 1820-1860* by Joseph Brennan (Washington, D.C., 1940); *Public to Republic* by Alfred De Grazia (New York: Alfred A. Knopf, 1951); *A Concise History of the Efforts to Obtain an Extension of Suffrage in Rhode Island from the Year 1811 to 1842* by Jacob Frieze (Providence: Benjamin F. Moore, 1842); *The Constitutional History of the United States, 1826-1876* by Arthur May Mowry (Providence: Preston & Rounds Company, 1901); and "Democrats and the Dorr Rebellion" by John B. Rae, in 9 *New England Quarterly* 476 (1936).

[5] Rae, *op. cit.*

[6] If the Rhode Island government was unconstitutional, so was the court, which was, of course, an organ of the government.

[7] 7 How. 21.

[8] 7 How. 21-26.

[9] 7 How. 19-20.

[10] 7 How. 16. The Rhode Island court had refused to consider this evidence.

[11] Quoted in Charles Warren, *The Supreme Court in United States History* (2 vols: Boston: Little, Brown and Co., 1926), II, 187.

[12] *Ibid.*

[13] 7 How. 31.

[14] *Ibid.*

[15] 7 How. 34.

[16] 7 How. 31-32.

[17] 7 How. 33.

[18] *Ibid.*

[19] *Gray* v. *Sanders,* 371 U.S. (1963). See below, p. 80.

[20] Warren, *op. cit.,* p. 190.

[21] *Ibid.*

[22] *Ibid.*

[23] 7 How. 35.

[24] 7 How. 36-37.

[25] 7 How. 37.

[26] 7 How. 38-39.

[27] 7 How. 39.

[28] *Ibid.*

[29] 7 How. 39-40.

[30] This argument becomes more understandable when it is considered in the light of Taney's states-rights ideology.

[31] 1 Cranch 137 (1803).

[32] 7 How. 40-41.

[33] 7 How. 41.

[34] 7 How. 42.

[35] 7 How. 42-44.

[36] 7 How. 44.

[37] 7 How. 44-45.

[38] 7 How. 46.

[39] *New York Courier,* January 4, 1849. Quoted in Warren, *op. cit.,* II, 193.

[40] *Boston Post,* January 5, 1849. Quoted in Warren, *op. cit.,* II, 194.

[41] *Pennsylvanian,* January 27, 1849. Quoted in Warren, *ibid.*

[42] Dean Pound has stated that the consequences of proclaiming a functioning state government as possessing no legal existence was the *ratio decidendi* of *Luther* v. *Borden.* Pound, *op. cit.,* pp. 659-60.

[43] Cf. Warren, *op. cit.,* II, 186; Williamson, *op. cit.,* p. 266; Rae, *op. cit., passim.*

[44] The Court of 1849 was already the center of a storm created by abolitionists, who were busily engaged in an attempt to denigrate it. Cf. Walter P. Murphy, *Congress and the Court* (Chicago: University of Chicago Press, 1962), p. 28.

[45] Here Ehrlich's view of the judiciary as the mechanism by which the more important social norms are translated into enforceable legal rules becomes important. If only to ensure the perpetuation of their own power, the judiciary and the other branches of government will not attempt to promulgate a law unless it is a widely accepted norm or unless the societal atmosphere is such that the law has grown naturally out of it and can expect to be widely accepted within it. Cf. Eugen Ehrlich, *Fundamental Principles of the Sociology of Law* (Boston: Harvard University Press, 1936).

⁴⁶ One appeared in 1900: see *Taylor & Marshall* v. *Beckham,* 178 U.S.548 (1900).

⁴⁷ One commentator, however, has suggested that the Court "might have invited armed conflict" had it handed down a substantive decision. Frank, *op. cit.,* p. 40.

⁴⁸ 7 Wall. 700, 729 (1869).

⁴⁹ 4 Wall. 475 (1866). See p. 134.

⁵⁰ 6 Wall. 50 (1867). See p. 171 n. 34.

⁵¹ 11 Wall. 113 (1870).

⁵² 11 Wall. 126.

⁵³ The decision in this case, but not its comments on the necessity of judges, was overruled in *Graves* v. *New York ex. rel. O'Keefe,* 306 U.S. 466 (1939).

⁵⁴ *Minor* v. *Happersett,* 21 Wall. 162 (1874).

⁵⁵ The vote was 40,007 for, 135,957 against. For a fuller examination of this subject, see Ida Husted Harper, *A Brief History of the Movement for Woman Suffrage in the United States* (New York: National Woman Suffrage Publishing Company, Inc., 1917); Sophonisba P. Breckinridge, *Women in the Twentieth Century* (New York: McGraw-Hill Book Company, Inc., 1933); and Kirk H. Porter, *A History of Suffrage in the United States* (Chicago: University of Chicago Press, 1918), pp. 137-244.

⁵⁶ Article II Section 18: "Every male citizen of the United States shall be entitled to vote."

⁵⁷ 21 Wall. 175.

⁵⁸ 21 Wall. 175-176.

⁵⁹ 16 Stat. 1131.

⁶⁰ In a later case, the Court of 1891 chose to make specific what Taney had implied by stating that the "distinguishing feature" of the republican form of government is "the right of the people to choose their own officers for governmental administration, and pass their own laws in virtue of the legislative power reposed in the representative bodies . . . their governments, National and State, have been limited by written constitutions, and they have themselves thereby set bounds to their own power, as against the sudden impulses of mere majorities." As this definition is no more extensive than one found in any dictionary, its inclusion in a Court decision could hardly be considered controversial. *In re Duncan,* 139 U.S.449,461. See p. 101.

⁶¹ 92 U.S. 542 (1875).

⁶² 92 U.S. 552.

⁶³ In the case of *Taylor & Marshall* v. *Beckham,* the Court refused to consider Taylor & Marshall's contention that Kentucky would lose its republican form of government if Beckham was installed as governor. Chief Justice Fuller cited *Luther* as controlling. This refusal was merely part of the unwillingness of the Court to become involved in an impossible situation. (See p. 113) In formal procedural terms, the Court said that the guarantee didn't give it the power to review a decision of a state court sustaining an election determination made by a state legislature under the authority of a state constitution. Other pertinent cases include *O'Neill* v. *Leamer,* 239 U.S.244 (1915), in which a claim that the delegation to a court of the power to form drainage districts negated republican government was held "futile"; *Mountain Timber Co.* v. *Washington,* 243 U.S. 219 (1917), when a claim that workmen's compensation legislation in Washington violated republican government was held to be nonjusticiable; and *Highland Farms Dairy* v. *Agnew,* 300 U.S. 608 (1937), which rejected a claim that delegation to an agency of the power to

control milk prices violated republican government. Also see *Cochran* v. *Board of Education,* 281 U.S. 370 (1930), which incidentally affirmed the political nature of this clause.

[64] DeGrazia, *op. eit.,* p. 58. Other important sources in this area are: *The Initiative, Referendum, and Recall,* Vol. XLIII of the Annals of the *American Academy of Political and Social Science* (1912); James D. Barnett, *The Operation of the Initiative, Referendum and Recall in Oregon* (New York: The Macmillan Company, 1915); Charles A. Beard and Birl E. Schultz, *Documents on the State-wide Initiative, Referendum and Recall* (New York: The Macmillan Company, 1913); Gilbert L. Hedges, *Where the People Rule* (San Francisco: Bender-Moss Company, 1914); and Benjamin V. Hubbard, *Making America Safe for Democracy: The Referendum as an Instrument of Government* (Chicago: Legal News Co., 1926). Also see relevant sections of Eric P. Goldman, *Rendezvous with Destiny* (New York: Alfred A. Knopf, Inc., 1952), and Richard Hofstadter, *The Age of Reform* (New York: Alfred A. Knopf, Inc., 1955).

[65] Beard and Schultz, *op. cit.,* pp. 15-18.

[66] G. B. Galbreath, "Provisions for State-wide Initiative and Referendum," *Annals, op. cit.,* p. 87.

[67] Article IV Section 1 of the Oregon Constitution, adopted June 2, 1902, by a vote of 62,024 to 5,668: "The legislative authority of the State shall be vested in a Legislative Assembly, consisting of a Senate and House of Representatives, but the people reserve to themselves the power to propose laws and amendments to the Constitution and to enact or reject the same at the polls, independent of the Legislative Assembly, and also reserve power at their own option to approve or reject at the polls any act of the Legislative Assembly. The first power reserved by the people is the initiative, and not more than eight per cent of the legal voters shall be required to propose any measure by such petition, and every such petition shall include the full text of the measure to be proposed. Initiative petitions shall be filed with the Secretary of State not less than four months before the election at which they are to be voted upon. The second power is the referendum, and it may be ordered (except as to laws necessary for the immediate preservation of the public peace, health, or safety), either by the petition signed by five per cent of the legal voters, or by the Legislative Assembly, as other bills are enacted. . . . The veto power of the Governor shall not extend to measures referred to the people. All elections on measures referred to the people of the State shall be had at the biennial regular general elections, except when the Legislative Assembly shall order a special election. Any measure referred to the people shall take effect and become the law when it is approved by a majority of the votes cast thereon, and not otherwise. . . . The whole number of votes cast for Justice of the Supreme Court at the regular election last preceding the filing of any petition for the initiative or for the referendum shall be the basis on which the number of legal voters necessary to sign such petition shall be counted. . . ." Section 1a was proposed by initiative petition and declared effective on June 4, 1906. The vote was 47,678 to 16,735. The section reads in part: ". . . The initiative and referendum powers reserved to the people by this Constitution are hereby further reserved to the legal voters of every municipality and district, as to all local, special and municipal legislation, of every character, in or for their respective municipalities and districts . . . . Not more than ten per

cent of the legal voters may be required to order the referendum nor more than fifteen per cent to propose any measure, by the initiative, in any city or town." Other states followed this wording fairly closely.

[68] Galbreath, *op. cit.,* pp. 93-96.

[69] Hedges, *op. cit.,* p. 37.

[70] *Pacific States Telephone and Telegraph Co.* v. *Oregon,* 223 U.S. 118, 119-129 (1912). The Company's argument that the Oregon government had become invalid because it had permitted the passage of an unconstitutional act is necessarily fallacious. Judicial review would be no more than an invitation to anarchy if the Court's declaration that a law is unconstitutional automatically implied that the government which sponsored it is no longer legitimate. The Company overlooked the important question: namely, can the people amend their Constitution in such a way that the addition changes the tenor of the entire document? And if not, were the initiative and referendum amendments basic alterations? But more sophisticated legal thinking would have gotten the Company no further than its original objections, since this was one case the Court was determined not to decide.

[71] 223 U.S. 126.

[72] 223 U.S. 129-133.

[73] *Kadderly* v. *Portland,* 74 Pac. 710 (1903). Also see *Farrell* v. *Port of Portland,* 52 Or. 582, 98 Pac. 145. In 1908, the Oklahoma Supreme Court had found that state's initiative and referendum provisions consistent with republican government. *Ex parte Wagner,* 95 Pac. 435. Both the Circuit Court and the Oregon Supreme Court had agreed with this decision in judging the *Pacific Telephone and Telegraph* case. 52 Or. 163; 99 Pac. 427 (1909).

[74] *Straw* v. *Harris,* 54 Or. 424, 103 Pac. 777; *Haines* v. *City of Forest Grove,* 54 Or. 424, 103 Pac. 775: *Kiernan* v. *Portland,* 54 Or. 454; *State* v. *Langworthy,* 104 Pac. 424; *State* v. *Cochrane,* 105 Pac. 884.

[75] Gustavus Myers, *History of the Supreme Court of the United States* (Chicago: Charles H. Kerr and Co., 1912), p. 781.

[76] 223 U.S. 133.

[77] 223 U.S. 141.

[78] *Ibid.*

[79] 223 U.S. 141-142.

[80] 223 U.S. 142.

[81] *Ibid.*

[82] 223 U.S. 143.

[83] 223 U.S. 143-148.

[84] 223 U.S. 150.

[85] *Ibid.*

[86] 223 U. S. 150-151.

[87] 223 U.S. 151 (1912).

[88] See p. 151, note 67.

[89] 223 U.S. 164. In 1913, the Court incidentally reaffirmed the rule of *Pacific* v. *Oregon.* It held nonjusticiable a claim that Indiana's constitutional amendment procedure negated republican government in that state. *Marshall* v. *Dye,* 231 U.S. 250, 256 (1913).

[90] 241 U.S. 565 (1916).

[91] Article II, Sections 1-lg.

[92] "The Time, Places and Manner of holding Elections for Senators and Representatives, shall be prescribed in each State by the Legislature thereof. . . ."

[93] The Act of 1911 said that existing Congressional districts would continue in force until they were redistricted by the State "in the manner provided by the laws thereof," whereas the Act of 1891 had said "until the legislature of such State in the manner herein prescribed shall redistrict such state." Act of Feb. 7, 1891, c. 116, 26 Stat. 735. As indicated by White in his opinion, legislative history indicates that the difference was the direct result of the appearance of referendum amendments in various states. Cf. *Congressional Record*, Vol. 47, pp. 3436, 3437, 3507.

[94] 241 U.S. 569, citing *Pacific Telephone and Telegraph.*

[95] Article I Section 4: ". . . the Congress may at any time by Law make or alter such [Election] Regulations, except as to the Places of choosing Senators."

[96] *Hawke* v. *Smith No. 1*, 253 U.S. 221 (1920).

[97] Constitution of Ohio, Article II Section I Paragraph 2: "The people also reserve to themselves the legislative power of the referendum on the action of the General Assembly ratifying any proposed amendment to the Constitution of the United States." Adopted November 5, 1918.

[98] 253 U.S. 230.

[99] 253 U.S. 227-228.

[100] 253 U.S. 230.

[101] *Hawke* v. *Smith No. 2*, 253 U.S. 231, treated Hawke's challenge of the proposed referendum on the Nineteenth Amendment, on the same grounds, in a similar fashion.

[102] Justice Frankfurter, for example, thought that reapportionment cases could be argued only on the grounds that unequal apportionment constituted a violation of republican government. *Baker* v. *Carr*, 369 U.S. 186, 297, 301 (1962).

NOTES—CHAPTER 3

[1] United States Constitution, Fourteenth Amendment, Section 2.

[2] Article I, Section 2, Paragraph 3.

[3] Act of August 8, 1911, c.5, 27 Stat. 13.

[4] Otto Kerner, Jr., "Recent Cases: 'Constitutional Law—Congressional Redistricting,'" 27 *Illinois Law Review* 445, 446 (1932).

[5] 285 U.S. 355 (1932).

[6] The reason for Governor Floyd B. Olsen's veto may be gathered from his announcement, after the Court handed down its decision, that he would not invoke an extraordinary session of the Minnesota legislature to redistrict. Olsen's party, Farmer-Labor, expected to benefit from elections at large. *The New York Times*, April 12, 1932, p. 1, col. 5; cf. p. 14, col. 2.

[7] 285 U.S. 362.

[8] 8-0. Justice Cardozo did not participate in these cases, apparently because as the Chief Justice of the New York Court of Appeals, he had heard and written

that Court's opinion in *Koenig* v. *Flynn*. The Supreme Court's three decisions followed the reasoning in that opinion.

⁹ 285 U.S. 366-367.

¹⁰ 285 U.S. 373-374.

¹¹ 285 U.S. 367-369, 373, 375.

¹² 285 U.S. 374-375.

¹³ 285 U.S. 375 (1932).

¹⁴ It is of some historical interest that he was supported by the New York State Democratic organization which, under the guidance of chairman James A. Farley, handled the litigation. *The New York Times,* April 12, 1932, p. 1, col. 5; p. 14, col. 5, 6.

¹⁵ The future Court-packer was quoted as being "extremely gratified" by the Court's action. *The New York Times,* April 12, 1932, p. 14, col. 5.

¹⁶ 285 U.S. 376-377. This argument had been employed by Holm in the *Smiley* case, where it was ignored by the Court, in spite of its having been accepted by the Minnesota courts.

¹⁷ 285 U.S. 380 (1932).

¹⁸ Quoted at 285 U.S. 382.

¹⁹ 287 U.S. 1 (1932).

²⁰ 287 U.S. 6-8.

²¹ See above, p. 37. As *The New York Times* commented, whether or not Hughes' view was legally "correct," it was "generally conceded that the opinion meant that . . . the gerrymandering could proceed as the party controlling the Legislature saw fit." October 19, 1932, p. 3, col. 3.

²² 287 U.S. 2.

²³ 287 U.S. 3.

²⁴ 287 U.S. 8, 9.

²⁵ 328 U.S. 549 (1946).

²⁶ David O. Walter, "Reapportionment of State Legislative Districts," 37 *Illinois Law Review,* 20, 21 (1942).

²⁷ Gordon E. Baker, *State Constitutions: Reapportionment* (New York: National Municipal League, 1960), p. 19.

²⁸ Quoted *ibid.*

²⁹ Austin Ranney, *Illinois Politics* (New York: New York University Press, 1960), p. 506.

³⁰ Gilbert Y. Steiner and Samuel K. Gove, *The Legislature Redistricts Illinois* (Urbana: University of Illinois Institute of Government and Public Affairs, 1956) p. 7.

³¹ Neil F. Garvey, *The Government and Administration of Illinois* (New York: Thomas Y. Crowell Co., 1958). pp. 32-33.

³² *Fergus* v. *Marks,* 321 Ill. 510, 152 N.E. 557 (1926).

³³ *Fergus* v. *Kinney,* 331 Ill. 437, 164 N.E. 665 (1928).

³⁴ *Fergus* v. *Blackwell,* 342 Ill. 223, 173 N.E. 750 (1930).

³⁵ *Keogh* v. *Neeley,* 20 Fed. (2d) 685 (1931).

³⁶ *Moran* v. *Bowley,* 247 Ill. 148, 179 N.E. 526 (1932).

³⁷ *Daly* v. *County of Madison,* 378 Ill. 357, 38 N.E. (2d) 160 (1942).

³⁸ Anthony Lewis, "Legislative Apportionment and the Federal Courts," 71 *Harvard Law Review* 1057 (1958).

[39] The case took its name from Kenneth W. Colegrove, chairman of the political science department at Northwestern University and secretary-treasurer of the American Political Science Association.

[40] 64 F. Supp. 632.

[41] 328 U.S. 551.

[42] 328 U.S. 552.

[43] *Ibid.* Charles L. Black has commented that the wrong was not suffered by Illinois as a polity, but "by individuals—numerous, to be sure, but what of that?—in consequence of certain public arrangements for Illinois." Black, "Inequities in Districting for Congress: Baker v. Carr and Colegrove v. Green," 72 *Yale Law Journal* 13 (1962).

[44] 328 U.S. 553.

[45] 328 U.S. 553.

[46] 328 U.S. 553-554.

[47] *Nixon v. Herndon,* 273 U.S. 536 (1927); *Nixon v. Condon,* 286 U.S. 73 (1932); *Smith v. Texas,* 311 U.S. 128 (1940); *U.S. v. Classic,* 313 U.S. 299 (1941); *Lane v. Wilson* (below p. 51); *Guinn v. U.S.* (below, p. 51); *Smith v. Allwright,* 321 U.S. 649 (1944); *Rice v. Elmore,* 333 U.S. 875 (1947); etc.

[48] 328 U.S. 554. ". . . is this a practicable suggestion, when the wrong complained of is the corruption of the electoral process?" Black, *op. cit.,* p. 14.

[49] See below, p. 132.

[50] See below, p. 134.

[51] See above, p. 30.

[52] 328 U.S. 556.

[53] 328 U.S. 555.

[54] 328 U.S. 557-559.

[55] 328 U.S. 560-563. Franklin H. Burdette has pointed out that Illinois' districts were "the most inequitable . . . in the Union," at least twice as much so as those of any other state. "The Illinois Congressional Redistricting Case," 40 *American Political Science Review* 958 (1946).

[56] 328 U.S. 564.

[57] 328 U.S. 565.

[58] See below, p. 53.

[59] 328 U.S. 565-566.

[60] 328 U.S. 566.

[61] *Ibid.*

[62] 328 U.S. 566-567.

[63] 328 U.S. 567.

[64] 328 U.S. 568-569.

[65] 328 U.S. 569, 571-572.

[66] 328 U.S. 570-572.

[67] 328 U.S. 574.

[68] 328 U.S. 572-573.

[69] 328 U.S. 574. For further comments and information about *Colegrove v. Green* and the circumstances leading to it, see the following Notes and Comments: 2 *American Law Reports* 1337 (1919); 46 *American Law Reports* 964 (1927); 16 *Minnesota Law Review* 850 (1932); 30 *Michigan Law Review* 969 (1932); 30 *Michigan Law Review* 1337 (1932); 17 *Cornell Law Quarterly* 466 (1932; 30 *Minnesota Law*

Review 37 (1945); 18 *Mississippi Law Journal* 170 (1946); 26 *Nebraska Law Review* 119 (1946); 20 *Southern California Law Review* 284 (1947); 35 *California Law Review* 296 (1947); 45 *Michigan Law Review* 368 (1947); 15 *George Washington Law Review* 359 (1947); 26 *Notre Dame Lawyer* 122 (1950); 35 *Illinois Bar Journal* 263 (1947); 56 *Yale Law Journal* 127 (1946). Also: 17 *Law and Contemporary Problems* (Spring 1952): entire issue devoted to Legislative Reapportionment; Harold M. Bowman, "Congressional Redistricting and the Constitution," 31 *Michigan Law Review* 149 (1932); Zechariah Chafee, Jr., "Congressional Reapportionment," 42 *Harvard Law Review* 1015 (1929); Samuel K. Gove (ed.), *State and Local Government in Illinois: A Bibliography* (Urbana: University of Illinois, 1953); Elmer C. Griffith, *The Rise and Development of the Gerrymander* (Chicago: Scott, Foresman and Company, 1907); V.O. Key, Jr., "Procedures in State Legislative Apportionment," 26 *American Political Science Review* 1050 (1932); Laurence F. Schmeckebier, *Congressional Apportionment* (Washington, D.C.: The Brookings Institution, 1941); David O. Walter, "Reapportionment of State Legislative Districts," 37 *Illinois Law Review* 20 (1942).

[70] *U.S.* v. *Cruikshank,* above, p. 27.

[71] *Ex parte Yarbrough,* 110 U.S. 651 (1884).

[72] *Giles* v. *Harris,* 189 U.S. 475 (1903.

[73] 189 U.S. 485-487.

[74] 189 U.S. 487-488.

[75] 189 U.S. 482-484.

[76] 189 U.S. 485.

[77] 273 U.S. 536 (1927).

[78] *Lane* v. *Wilson,* 307 U.S. 268 (1939).

[79] *Guinn* v. *United States,* 238 U.S. 347 (1915).

[80] 307 U.S. 272-273, 277.

[81] *Nixon* v. *Herndon, Nixon* v. *Condon, United States* v. *Classic, Smith* v. *Allwright.*

[82] *United States* v. *Mosley,* 238 U.S. 383 (1915); *United States* v. *Saylor,* 322 U.S. 385 (1944).

[83] 335 U.S. 281 (1948).

[84] 330 U.S. 804 (1947). This was a futile attempt to have *Colegrove* v. *Green* reheard.

[85] 335 U.S. 281.

[86] *Progressive Party* v. *Flynn,* 400 Ill. 102, 79 N.E. 2d 516 (1948).

[87] *MacDougall* v. *Green,* 80 F. Supp. 725 (Ill., 1948). The background of this case is discussed more fully in Note: "Legal Barriers Confronting Third Parties," 16 *University of Chicago Law Review* 499 (1949).

[88] 335 U.S. 281.

[89] 335 U.S. 283.

[90] 335 U.S. 284.

[91] *Ibid.*

[92] *Colegrove* v. *Green,* 328 U.S. 549, 566.

[93] 335 U.S. 284.

[94] 335 U.S. 286. The case was decided on October 21.

[95] 335 U.S. 285-287.

[96] 335 U.S. 284-285.

[97] See Note, 16 *University of Chicago Law Review* 499 (1949) and *The New York*

Times, October 22, 1948, p. 1 col. 2-3. For further background information and comment, see Note, 62 *Harvard Law Review* 659, 660 (1949), Note 34 *Connell Law Quarterly* 620 (1949); Comment, 43 *Illinois Law Review* 832 (1949); Comment, *Michigan Law Review* 406 (1949).

[98] This leaves the impression that a system under which some such *attempt* was made would receive Douglas' approval, but he does not here discuss what would constitute an acceptable attempt.

[99] 335 U.S. 287, 289.

[100] 335 U.S. 290.

[101] 335 U.S. 288.

[102] *Ibid.*

[103] See below, p. 66.

[104] 335 U.S. 290-291. The political reason for the officials not having offered such an opinion is suggested above, p. 53.

[105] 335 U.S. 289.

[106] *Colegrove* v. *Green,* 328 U.S. 549, 553, 554.

[107] 328 U.S. 553.

[108] For the Court's rule preserving other portions of a statute which has been ruled unconstitutional in part, see *Pollock* v. *Farmers' Loan & Trust Co.,* 158 U.S. 429, 601 (1895).

[109] *Burroughs* v. *United States,* 290 U.S. 534 (1934) validated a statute designed to protect the choice of Electors from fraud or corruption.

[110] *South* v. *Peters,* below, p. 76; *Chicago & Southern Air Lines, Inc.* v. *Waterman Steamship Corp.,* 333 U.S. 103 (1948), but especially *Baker* v. *Carr,* below, p. 59.

[111] This is a supposition which this writer finds it impossible to accept. Justice Frankfurter could not have been unaware of the enforcement problem, but that is not to say that he was entirely motivated by it.

[112] See especially *Chicago & Southern* v. *Waterman.* Jackson must have voted with the majority in *Cook* v. *Fortson* and *Turman* v. *Duckworth,* below, p. 75, as only Black and Murphy chose to note probable jurisdiction in those cases.

[113] *The New York Times* estimated that, in 1910, only 40% of the American people lived in cities; by 1960, this number had increased to 69.9%. February 4, 1962, Section IV, p. 10, col. 7. Cited in Arthur L. Goldberg, "The Statistics of Malapportionment," 72 *Yale Law Journal* 90, 97 (1962). According to E. E. Schattschneider, urban dwellers constituted 4% of the population in 1790 and 70% in 1962. "Urbanization and Reapportionment," 72 *Yale Law Journal* 7 (1962).

[114] William J. D. Boyd (ed.), *Compendium on Legislative Apportionment* (New York: National Municipal League, 1962), p. ii.

[115] *Ibid.,* pp. iii-iv. "A study in 1955 concluded that Legislatures in three-fourths of the states were less representative of population than they had been twenty years earlier.

"In only six states today does the most populous district in either branch of the Legislature have less than twice the population of the least." Anthony Lewis, *The New York Times,* March 27, 1962, p. 21, col. 5.

[116] In 1960, only 42% of the House of Representatives was elected by the urban population. *The New York Times,* February 4, 1962, Section IV, p. 10, col. 77. cited in Goldberg, *op. cit.*

[117] Robert M. Brock and David H. Grubbs, "Tennessee," in Boyd, *op. cit.,* p. 2. of Tennessee article.

[118] Brief for Appellants in *Baker* v. *Carr,* p. 13.

[119] *Baker, op. cit.,* pp. 63-68. Cf. Appendix B, "Congressional Districting as of Baker v. Carr, 1962" in Robert G. Dixon, Jr.: *Democratic Representation: Reapportionment in Law and Politics* (New York: Oxford University Press, 1968), pp. 629-631.

[120] Brock and Grubbs, *op. cit.,* p. 1. Cf. Alexander M. Bickel, "The Great Apportionment Case," 146 *New Republic* 13, April 9, 1962.

[121] Wilder Crane, "Tennessee: Inertia and the Courts," *The Politics of Reapportionment,* ed. Malcolm C. Jewell (New York: The Atherton Press, 1962), p. 316.

[122] *Ibid.*

[123] *Ibid.,* p. 315. Cf. Brock and Grubbs, *op. cit.,* p. 1; Henry N. Williams "Legislative Apportionment in Tennessee," 20 *Tennessee Law Review* 235 (1948).

[124] The ten plaintiffs included, besides the Charles W. Baker whose name thus gained a measure of immortality, a former mayor of Memphis, the editor of the Knoxville *Journal,* and a Montgomery County judge. *The New York Times,* March 27, 1962, p. 21, col. 7.

[125] In 1955, taxpayers had brought an action in Chancery Court in Davidson County, charging that the apportionment situation violated the state constitution. They won, but lost on appeal to the Tennessee Supreme Court, which held that declaring the 1901 Act unconstitutional would leave the state without a legislature. *Kidd* v. *McCanless,* 200 Tenn. 282, 292 S.W.2d 40 (1956).

[126] 369 U.S. 186 (1962).

[127] It should have been; it is estimated that the six opinions totalled some 50,000 words. Jo Desha Lucas, "Legislative Apportionment and Repressive Government: The Meaning of Baker v. Carr," 61 *Michigan Law Review* 711 (1963).

[128] U.S. 339.

[129] 369 U.S. 340-349.

[130] 369 U.S. 190.

[131] 369 U.S. 201-204.

[132] 369 U.S. 202.

[133] *U.S.* v. *Classic; U.S.* v. *Mosley; Ex parte Siebold,* 100 U.S. 371 (1880); *U.S.* v. *Saylor.*

[134] 369 U.S. 208.

[135] 369 U.S. 210.

[136] 369 U.S. 209.

[137] Further reading, however, suggests that Brennan's remarks were meant to answer those of Justice Frankfurter. Cf. 369 U.S. 301.

[138] 369 U.S. 210.

[139] 369 U.S. 211.

[140] 369 U.S. 211-217.

[141] 369 U.S. 217.

[142] Justice Brennan himself apparently realized the inapplicability of his definition, for he cautiously stressed "the need for case-by-case inquiry" (369 U.S. 210-211) and "the necessity for discriminating inquiry into the precise facts and posture of the particular case, and the impossibility of resolution by any semantic cataloguing." (369 U.S. 217).

[143] 369 U.S. 227, 229-230.

[144] 369 U.S. 226.

[145] See the excellent article by E. E. Schattschneider, "Urbanization and Reapportionment," 72 *Yale Law Journal* 7 (1962).

[146] E. F. Roberts and Paul T. Schultz III: "The Reapportionment Cases: Cognitive Lag, the Malady and its Cure". 27 *University of Pittsburgh Law Review* 633, 645-6 (1966). The article makes the interesting argument that because it shored up popular belief in the viability of state boundaries, *Baker* was an extremely conservative decision.

[147] March 26, 1962, p. 21, col. 1.

[148] 369 U.S. 228-229, 234, 237.

[149] 369 U.S. 242, 245.

[150] 369 U.S. 247-250.

[151] 369 U.S. 241n.

[152] 369 U.S. 241-242n.

[153] 369 U.S. 246n.

[154] 369 U.S. 245.

[155] See below, p. 132.

[156] Cf. Justice Douglas' dissent in *New York* v. *O'Neill,* 359 U.S. 1 (1959).

[157] 369 U.S. 250n-251n.

[158] 369 U.S. 251.

[159] 369 U.S. 251-252.

[160] 369 U.S. 253-258; Table I, 369 U.S. 262-264.

[161] 369 U.S. 258.

[162] 369 U.S. 260.

[163] 369 U.S. 261.

[164] 369 U.S. 260.

[165] In oral dissent, the justice said, "Today the court begins a process of litigation that it requires no prophet to say—and Cassandra was sometimes right—will outlast the life of the youngest member of this court." Quoted in *The New York Times,* March 27, 1962, p. 21, col. 6.

[166] 369 U.S. 266-267.

[167] One might quarrel with his assumption that important political forces clash in the electoral process, or that they do not clash more directly and more significantly elsewhere.

[168] 369 U.S. 285-286. This belief explains Justice Frankfurter's opinion in *Gomillion* v. *Lightfoot,* 364 U.S. 339, 346 (1960), in which the Court struck down the Alabama legislature's redistricting of Tuskegee into a 28-sided monstrosity which excluded all but four or five black voters from the city's electorate. Cf. Bernard Taper: *Gomillion versus Lightfoot* (New York: McGraw-Hill, 1962), passim. Kenneth S. Tollett points out that Frankfurter inquired into the motives of the legislature and found an attempt to deprive citizens of their constitutional rights—something he refused to do in *Colegrove* and protested the Court's doing in *Baker.* "Political Questions and the Law," 42 *Detroit Law Journal* 439, 458 (1965).

[169] 369 U.S. 267.

[170] 349 U.S. 294 (1955).

[171] 369 U.S. 269-270.

[172] 340 U.S. 268, 285 (1951).

[173] Quoted in Lewis, *op. cit.* p. 1086. Cf. Lewis' contention that it is the function of courts "to decide cases in which precise standards are not, perhaps cannot, be fixed." pp. 1084, 1087.

[174] 369 U.S. 277-278.

[175] 369 U.S. 380-381.

[176] 369 U.S. 299.

[177] 369 U.S. 300.

[178] 369 U.S. 301.

[179] 369 U.S. 301-323.

[180] 369 U.S. 324,330.

[181] 369 U.S. 340-349.

[182] It could be argued that the major part of the Court's work, and certainly the most important part, consists of defining concepts which come close to defying such elucidation. Cases in point are "commerce among the states," "free speech," "due process," etc. Over the years, these phrases acquire a chameleon-like character, miraculously taking on the coloration decreed by successive generations.

[183] 369 U.S. 334-338.

[184] 369 U.S. 339.

[185] Comment, 36 *Iowa Law Review* 134 (1950).

[186] Morris B. Abram, "The County Unit System is Unconstitutional," 14 *Georgia Bar Journal* 28 (1951).

[187] Melvin C. Hughes, "Georgia," *County Government Across the Nation,* Paul W. Wager, ed. (Chapel Hill: University of North Carolina Press, 1950), p. 439.

[188] Cf. Cullen B. Gosnell, *Government and Politics of Georgia* (New York: Thomas Nelson & Sons, 1936), pp. 176-178.

[189] Cf. Comment, 99 *University of Pennsylvania Law Review* 413, 416 (1950).

[190] Comment, 36 *Iowa Law Review* 134, 140 (1950). A former Georgia lawyer has presented the argument that the system discriminated between rural citizens and between small counties as well. Abram, *op. cit.,* pp. 28-29, 34n. Be this as it may, it is certain the system did discriminate against urban whites in general and urban white laborers in particular, in addition to Negroes.

[191] Comment, 99 *University of Pennsylvania Law Review* 413, 415.

[192] Note, 47 *Columbia Law Review* 284, 285 (1947).

[193] Daniel Minchew, "Georgia," in Boyd, *op. cit.,* p. 1 of Georgia article.

[194] *Gates* v. *Long,* 172 Tenn. 471, 112 S.W. 2d 388 (1938).

[195] Cf. V. O. Key, Jr., *Southern Politics in State and Nation* (New York: Alfred A. Knopf, 1949), Ch. 6: "Georgia: Rule of the Rustics," pp. 112, 115.

[196] Gosnell, *op. cit.,* p. 179.

[197] Key, *Southern Politics,* p. 120.

[198] *Ibid.,* pp. 119-120.

[199] *The New York Times* reported that Carmichael polled more votes "than any other Georgia Governorship candidate had ever received." July 21, 1946, Section IV, p. 10, col. 5-8. Also see July 14, p. 12, col. 1; July 19, p. 36, col. 1; August 3, p. 3, col. 8; August 27, p. 14, col. 2-5.

[200] *Turman* v. *Duckworth,* 328 U.S. 675 (1946). Cf. Note: "Georgia County Unit Vote," 47 *Columbia Law Review* 284, 286-287 (1947).

[201] *Cook* v. *Fortson,* 329 U.S. 675 (1946).

[202] Although the court did not choose to mention the fact, the general election was imminent. The decision was handed down on October 28, and the Georgia Constitution required the election to be held on the Tuesday after the first Monday in November. If the Neill Act had been invalidated, there might not have been either nominees or machinery for the election fifteen days away.

[203] 68 F. Supp. 744, 747.

[204] 279 U.S. 812 (1928).

[205] 329 U.S. 678-679. In a technical argument, Rutledge also objected to the tacit opinion of the lower court that declaratory relief could not be given "beyond the boundaries fixed by the preexisting jurisdiction in equity." If injunctions could not have been issued in the instant cases, declaratory relief could. To interpret this in layman's language, no legal formulae prevented the lower and higher courts from deciding the cases on their merits. 328 U.S. 677, 678. Justices Black and Murphy, who thought that probable jurisdiction should have been noted, may have been aware of such considerations. 329 U.S. 675.

[206] 339 U.S. 276 (1950).

[207] 89 F. Supp. 672. The system was now being championed by Eugene Talmadge's heir, Governor Herman Talmadge.

[208] 339 U.S. 277.

[209] 339 U.S. 277.

[210] 339 U.S. 278.

[211] *Ibid.*

[212] 339 U.S. 279. This reasoning became the basis for Douglas' opinion in *Gray* v. *Sanders.* See below, p. 80.

[213] 339 U.S. 280.

[214] 339 U.S. 281.

[215] *Ibid.*

[216] For further information about these cases, see Note: "Georgia County Unit Vote," 27 *Columbia Law Review* 284 (1947); Recent Cases, 24 *Temple Law Quarterly* 239 (1950); Recent Cases, 19 *George Washington Law Review* 216 (1950); Recent Decision, 36 *Virginia Law Review* 678 (1950); Recent Decisions, 49 *Michigan Law Review* 271 (1950); David O. Stone, "Equality of Voting Power as a Constitutional Right," 2 *Syracuse Law Review* 73 (1950); Recent Cases, 4 *Vanderbilt Law Review* 691 (1957); *The New York Times* (the *Cook* and *Turman* cases), July 17, 1946, p. 12, col. 1; July 19, p. 36, col. 1; July 21, Section IV, p. 10, col. 5-8; August 3, p. 3, col. 8; August 27, p. 14, col. 2-5; (*South* v. *Peters*), February 26, 1950, Section IV, p. 7, col. 4-5; April 18, 1950, p. 1, col. 6-7.

[217] *The New York Times,* November 8, 1950, p. 11, col. 3.

[218] *Cox* v. *Peters,* 342 U.S. 937 (1952); 208 Ga. 498, 67 S.E. 2d 579. Probably seeking to avoid the "no equity" defense of similar cases, Cox brought this suit as an action at law for money damages.

[219] *The New York Times,* March 27, 1952, p. 23, col. 5-6.

[220] *Hartsfield* v. *Sloan,* 357 U.S. 916. Cf. *The New York Times,* March 16, 1958, p. 78, col. 5; March 23, p. 76, col. 1; April 21, p. 10, col. 4; May 18, p. 52, col. 1; June 17, p. 23, col. 1. In 1952, see March 4, p. 19, col. 3; March 27, p. 23, col. 5-6; April 8, p. 22, col. 6.

[221] *Sanders* v. *Gray,* 203 F. Supp. 158 (1962). *Gray* v. *Sanders,* 372 U.S. 368 (1963). The suit was actually brought against James H. Gray, chairman of the state Democratic Executive Committee and other committee and state officials. Cf. *The New York Times,* March 27, 1962, p. 21, col. 2-3.

[222] 372 U.S. 370, 371.

[223] Georgia Laws 1962, Ex. Sess., p. 1217; Ga. Code Ann. § 34-3212, 34-3213 (1962).

[224] 372 U.S. 388.

[225] 203 F. Supp. 158. In support of its decision, the court cited Douglas' opinion in *South* v. *Peters.*

[226] March 19, 1963, p. 4, col. 3.

[227] *The New York Times,* September 28, 1962, p. 24, col. 1-3; March 19, 1963 (Western Edition), p. 4, col. 3.

[228] 372 U.S. 378-380.

[229] 372 U.S. 378-379.

[230] 179 U.S. 58 (1900).

[231] 100 U.S. 371 (1880).

[232] 345 U.S. 461 (1953).

[233] 372 U.S. 378.

[234] 372 U.S. 379.

[235] 372 U.S. 381. This line of thought reflects Douglas' earlier opinion in *South* v. *Peters.* See above, p. 76.

[236] 372 U.S. 388-389.

[237] According to Harlan, as of November 1, 1962, thirty reapportionment and ten electoral cases had been brought in various courts. 372 U.S. 382.

[238] 372 U.S. 388.

[239] 372 U.S. 386-387.

[240] 372 U.S. 383-385.

[241] 372 U.S. 383.

[242] 372 U.S. 381-382.

[243] In his first appearance in any court, Attorney General Robert F. Kennedy argued the case for the government as *amicus curiae,* delivering his oral argument and answering questions from the bench without the aid of notes.

[244] Some segregationist forces, which had already been affected by *Gray* v. *Sanders,* and which of course had been attempting since 1954 to weaken the Court, were strong supporters of the proposals.

[245] See Robert B. McKay, "Court, Congress, and Reapportionment," 63 *Michigan Law Review* 255, 256, 257 (1964).

[246] *Wesberry* v. *Sanders,* 376 U.S. 1, 2-3 (1964).

[247] The court rejected the argument of nonjusticiability but agreed with Frankfurter's contention of want of equity. *Sanders* v. *Wesberry,* 206 F. Supp. 276, 285. The justiciability argument had been irretrievably damaged by *Baker* v. *Carr;* the court's substitution of the equity arguments suggests that for purposes of political questions, "justiciability" and "equity" are interchangeable recognitions of the enforcement problem.

[248] 376 U.S. 3-5.

[249] 376 U.S. 6, quoting 369 U.S. 232.

[250] "The Times, Places and Manner of holding Elections for Senators and Representatives, shall be prescribed in each State by the Legislature thereof; but the Congress may at any time by Law make or alter such Regulations, except as to the Place of chusing Senators . . ."

[251] 376 U.S. 7.

[252] 376 U.S. 6.

[253] The reaction to *Baker* v. *Carr* had shown Black that the State legislatures wouldn't fight back, and this would eliminate Justice Harlan's implied fear that Congress might. A Congress chosen from reapportioned districts would hardly question the decision responsible for its existence.

[254] "The House of Representatives shall be composed of Members chosen every second Year by the People of the several States . . ."

[255] 376 U.S. 7-8.

[256] 376 U.S. 8-15.

[257] 376 U.S. 13-17.

[258] *U.S.* v. *Mosley, Ex parte Yarbrough, U.S.* v. *Classic, U.S.* v. *Saylor.*

[259] 376 U.S. 18.

[260] 376 U.S. 4, 18.

[261] 376 U.S. 18-19.

[262] 376 U.S. 20.

[263] Cf. Douglas in *Baker,* 369 U.S. 242; Clark in *Baker,* id. at 253-258. Justices Clark and Stewart would return to this standard in a later series of landmark cases, with Justice Stewart suggesting the additional criterion of "ultimate effective majority rule," *Maryland Committee* v. *Tawes,* 377 U.S. 656, 677. See below, p. 93n. 305.

[264] 376 U.S. 20, 21.

[265] 376 U.S. 25.

[266] *Ibid.*

[267] 376 U.S. 26.

[268] 376 U.S. 27.

[269] 376 U.S. 27-30.

[270] 376 U.S. 29-30.

[271] 376 U.S. 30-42.

[272] 376 U.S. 42.

[273] *Ibid.*

[274] 376 U.S. 46-47.

[275] 376 U.S. 48.

[276] *Ibid.*

[277] Justice Stewart also dissented. He agreed with Harlan's opinion, except that he felt the issues were justiciable, and wanted to make the point explicit. 376 U.S. 50-51.

[278] *The New York Times,* February 23, 1964, Section IV, page 6E, columns 2, 3.

[279] Robert B. McKay, "The Reapportionment Decisions: Retrospect and Prospect," 51 *American Bar Association Journal* 128, 131 (1965).

[280] 377 U.S. 533.

[281] 377 U.S. 533 at 545.

[282] Annotation: "Inequalities in population of election districts or voting units as rendering apportionment unconstitutional—federal cases", 12 L. ed. 2d 1282, 1288 (1965).

[283] 377 U.S. 533, 547, 549-550.

[284] *Sims* v. *Frink,* 208 F. Supp. 431 (DCMD) Ala. (1962).

[285] 377 U.S. 552.

[286] 377 U.S. 553.

[287] The vote to affirm was 8-1 (6-2-1) or 7-2, depending on whether one interprets Justice Stewart's opinion as indicating agreement or dissent. 377 U.S. 588. Cf. his related dissent in *Lucas* v. *Colorado General Assembly,* 377 U.S. 713, 744. Justice Clark concurred in the result but not in the Court's opinion. 377 U.S. 587.

[288] 377 U.S. 561.

[289] *Ibid.*

[290] 377 U.S. 562-563.

[291] 377 U.S. 567.

[292] 377 U.S. 566.

[293] 377 U.S. 568.

[294] *Ibid.*

[295] Perhaps "lethargy" would be more accurate than "acceptance".

[296] 377 U.S. 564-565.

[297] 377 U.S. 576-577.

[298] 377 U.S. 578-581.

[299] 377 U.S. 583-584.

[300] 377 U.S. 585-587.

[301] 377 U.S. 589.

[302] 377 U.S. 615-621.

[303] 377 U.S. 624.

[304] 377 U.S. 623-624.

[305] *WMCA* v. *Lomenzo,* 377 U.S. 633; *Maryland Committee* v. *Tawes,* 377 U.S. 656; *Davis* v. *Mann,* 377 U.S. 678; *Roman* v. *Sincock,* 377 U.S. 695; *Lucas* v. *Colorado General Assembly,* 377 U.S. 713.

[306] *Lucas* v. *Colorado General Assembly,* 377 U.S. 713, 736-737. It is not suggested that this is a sufficient summary of *Lucas* or that *Reynolds* or any other case has been thoroughly briefed from a legal point of view. The only aspects of the cases dealt with here are those which shed a light on the problem of "political questions".

[307] *Beadle* v. *Scholle,* 377 U.S. 990; *Marshall* v. *Hare,* 378 U.S. 561; *Meyers* v. *Thigpen,* 378 U.S. 554; *Williams* v. *Moss,* 378 U.S. 558; *Germano* v. *Kerner,* 378 U.S. 560; *Hearne* v. *Smylie,* 378 U.S. 563; *Pinney* v. *Butterworth,* 378 U.S. 556; *Hill* v. *Davis,* 378 U.S. 565.

[308] Alabama, New York, Maryland, Virginia, Delaware, Colorado, Michigan, Washington, Oklahoma, Illinois, Idaho, Connecticut, Florida, Ohio, Iowa.

[309] Robert G. Dixon, Jr.: "Reapportionment in the Supreme Court and Congress: Constitutional Struggle for Fair Representation", 63 *Michigan Law Review* 209 (1964).

[310] For a discussion of many of them, see Dixon, *op. cit.* pp. 214-217.

[311] The defeated Dirksen "rider," Representative McCulloch's proposed Constitutional amendment, and other attempted measures and their demise are chronicled in Dixon, *op. cit.* pp. 231-232, 237; McKay, *op. cit.*, passim; Note, "Reapportionment," 79 *Harvard Law Review* 1228, 1232-1237 (1966); and Robert G. Dixon, Jr.: *Democratic Representation: Reapportionment in Law and Politics* (New York: Oxford University Press, 1968), chs. xv and xvi. McKay points out elsewhere that what murmurs of discontent existed disappeared by 1968, with reapportionment as an issue being ignored in the anti-Court rhetoric of the 1968 Presidential campaign. Robert B. McKay: "Reapportionment: Success Story of the Warren Court," 67 *Michigan Law Review* 223, 228 (1968). Perhaps the death of Congressional interest in the issue reflects the lack of any significant policy changes resulting from reapportionment. Cf. Ward Elliott: "Prometheus, Proteus, Pandora, and Procrustes Unbound: The Political Consequences of Reapportionment," 37 *Chicago Law Review* 474 (1970). This assessment is challenged by McKay, *op. cit.*, p. 230-231.

[312] Cf., e.g., *Kirkpatrick* v. *Presiler*, 394 U.S. 526 (1969); *Wells* v. *Rockefeller*, 394 U.S. 542 (1960). Applications by the Court and lower courts of the one man-one vote doctrine to other governmental units are summarized in *Annotation*, 18 L. ed. 2d 1537 (1967) and *Later Case Service*, L. ed. 2d 430 (1971).

[313] *Bode* v. *National Democratic Party*, cert. den., 30 L. ed. 2d 668 (1972). Relying on the decision in *Baker* and subsequent apportionment decisions as well as the Court's voting rights decisions, a Note in the *Yale Law Journal* argued that the Equal Protection clause's mandate of one man-one vote should be applied to party conventions. Note: "Constitutional Safeguards in the Selection of Delegates to Presidential Nominating Conventions," 78 *Yale Law Journal* 1228 (1969). The opposite opinion can be found in Note: "One Man, One Vote and Selection of Delegates to National Nominating Conventions," 37 *Chicago Law Review* 536 (1970). Whatever the Constitutional argument, it seems clear that Court involvement in delegate selection would be met with great hostility from both parties. In addition, at the time the Court refused certiorari, the Democratic Party was about to begin delegate selection under its relatively democratic post-1968 reforms and the Republican Party had pledged itself to a major effort to increase representation among delegates of women, youth, and minority groups. Thus the Court may have felt that this particular problem would be solved satisfactorily without Court intervention.

NOTES—CHAPTER 4

[1] For the converse situation, accepted as justiciable by the Court, see *Smiley* v. *Holm*, 285 U.S. 355 (1932); *Koenig* v. *Flynn*, 285 U.S. 375 (1932); and *Carroll* v. *Becker*, 285 U.S. 380 (1932); all discussed above, pp. 37-40.

[2] 6 Wall. 499 (1867).

[3] 6 Wall. 506-507.

[4] 6 Wall, 508-511.

[5] *White* v. *Hart*, 13 Wall. 646 (1871).

[6] 13 Wall. 649.

[7] 92 U.S. 130 (1875).

[8] 92 U.S. 133.

[9] *Field* v. *Clark,* 143 U.S. 649 (1891).

[10] The Act was also challenged as an unconstitutional delegation of legislative power to the executive.

[11] 143 U.S. 670. Underlined words are italicized in the original.

[12] 143 U.S. 672.

[13] 143 U.S. 673.

[14] 143 U.S. 672.

[15] Harlan went on to say that the Act was not an unconstitutional delegation of power. Justice Lamar and Chief Justice Fuller concurred on the political point but thought the delegation unconstitutional. 143 U.S. 697. Five years later, the *Field* doctrine was extended to laws governing United States Territories. *Harwood* v. *Wentworth,* 162 U.S. 547 (1896).

[16] *In re Duncan,* 139 U.S. 449 (1891).

[17] 139 U.S. 450-451.

[18] 139 U.S. 451.

[19] 139 U.S. 461-462, 454-456.

[20] 139 U.S. 454-455, 459-460.

[21] 139 U.S. 459.

[22] 253 U.S. 350 (1920).

[23] 253 U.S. 385, 386.

[24] *Dillon* v. *Glass,* 256 U.S. 368 (1921).

[25] 256 U.S. 376.

[26] 256 U.S. 375-376.

[27] *Leser* v. *Garnett,* 258 U.S. 130 (1922).

[28] 258 U.S. 136.

[29] 258 U.S. 137.

[30] 282 U.S. 716 (1931).

[31] The argument of the two plaintiffs, who had been indicted for transporting fifty half-barrels of beer, was accepted by the District Court in New Jersey which heard the suit. Apparently the case caught the imagination of the average parched citizen: "The Supreme Court's decision was not unexpected, but great interest centered in it, especially as the government had asked the court to act speedily because there was so great a question in the public mind that prohibition enforcement was made more difficult." *The New York Times,* February 25, 1931, p. 1, col. 6. The decision was handed down along with others penalizing offenders of the prohibition laws.

[32] 282 U.S. 734.

[33] 282 U.S. 731, 732.

[34] 307 U.S. 433 (1939).

[35] *Hammer* v. *Dagenhart,* 247 U.S. 251 (1918).

[36] 146 Kan. 390; 71 P. 2d 518 (1937).

[37] Edward S. Corwin (ed.), *The Constitution of the United States of America: Analysis and Interpretation* (Washington: Government Printing Office, 1953), p. 51n.

[38] *Wise* v. *Chandler,* 270 Ky. 1 (1937).

[39] 307 U.S. 438, 441-446.

[40] 307 U.S. 441-446.

[41] 307 U.S. 460, 464-470.

[42] 307 U.S. 447.

[43] 307 U.S. 449.

[44] 307 U.S. 450, 452.

[45] 307 U.S. 452-453.

[46] 307 U.S. 453-454.

[47] 307 U.S. 454-455.

[48] 307 U.S. 458.

[49] *Ibid.*

[50] 307 U.S. 459-460.

[51] 307 U.S. 460, 464.

[52] 307 U.S. 464-467.

[53] 273 U.S. 536, 540 (1927).

[54] 307 U.S. 469-470.

[55] See Frankfurter's opinions in *Colegrove* v. *Green* and *Baker* v. *Carr,* above, pp. 44, 68.

[56] 369 U.S. 241n1., 242-243n., 246-248n. See above, p. 67.

[57] 307 U.S. 461.

[58] See above, p. 51.

[59] See above, p. 76.

[60] 395 U.S. 486 (1969).

[61] 143 U.S. 135 (1892).

[62] 143 U.S. 185-186.

[63] Chief Justice Fuller's optimistic estimate of the instant situation was warranted. *The New York Times* reported that enthusiasm in Nebraska was "at a high pitch" when the decision was handed down. A month earlier, when the *Times* had managed to publish the Court's vote before it was officially announced, Thayer had said that he "would at once and cheerfully" vacate the governor's office. *The New York Times,* February 2, 1891, p. 1, col. 7; p. 2, col. 1.

[64] 146 U.S. 1 (1892).

[65] "Each State shall appoint, in such Manner as the Legislature thereof shall direct, a Number of Electors, equal to the whole number of Senators and Representatives to which the State may be entitled in the Congress. . . ."

[66] 146 U.S. 21-22.

[67] 146 U.S. 22-42.

[68] *Taylor & Marshall* v. *Beckham,* 178 U.S. 548 (1900).

[69] Otto Kirchheimer, *Political Justice* (Princeton: Princeton University Press, 1961), p. 56. For a more complete account of the background events and an examination of the case itself, cf. pp. 54-60.

[70] 178 U.S. 571-573.

[71] This contention was disputed by Justices Brewer and Brown in a dissenting opinion.

[72] 178 U.S. 576-581.

[73] 178 U.S. 580.

[74] Harlan was a conservative Kentucky Republican, who had run for governor twice, and served as attorney general of Kentucky for four years. Kirchheimer, *op. cit.,* p. 57 n17.

[75] In 1944, the Court confirmed the ruling in *Taylor & Marshall* v. *Beckham*, holding that "an unlawful denial by state action of a right to state political office is not a denial of a right of property or of liberty secured by the due process clause." *Snowden* v. *Hughes,* 321 U.S. 1, 7 (1944). *Taylor & Marshall* v. *Beckham* did not end the problem for Kentucky; with the Democrats firmly in office, top Republican officials were tried and convicted, on extremely shaky evidence, for Geobel's murder. Cf. Kirchheimer, *op. cit.*, pp. 57-60.

[76] 124 U.S. 200, 210, 212 (1888).

[77] Also see *Cave* v. *Newell,* 246 U.S. 650 (1917).

[78] *Walton* v. *House of Representatives of the State of Oklahoma,* 265 U.S. 487 (1924).

[79] *Bond* v. *Floyd,* 251 F. Supp. 333 (1966).

[80] *Bond* v. *Floyd,* 385 U.S. 116 (1966). The facts of the case along with the SNCC statement and Bond's endorsement are to be found in the opinion of the Court. 385 U.S. 116, 118-125.

[81] Charles P. Kindregan: "The Cases of Adam Clayton Powell, Jr. and Julian Bond: The Right of Legislative Bodies to Exclude Members-Elect," 2 *Suffolk University Law Review* 58, 59 (1968).

[82] Quoted in the *New York Times,* April 5, 1972, p. 1 c. 5- p. 30 c. 1. Cf. Powell's statement during the debate leading to his non-seating: "There is no one here who does not have a skeleton in his closet. I know, and I know them by name." 113 Cong. Rec. 23, 90th Cong. 1st Sess.

[83] Kent M. Weeks: *Adam Clayton Powell and the Supreme Court* (New York: Dunellen, 1971), pp. 3-4. As of this writing, this is the best source for information about the events leading to the case, and I am indebted to it for much of the account below.

[84] Quoted in P. Allan Dionisopoulos: *Rebellion, Racism, and Representation: The Adam Clayton Powell Case and Its Antecedents* (Dekalb: Northern Illinois University Press, 1970), p. 155.

[85] H. Res. 1021, Sept. 22, 1966. 112 Cong. Rec. 23741, 89th Cong. 2d Sess.

[86] House Report 2349. Special Subcommittee on Contracts. 89th Cong. 2d Sess., 6-7 (1966).

[87] All of the suits and judgments are detailed in *In re Adam Clayton Powell: Hearings before Select Committee Pursuant to* H. Res. 1, 90th Cong. 1st sess. 114-120 (1967); hereinafter referred to as *In re Powell.*

[88] 113 Cong. Rec. 26-27, 90th Cong., 1st sess. 1967.

[89] The full list can be found in *In re Powell,* p. 1.

[90] The extensive briefs submitted by counsel can be found in three sections in *In re Powell,* beginning on pgs. 7, 31, and 255.

[91] *In re Powell,* pp. 114-127.

[92] *Ibid.*, pp. 172-196.

[93] *Ibid.*, p. 204.

[94] H. Res. 278, Mar. 1, 1967. 113 Cong. Rec. 4997, 90th Cong. 1st Sess.

[95] 113 Cong. Rec. 5037, 90th Cong. 1st Sess. (1967).

[96] 23 L Ed 2d 910-912 (1969).

[97] . . . for any Speech or Debate in either House, they (the Senators and Representatives) shall not be questioned in any other Place.

[98] Summarized in *Powell* v. *McCormack,* 395 U.S. 486, 493-494. Also see 23 L Ed 2d 912-914 (1969).

[99] *Powell* v. *McCormack,* 266 F Supp 354 (DC DC 1967).

[100] *Powell* v. *McCormack,* 129 US App DC 354, 395 F 2d 577 (1968).

[101] 115 Cong. Rec. 16, 91st Cong. 1st sess. (1969).

[102] *Ibid.*

[103] 115 Cong. Rec. 16-34, passim.

[104] 115 Cong. Rec. 34.

[105] 395 U.S. 486, 533.

[106] 395 U.S. 496-500.

[107] 395 U.S. 502-506.

[108] 395 U.S. 508.

[109] Robert C. Eckhardt: "The Adam Clayton Powell Case," 45 *Texas Law Review* 1205, 1209 (1967), cited by the Court at 395 U.S. 510-511.

[110] 395 U.S. 508-510.

[111] 395 U.S. 512.

[112] 395 U.S. 512-516.

[113] 395 U.S. 516-517.

[114] 395 U.S. 517-518.

[115] 395 U.S. 518-519 (quoting *Baker* v. *Carr,* 369 U.S. 217).

[116] 395 U.S. 522.

[117] 395 U.S. 522-527.

[118] 395 U.S. 527-531.

[119] 395 U.S. 541-546.

[120] 395 U.S. 547.

[121] 395 U.S. 547.

[122] 395 U.S. 547-548.

[123] 395 U.S. 549.

[124] 395 U.S. 549.

[125] 395 U.S. 550.

[126] 395 U.S. 551, 553.

[127] 395 U.S. 554-559.

[128] 395 U.S. 559-572.

[129] Annotation: "Federal Court's Power to Determine Election or Qualifications of Members of Legislative Body," 17 L. ed. 2d 911, 912 (1966).

[130] Note: "Adam Clayton Powell's Exclusion from Congress: Increased Judicial Review of Legislative Action," 24 *University of Miami Law Review* 389, 397 (1970).

[131] Lewis Donald Asper and Sanford Jay Rosen: "Comment on Powell v. McCormack," 17 *University of California at Los Angeles Law Review* 58, 62-63 (1969).

[132] The leading article is P. Allan Dionisopoulos: "A Commentary on the Constitutional Issues in the Powell and Related Cases," 17 *Journal of Public Law* 103 (1968). This is expanded in Dionisopoulos: *Rebellion, Racism, and Representation, op. cit.,* ch. II-VI. Also see "Congressional Power to Exclude Members-Elect," 83 *Harvard Law Review* 62, 72-75 (1969); Dousey D. Ellis, Jr.: "Powell v. McCormack and the Power to Expel," 5 *Georgia Law Review* 203 (1971).

[133] The words are Chief Justice Earl Warren's and refer to the investigations conducted by the House Committee on Un-American Activities during the McCarthy era. *Watkins* v. *United States,* 354 U.S. 178, 197 (1957).

[134] Dionisopoulos: *Rebellion, Racism, and Representation, op. cit.,* p. 156.

[135] Quoted in Weeks, *op. cit.,* p. 134.

[136] 113 Cong. Rec. 5028, 90th Cong. 1st Sess. (1967).

[137] 133 Cong. Rec. 5007, 90th Cong. 1st Sess. (1967).

[138] Weeks, *op. cit.* p. 13. Weeks also suggests that part of the reason for the Court's decision may be found in Bruce Bromley's oral argument before the high tribunal. In the face of extensive questioning by the justices, Bromley maintained that even if a Congressional decision to exclude or expel was based on clearly unconstitutional grounds such as race or religion, the speech and debate clause would preclude judicial review. Weeks, p. 180, 182-185: The oral arguments of both sides are to be found in "*Powell* v. *McCormack:* Oral Argument," 24 *Rutgers Law Review* 193 (1970).

[139] Dionisopoulos, *op. cit.* p. 157.

[140] *Powell* v. *McCormack,* cert. denied, 387 U.S. 933 (1967).

[141] *New York Law Journal,* Sept. 30, 1969, p. 1, c. 3.

[142] The letter is reprinted in Robert B. McKay: "Comment on Powell v. McCormack," 17 *University of California at Los Angeles Law Review* 117, 125 (1969).

[143] *Powell* v. *Hart,* 396 U.S. 1055 (1970).

[144] Dionisopoulos, *op. cit.*, p. 161.

[145] Cf., for example, *Manion* v. *Holzman,* 379 F 2d 843, cert. denied 389 U.S. 976 (1967). Manion claimed that a Congressional election in Illinois was stolen from him through fraudulent vote-counting. By the time the case reached the District Court, his opponent had been seated in Congress. Both the District Court and the Court of Appeals said they had no jurisdiction in the matter. In spite of *Powell* v. *McCormack,* were a similar case (i.e. the opponent already seated) to arise today, the Supreme Court would again deny certiorari.

[146] Election cases which are brought to the Court by a winner, in firm control of the political machinery, who merely wishes to acquire a judicial imprimatur, do not become political questions. Cf. *Boyd* and *McPherson,* above.

[147] Supra, p. 113.

NOTES—CHAPTER 5

[1] 1 Cranch 137, 170 (1803). Marshall, of course, did not employ the political question technique in *Marbury* because he devised a cleverer method which achieved the result of non-interference while permitting him to set a firm precedent for judicial review.

[2] *Youngstown Co.* v. *Sawyer,* 343 U.S. 579 (1952). Also see *United States* v. *United States,* 407 U.S. 297 (1972).

[3] *Kentucky* v. *Dennison,* 24 How. 66 (1860).

[4] "A Person charged in any State with Treason, Felony, or other Crime, who shall flee from justice, and be found in another State, shall on Demand of the executive Authority of the State from which he fled, be delivered up, to be removed to the State having Jurisdiction of the Crime."

[5] Act of Feb. 12, 1793: "That whenever the Executive authority of any state in the Union . . . shall demand any person as a fugitive from justice of the Executive authority of any such State . . . to which such person shall have fled, and shall, moreover, produce the copy of an indictment found, . . . charging the person so

demanded with having committed treason, felony, or other crime. . . . it shall be the duty of the Executive authority of the State . . . to which such person shall have fled to cause him or her to be arrested and secured, . . . and to cause the fugitive to be delivered to such agent when he shall appear. . . ."

[6] 24 How. 90.

[7] 24 How. 84.

[8] *Dred Scott* v. *Sandford,* 19 How. 393 (1857).

[9] 24 How. 99-103.

[10] 4 Wheat. 316, 414 (1819).

[11] 24 How. 103.

[12] 24 How. 104.

[13] 24 How. 106.

[14] 24 How. 107.

[15] 24 How. 108.

[16] 24 How. 107.

[17] 24 How. 107-108.

[18] 24 How. 109.

[19] 24 How. 109-110.

[20] Carl Brent Swisher, *Roger Taney* (New York: The Macmillan Co., 1935), p. 545.

[21] 4 Wall. 475 (1866).

[22] Warren, *op. cit.,* II, 178-179, 181n.

[23] 4 Wall. 476.

[24] 4 Wall. 477, 479, 480. Mississippi cited *Kendall* v. *U.S.,* 12 Peters 524 (1838), which involved the Postmaster General, and in which the Court held that it could issue a mandamus to the head of an executive department, ordering the performance of a purely ministerial act; and *U.S.* v. *Guthrie,* 17 How. 284 (1854), involving the Secretary of Treasury.

[25] 4 Wall. 481, 484-485.

[26] 4 Wall. 483.

[27] Underlined word italicized in the original.

[28] 4 Wall. 483.

[29] 4 Wall. 486.

[30] 4 Wall. 487.

[31] 4 Wall. 488.

[32] Quoted in Warren, *op. cit.,* p. 181.

[33] 4 Wall. 498-500.

[34] 4 Wall. 500-501. The South persisted, with Georgia taking up the cudgels: in 1867, it filed a bill against Stanton, Secretary of War; General Grant, and Major-General Pope; asking that they be enjoined from carrying out the Reconstruction Acts. Mr. Stanbery argued that equity could not secure the political rights involved, and Justice Nelson agreed that courts in law and equity could handle only rights "of persons or property," not those "of sovereignty, of political jurisdiction, of government, of corporate existence as a state." He chose to ignore Georgia's contention that the United States had done precisely what Dorr had not been allowed to do in Rhode Island. *Georgia* v. *Stanton,* 6 Wall. 50, 56-59, 76, 77, 85. A final attempt, again undertaken by Mississippi, was dismissed *per curiam* on the basis

of *Georgia* v. *Stanton. Mississippi* v. *Stanton and Grant,* 154, U.S. 554 (1868). The Court paid no heed to Georgia's assertion that both political and property rights were involved in her case.

³⁵ 12 Pet. 524 (1838).

³⁶ Warren, *op. cit.,* II, 44.

³⁷ *Ibid.*

³⁸ 12 Pet. 609.

³⁹ For his pains, Taney was criticized as being more interested in protecting Jackson's Postmaster-General than he was in the legal issues. Cf. Samuel Tyler, *Memoir of Roger Brooke Taney, LL.D.* (Baltimore: John Murphy & Co., 1872), p. 306.

⁴⁰ Quoted in Warren, *op. cit.,* II, 48.

⁴¹ 14 Peters 497 (1840).

⁴² 14 Peters 499-500.

⁴³ 14 Peters 516.

⁴⁴ 6 How. 92 (1848).

⁴⁵ 6 How. 100.

⁴⁶ 6 How. 102.

⁴⁷ Cf. e.g., *U.S. ex rel. Goodrich* v. *Guthrie,* 17 How. 284 (1854), in which President Taylor's removal of the Chief Justice of the Territory of Minnesota was held to be discretionary; *Gaines* v. *Thompson,* 7 Wall. 347 (1868), *U.S. ex rel. Riverside Oil Company* v. *Hitchcock,* 190 U.S. 316 (1903), and *Ness* v. *Fisher,* 223 U.S. 683 (1912), which held the Secretary of the Interior's decisions in land ownership cases to be discretionary; *Louisiana* v. *McAdoo,* 234 U.S. 627 (1914), which turned down Louisiana's request to order Secretary of the Treasury McAdoo to review his action on sugar tariffs, on the grounds that his action had been discretionary. Cf. also *Ex parte Nennen,* 13 Pet. 230 (1839); *Commissioner of Patents* v. *Whitelye,* 4 Wall. 522 (1866); *U.S. ex rel. Dunlap* v. *Black,* 128 U.S. 40 (1888); *Keim* v. *U.S.,* 177 U.S. 290 (1899).

NOTES–CHAPTER 6

¹ Pound, *op. cit.,* p. 660.

² Robert G. McCloskey, "The Supreme Court 1961 Term: Foreword: The Reapportionment Case", 76 *Harvard Law Review* 54, 67 (1963).

³ John P. Frank, "Political Questions," *Supreme Court and Supreme Law,* ed. Edmund Cahn (Bloomington: Indiana University Press, 1964), p. 46.

⁴ "The Congress shall have Power . . . To declare War . . ." See, e.g., *Sarnoff* v. *Shultz,* 457 F. 2d 809 (9th Cir. 1971); *Massachusetts* v. *Laird,* 327 F. Supp. 378 (1971); *Davi* v. *Laird,* 318 F. Supp. 478 (W.D.Va. 1970); *Luftig* v. *McNamara,* 126 U.S. App. D.C. 4, 373 F. 2d 664 (D.C. Cir. 1967); *United States* v. *Mitchell,* 369 F. 2d 323 (2d Cir. 1966).

⁵ See, e.g., *Holtzman* v. *Schlesinger,* 38 L.Ed.2d 18 (1973); *Schlesinger* v. *Holtzman,* 38 L.Ed.2d 33 (1973); *Atlee* v. *Richardson,* 36 L.Ed. 2d 304 (1973); *DaCosta* v. *Laird,* 405 U.S. 979 (1972); *Perkins* v. *Laird,* 405 U.S. 965 (1972); *Sarnoff* v. *Shultz,* 34 L. Ed. 2d 186 (1972); *Orlando* v. *Laird,* 404 U.S. 869 (1971); *Massachusetts*

v. *Laird,* 400 U.S. 886 (1970); *United States* v. *Sisson,* 399 U.S. 267 (1970); *Velvel* v. *Nixon,* 396 U.S. 1042 (1970); and cases cited by Douglas, dissenting, in all of the above.

⁶ The 1973 Congress found itself unable to override a Presidential veto of its bill forbidding the use of appropriations for continued bombing in Cambodia. The impasse was resolved only when the Congress agreed to extend appropriations through August 15, 1973, and the President promised to seek explicit Congressional approval for any military action taken in Indochina after that date.

⁷ Recognition of this political reality was taken by Judge Wyzanski in *Mitchell* v. *Laird,* 476 F. 2d 533 (D.C. Cir. 1973).

⁸ See, e.g., *DaCosta* v. *Laird,* 448 F. 2d 1368 (2d Cir. 1971); *Orlando* v. *Laird,* 443 F. 2d 1039 (2d Cir. 1971); *Mottola* v. *Nixon,* 318 F. Supp. 538 (N.D. Cal. 1970); *Berk* v. *Laird,* 317 F. Supp. 715 (E.D.N.Y. 1970), 429 F. 2d 303 (2d Cir. 1970).

⁹ Fritz W. Scharpf, rejecting the idea of the political question doctrine as reflecting enforcement problems, has argued that the Court will not apply the doctrine "where important individual rights are at stake." Fritz W. Scharpf, "Judicial Review and the Political Question: A Functional Analysis," 75 *Yale Law Journal* 517, 584 (1966). Scharpf thus maintains that enforcement difficulties will not deter the Court from its job of upholding basic rights. If the Court was not deterred by the enforcement-basic American axiom problem, it is difficult to see why it refused to grant certiorari in any of these cases. As Justice Douglas points out in his dissent in *DaCosta* v. *Laird,* the circuit courts were in conflict about the justiciability of the constitutional questions raised. 31 L Ed 2d255. The Court does not always grant certiorari when circuit courts disagree, but, especially in cases involving rights, it does so frequently enough to make an exception noticeable. The Court would appear to have used the power to deny certiorari in the same way and for the same purpose that it uses its power to declare the existence of a political question. Surely no rights could be more "important" than those of physical liberty and of life itself, which were precisely the rights at stake in the war cases.

BIBLIOGRAPHY

Books

Baker, Gordon E. *State Constitution: Reapportionment.* New York: National Municipal League, 1960.

Barnett, James D. *The Operation of the Initiative Referendum, and Recall in Oregon.* New York: The Macmillan Company, 1915.

Beard, Charles A., and Schultz, Birl E. *Documents on the State-wide Initiative, Referendum and Recall.* New York: The Macmillan Company, 1912.

Bickel, Alexander. *The Least Dangerous Branch.*

Black, Charles L., Jr. *The People and the Court: Judicial Review in a Democracy.* New York: The Macmillan Company, 1960.

Boyd, William J.D. (ed.). *Compendium on Legislative Apportionment.* New York: National Municipal League, 1962.

Breckinridge, Sophonisba P. *Women in the Twentieth Century.* New York: McGraw-Hill Book Company, Inc. 1933.

Brennan, Joseph. *Social Conditions in Industrial Rhode Island, 1820-1860.* Washington, D.C.: n.p., 1940.

Chafee, Zechariah, Jr., and Re, Edward D. *Cases and Materials on Equity.* Brooklyn: The Foundation Press, Inc.

DeGrazia, Alfred. *Public and Republic.* New York: Alfred A. Knopf, 1951.

Dionisopoulos, P. Allan. *Rebellion, Racism, and Representation: The Adam Clayton Powell Case and Its Antecedents.* DeKalb: Northern Illinois University Press, 1970.

Dixon, Robert G., Jr. *Democratic Representation: Reapportionment in Law and Politics.* New York: Oxford University Press, 1968.

Duguit, Leon. *Law in the Modern State.* New York: B. W. Huebsch, 1919.

Ehrlich, Eugen. *Fundamental Principles of the Sociology of Law.* Cambridge: Harvard University Press, 1936.

Frieze, Jacob. *A Concise History of the Efforts to Obtain an Extension of Suffrage in Rhode Island from the Year 1811 to 1842.* Providence: Benjamin F. Moore, 1842.

Garvey, Neil F. *The Government and Administration of Illinois.* New York: Thomas Y. Crowell Co., 1958.

Godley, Leon Grant. *Outline of Equity.* 2d. ed. Brooklyn: n.p. 1931.

Goldman, Eric F. *Rendezvous with Destiny.* New York: Alfred A. Knopf, Inc., 1952.

Goldwin, Robert A. (ed.). *Representation and Misrepresentation: Legislative Reapportionment in Theory and Practice.* Chicago: Rand, McNally, 1968.

Gosnell, Cullen B. *Government and Politics of Georgia.* New York: Thomas Nelson & Sons, 1936.

Gove, Samuel K. (ed.). *State and Local Government in Illinois: A Bibliography.* Urbana: University of Illinois Press, 1953.

Griffith, Elmer C. *The Rise and Development of the Gerrymander.* Chicago: Scott, Foresman and Company, 1907.

Harper, Ida Husted. *A Brief History of the Movement for Woman Suffrage in the United States.* New York: National Woman Suffrage Publishing Co., Inc., 1917.

Hedges, Gilbert L. *Where the People Rule.* San Francisco: Bender-Moss Company, 1914.

Hockett, Homer Gary. *The Constitutional History of the United States, 1826-1876.* New York: The Macmillan Company, 1939.

Hofstadter, Richard. *The Age of Reform.* New York: Alfred A. Knopf, Inc., 1955.

Hubbard, Benjamin V. *Making America Safe for Democracy: The Referendum as an Instrument of Government.* Chicago: Chicago Legal News Company, 1926.

In re Adam Clayton Powell: Hearings before Select Committee Pursuant to H. Res. I, 90th Congress, 1st sess. Washington: U.S. Government Printing Office, 1967.

Jewell, Malcolm C. (ed.). *The Politics of Reapportionment.* New York: The Atherton Press, 1962.

Kettleborough, Charles. *The State Constitutions.* Indianapolis: B. F. Bowen & Co., 1918.

Key, V. O., Jr. *Southern Politics in State and Nation.* New York: Alfred A. Knopf, Inc. 1949.

Kirchheimer, Otto. *Political Justice.* Princeton: Princeton University Press, 1961.

Larson, James E. *Reapportionment and the Courts.* University, Alabama: University of Alabama Press, 1962.

McGovney, Dudley O. *The American Suffrage Medley.* Chicago: University of Chicago Press, 1949.

McLaughlin, Andrew C. *A Constitutional History of the United States.* New York: Appleton-Century-Crofts, Inc. 1935.

Mason, Alpheus Thomas: *The Supreme Court from Taft to Warren.* Baton Rouge: Louisiana State University Press, 1958.

Mott, Rodney L., and Hindman, Wilbert L. (eds.). *Constitutions of the States and United States.* New York State Constitutional Convention Committee, 1938.

Mowry, Arthur May. *The Dorr War.* Providence: Preston & Rounds Company, 1901.

Murphy, Walter P. *Congress and the Court.* Chicago: University of Chicago Press, 1962.

Myers, Gustavus. *History of the Supreme Court of the United States.* Chicago: Charles H. Kerr & Co., 1912.

Pomeroy, John Norton. *A Treatise on Equity Jurisprudence* 2d ed. 3 vols. San Francisco: Bancroft-Whitney Company, 1899.

Porter, Kirk H. *A History of Suffrage in the United States.* Chicago: University of Chicago Press, 1918.

Post, Charles Gordon, Jr. *The Supreme Court and Political Questions.* Baltimore: Johns Hopkins Press, 1936.

Ranney, Austin. *Illinois Politics.* New York: New York University Press, 1960.

Schmeckebier, Laurence F. *Congressional Apportionment.* Washington, D. C.: The Brookings Institution, 1941.

Steiner, Gilbert Y., and Gove, Samuel K. *The Legislature Redistricts Illinois.* Urbana: University of Illinois Institute of Government and Public Affairs, 1956.

Swisher, Carl Brent. *Roger B. Taney.* New York: The Macmillan Company, 1935.

Tyler, Samuel. *Memoir of Roger Brook Taney, LL.D.* Baltimore: John Murphy & Co., 1872.

Wagner, Paul W. (ed.). *County Government Across the Nation.* Chapel Hill: The University of North Carolina Press, 1950.

Warren, Charles. *The Supreme Court in United States History.* Boston: Little, Brown and Company, 1926. 2 vol.

Weeks, Kent M. *Adam Clayton Powell and the Supreme Court.* New York: Dunellen, 1971.

Williamson, Chilton. *American Suffrage.* Princeton: Princeton University Press, 1960.

Articles and Periodicals

Albertsworth, E. F. "Constitutional Duties and Inadequate Enforcement Machinery," 17 *American Bar Association Journal* 153 (1931).

Armstrong, David H. "Constitutional Law—Equal Protection—State Restrictions in Nominations of Candidates," 47 *Michigan Law Review* 406 (1949).

Atleston, James B. "The Aftermath of Baker v. Carr—An Adventure in Judicial Experimentation," 51 *California Law Review* 535 (1963).

Auerbach, Carl A. "The Reapportionment Cases: One Person, One Vote—One Vote, One Value," in Philip B. Kurland, ed.: *The Supreme Court Review 1964* (Chicago: University of Chicago Press, 1964), p. 1.

Bannon, A. Jay. "Constitutional Law—Political Questions—Congressional Apportionment," 25 *Texas Law Review* 419 (1949).

Barron, Jerome A. "The Ambiguity of Judicial Review: A Response to Professor Bickel," 1970 *Duke Law Journal* 591 (1970).

Basye, Wendell M. "The Scope of Judicial Power in Matters of a Political Nature," 33 *Virginia Law Review* 625 (1947).

Bellamy, Calvin: "Applicability of the 14th Amendment to the Allocation of Delegates to the Democratic National Convention," 38 *George Washington Law Review* 892 (1970).

Bickel, Alexander M. "The Durability of Colegrove v. Green," 72 *Yale Law Journal* 39 (1962).

——. "The Great Apportionment Case," 146 *New Republic* 13 (April 9, 1962).

——. "The Supreme Court 1960 Term: Foreword: The Passive Virtues," 75 *Harvard Law Review* 40 (1961).

Black, Charles L. "Inequities in Districting for Congress: Baker v. Carr and Colegrove v. Green," 72 *Yale Law Journal* 13 (1962).

Bonfield, Arthur Earl. "Baker v. Carr: New Light on the Constitutional Guarantee of Republican Government" 50 *California Law Review* 245 (1962).

——. "The Guarantee Clause of Article IV, Section 4: A Study in Constitutional Desuetude," 46 *Minnesota Law Review* 513 (1962).

Bowman, Harold M. "Congressional Redistricting and the Constitution," 31 *Michigan Law Review* 149 (1932).

Brock, Robert M., and Grubbs, David H. "Tennessee," *Compendium on Legislative Apportionment,* William J. D. Boyd, editor (New York: National Municipal League, 1962).

Brody, Lee B. "Constitutional Law–State Apportionment for Congressional Elections–Justiciability of Issue," 45 *Michigan Law Review* 368 (1947).

Burdette, Franklin L. "The Illinois Congressional Redistricting Case," 40 *American Political Science Review* 958 (1946).

Caruso, Lawrence R. "The Lucas Case and the Reapportionment of State Legislatures," 37 *University of Colorado Law Review* 433 (1965).

———. "The Rocky Road from Colegrove to Wesberry: Or, You Can't Get There from Here," 36 *Tennessee Law Review* 621 (1969).

Cauley, John J. "Political Questions As Distinguished from Judicial Questions," 24 *Notre Dame Lawyer* 231 (1949).

Chafee, Zechariah, Jr. "Congressional Reapportionment," 42 *Harvard Law Review* 1015 (1929).

———. "The Internal Affairs of Associations not for Profit," 43 *Harvard Law Review* 993 (1930).

Conner, Francis D. "Constitutional Law–Refusal of Court to Compel Reapportionment of Congressional Districts," 35 *Illinois Bar Journal* 263 (1947).

Conron, Michael A. "Law, Politics, and Chief Justice Taney: A Reconsideration of the Luther v. Borden Decision," 11 *American Journal of Legal History* 377 (1967).

Crane, Wilder. "Tennessee: Inertia and the Courts," *The Politics of Reapportionment,* Malcolm C. Jewell, editor (New York: The Atherton Press, 1962).

Curtis, Thomas B. "The Power of the House of Representatives to Judge the Qualifications of its Members," 45 *Texas Law Review* 1199 (1967).

Dionisopoulos, P. Allan. "A Commentary on the Constitutional Issues in the Powell and Related Cases," 17 *Journal of Public Law* 103 (1968).

Dixon, Robert G., Jr. "Reapportionment in the Supreme Court and Congress: Constitutional Struggle for Fair Representation," 63 *Michigan Law Review* 209 (1964).

Dixon, Rogert G., Jr. "The Warren Court Crusade for the Holy Grail of 'One Man-One Vote'," in Philip B. Kurland, ed.: *The Supreme Court Review 1969* (Chicago: University of Chicago Press, 1969), p. 219.

Dodd, Walter F. "Judicially Non-Enforceable Provisions of Constitutions," 80 *University of Pennsylvania Law Review* 54 (1931).

Eckhardt, Robert C. "The Adam Clayton Powell Case," 45 *Texas Law Review* 1205 (1967).

Eisenhart, Earl E., Jr. "Judicial Power–Political Question–Black Tom Award Cases," 9 *George Washington Law Review* 967 (1941).

Elliott, Ward. "Prometheus, Proteus, Pandora and Procrustes Unbound: The Political Consequences of Reapportionment," 37 *University of Chicago Law Review* 474 (1970).

Ellis, Dousey D., Jr. "Powell v. McCormack and the Power to Expel," 5 *Georgia Law Review* 203 (1971).

Emerson, Thomas I. "Malapportionment and Judicial Power," 72 *Yale Law Journal* 64 (1962).

Fahy, Charles. "Judicial Review of Executive Action," 50 *Georgetown Law Journal* 709 (1962).

Ferguson, Clarence C. "The Inherent Justiciability of the Constitutional Guaranty Against Domestic Violence," 13 *Rutgers Law Review* 407 (1959).

Field, Oliver P. "The Doctrine of Political Questions in the Federal Courts," 8 *Minnesota Law Review* 485 (1924).

Finkelstein, Maurice. "Further Notes on Judicial Self-Limitation," 39 *Harvard Law Review* 221 (1925).

⸺ "Judicial Self-Limitation," 37 *Harvard Law Review* 339 (1924).

Frank, John P. "Political Questions," *Supreme Court and Supreme Law*, Edmund Cahn, editor (Bloomington: Indiana University Press, 1954).

Frankino, Steven P., and Wyss, Garrett N. "Baker v. Carr," 11 *Catholic University Law Review* 96 (1962).

Freund, Paul A. "New Vistas in Constitutional Law," 112 *University of Pennsylvania Law Review* 631 (1964).

Galbreath, C. B. "Provisions for State-wide Initiative and Referendum," 43 *Annals of the American Academy of Political and Social Science* 81 (1912).

Gold, A. E. "Constitutional Law: Jurisdiction of the Supreme Court over Political Questions: What is a Political Question?", 9 *Cornell Law Quarterly* 50 (1923).

Goldberg, Arthur L. "The Statistics of Malapportionment," 72 *Yale Law Journal* 90 (1962).

Gunther, Gerald. "The Subtle Vices of the 'Passive Virtues'—A Comment on Principle and Expediency in Judicial Review," 64 *Columbia Law Review* 1 (1964).

Hochman, Charles B. "Judicial Review of Administrative Processes in Which the President Participates," 74 *Harvard Law Review* 684 (1961).

Hohfield, Wesley Newcomb. "The Relations Between Equity and Law," 9 *Michigan. Law Review* 537 (1913).

Hughes, Graham. "Civil Disobedience and the Political Question Doctrine," 43 *New York University Law Review* 1 (1968).

Hughes, Melvin C. "Georgia," *County Government Across the Nation*, Paul W. Wager, editor. (Chapel Hill: The University of North Carolina Press, 1950).

The Initiative, Referendum and Recall, Vol. XLIII, *Annals of the American Academy of Political and Social Science* (1912).

Irwin, William P. "Representation and Election: the Reapportionment Cases in Retrospect," 67 *Michigan Law Review* 729 (1969).

Jackson, Robert H. Statement, 20 *United States News* 81 (June 21, 1946).

Jaffe, Louis L. "Standing to Secure Judicial Review: Private Actions," 75 *Harvard Law Review* 255 (1961).

⸺ "Standing to Secure Judicial Review: Public Actions," 74 *Harvard Law Review* 1265 (1961).

Kerner, Otto, Jr. "Constitutional Law—Congressional Redistricting," 27 *Illinois Law Review* 445 (1932).

Key, V. O., Jr. "Procedures in State Legislative Apportionment," 26 *American Political Science Review* 1050 (1932).

Kindregan, Charles P. "The Cases of Adam Clayton Powell, Jr. and Julian Bond: The Right of Legislative Bodies to Exclude Members-Elect," 2 *Suffolk University Law Review* 58 (1968).

Legislative Reapportionment, Vol. XVII, *Law and Contemporary Problems* (1952).

Lewis, Anthony. "Legislative Apportionment and the Federal Courts," 71 *Harvard Law Review* 1057 (1958).

Lucas, Jo Desha. "Legislative Apportionment and Representative Government: The Meaning of Baker v. Carr," 61 *Michigan Law Review* 711 (1963).

McCloskey, Robert G. "The Supreme Court 1961 Term: Foreword: The Reapportionment Case," 76 *Harvard Law Review* 54 (1963).

McConnell, Edward B. "Constitutional Law—Validity of Illinois Law," 26 *Nebraska Law Review* 119 (1946).

McGraw Bernard James. "Constitutional Law—Exercise of Equitable Powers of Federal Courts in Political Questions—Disproportionate Voting System of State," 26 *Notre Dame Lawyer* 122 (1950).

McKay, Robert B. "Court, Congress, and Reapportionment," 63 *Michigan Law Review* 255 (1964).

_____. "Political Thickets and Crazy Quilts: Reapportionment and Equal Protection," 61 *Michigan Law Review* 645 (1963).

_____. "Reapportionment: Success Story of the Warren Court," 67 *Michigan Law Review* 223 (1968).

_____. "Stability and Change in Constitutional Law," 17 *Vanderbilt Law Review* 203 (1963).

McKay, Robert B. "The Reapportionment Decisions: Retrospect and Prospect," 51 *American Bar Association Journal* 128 (1965).

Meshon, Max. "Constitutional Law—Georgia County Unit System," 24 *Temple Law Quarterly* 239 (1950).

Miller, Arthur Selwyn and Alan W. Scheflin. "The Power of the Supreme Court in the Age of the Positive State: A Preliminary Excursus—Part One," 1967 *Duke Law Journal* 273 (1967).

Miller, Sam S. "Constitutional Law—Reapportionment—State Legislatures," 36 *Tulane Law Review* 853 (1962).

Minar, David W. "Equilibrium in Illinois," *The Politics of Reapportionment*, Malcolm C. Jewell, editor (New York: The Atherton Press, 1962).

Mitchell, Stephen R. "Judicial Self-Restraint: Political Questions and Malapportionment," 39 *Washington Law Review* 761 (1964).

Moore, William G. "Legislative Reapportionment," 1949 *Wisconsin Law Review* 761 (1949).

Myneder, Charles. "Constitutional Law—Equal Protection Clause—County Unit Vote," 49 *Michigan Law Review* 271 (1950).

Nagel, Stuart S. "Court-Curbing Periods in American History," 18 *Vanderbilt Law Review* 925 (1965).

Nathanson, Nathaniel L. "The Supreme Court as a Unit of the National Government: Herein of Separation of Powers and Political Questions," 6 *Journal of Public Law* 331 (1957).

Neal, Phil C. "Baker v. Carr: Politics in Search of Law," *The Supreme Court Review,* 1962, Philip B. Kurland, editor (Chicago: University of Chicago Press, 1962), p. 252.

The New York Times.

Nilsen, Sylvia E. "Constitutional Law—Legislative Apportionment—Failure to Apportion—Effect of Change in Population," 15 *George Washington Law Review* 359 (1947).

Norquist, Griffin. "Constitutional Law—Political Question—Apportionment," 18 *Mississippi Law Journal* 170 (1946).

Notes, Comments, and Annotations:

"The Alabama Franchise Case," 17 *Harvard Law Review* 130 (1903).

"Baker v. Carr and Legislative Apportionments: A Problem of Standards," 72 *Yale Law Journal* 968 (1963).

"Comments on Powell v. McCormack," 17 *University of California-Los Angeles Law Review* 1-191 (1969).

"Congress in the Thicket: The Congressional Redistricting Bill of 1967," 36 *George Washington Law Review* 224 (1967).

"Congressional Exclusion: A Test of Judicial Supremacy," 15 *New York Law Forum* 921 (1969).

"Congressional Power to Exclude Members-Elect," 83 *Harvard Law Review* 62 (1969).

"Constitutional Law—Congressional Power to Exclude When Constitutional Qualifications for Membership are Satisfied," 16 *Loyola Law Review* 483 (1969-70).

"Constitutional Law—Construction and Operation—Independent Power of State Legislature to Create Congressional Election Districts," 16 *Minnesota Law Review* 850 (1932).

"Constitutional Law—Construction, Operation and Enforcement of Constitutions," 30 *Harvard Law Review* 184 (1916).

"Constitutional Law—Federal Jurisdiction of Political Issues—County Unit System of Voting," 36 *Iowa Law Review* 134 (1950).

"Constitutional Law—Is Redistricting of a State for Congressional Elections an Exercise of the Lawmaking Power of a State?", 30 *Michigan Law Review* 969 (1932).

"Constitutional Law—Judicial Self-Limitation—Political Question," 32 *Virginia Law Review* 647 (1946).

"Constitutional Law—Legislative Apportionment—Failure to Apportion—Effect of Change of Population," 30 *Minnesota Law Review* 37 (1945).

"Constitutional Law—Political Questions—Georgia County Unit Vote System," 4 *Vanderbilt Law Review* 691 (1957).

"Constitutional Law—Redistricting for Congressional Elections—Lawmaking Power of the State," 30 *Michigan Law Review* 1337 (1932).

"Constitutional Law—Suit to Enjoin Enforcement," 1 *Rutgers Law Review* 152 (1947).

"Constitutional Law—Voting—Comparative Weight of Each Vote in Primary Elections," 36 *Virginia Law Review* 678 (1950).

"Constitutional Law—Voting—Constitutionality of Georgia County Unit System," 99 *University of Pennsylvania Law Review* 413 (1950).

"Constitutional Right to Congressional Districts of Equal Population," 56 *Yale Law Journal* 127 (1946).

"Constitutional Safeguards in the Selection of Delegates to Presidential Nominating Conventions," 78 *Yale Law Journal* 1228 (1969).

"Federal Court's Power to Determine Election or Qualifications of Member of Legislative Body," 17 L. ed. 2d 911 (1966).

"Georgia County Unit Vote," 47 *Columbia Law Review* 284 (1947).

"The Gerrymander and Judicial Abstention," 26 *Indiana Law Journal* 259 (1951).

"Inequality of Population or Lack of Compactness of Territory as Invalidating Apportionment of Representatives," 2 *American Law Reports* 1337 (1919).

"Injunctive Protection of Political Rights in the Federal Courts," 62 *Harvard Law Review* 659 (1949).

"Legal Barriers Confronting Third Parties: The Progressive Party in Illinois," 16 *University of Chicago Law Review* 499 (1949).

"Legal Obstacles to Minority Party Success," 57 *Yale Law Journal* 1276 (1948).

"Legislative Exclusion: Julian Bond and Adam Clayton Powell," 35 *University of Chicago Law Review* 151 (1966).

"Limiting Judicial Review of Congressional Exclusion with the Political Question Doctrine," 1969 *Utah Law Review* 182 (1969).

"Minority Government," 146 *New Republic* 8 (April 9, 1962).

"One Man, One Vote and Selection of Delegates to National Nominating Conventions," 37 *University of Chicago Law Review* 536 (1970).

"Political Questions—Classical or Discretionary Applications of Judicial Review?" 4 *Suffolk University Law Review* 127 (1969).

"Power of Judiciary to Compel Legislature to Make Apportionment of Representatives or Election Districts as Required by Constitution," 46 *American Law Reports* 964 (1927).

"Reapportionment of Congressional Districts in Illinois," 41 *Illinois Law Review* 578 (1946).

"The Julian Bond Case," 52 *Virginia Law Review* 1309 (1966).

"The Power of a House of Congress to Judge the Qualifications of its Members," 81 *Harvard Law Review* 673 (1968).

"The Right to Form a Political Party," 43 *Illinois Law Review* 832 (1949).

"Threat of Enforcement—Prerequisite of a Justiciable Controversy," 62 *Columbia Law Review* 106 (1962).

"Viet-Nam in the Courts of the United States: 'Political Questions'," 63 *American Journal of International Law* 284 (1969).

"Wright v. Rockefeller and Legislative Gerrymanders," 72 *Yale Law Journal* 1041 (1963).

Perrin, Noel. "In Defense of Country Votes," 52 *Yale Review* 17 (1962).

Pollak, Louis H., "Judicial Power and 'The Politics of the People'," 72 *Yale Law Journal* 81 (1962).

Pound, Roscoe. "Judicial Review: Its Role in Intergovernmental Relations: Foreword," 50 *Georgetown Law Journal* 653 (1962).

Rae, John B. "Democrats and the Dorr Rebellion," 9 *New England Quarterly* 476 (1936).

Rankin, J. Lee. "The High Price Exacted for Not Entering the Political Thicket," 15 *American University Law Review* 1 (1965).

Reapportionment, Vol. 72, No. 1, *Yale Law Journal* (1962).

Rolston, Robert. "Constitutional Law—Congressional Districts—Suit Questioning Validity," 20 *Southern California Law Review* 284 (1947).

Roche, John P. "Judicial Self-Restraint," 49 *American Political Science Review* 762 (1955).

Rodell, Fred. "For Every Justice, Judicial Deference is a Sometime Thing," 50 *Georgetown Law Journal* 700 (1962).

Russell, Denver L. "Constitutional Law—Political Issue—Equal Protection of the Laws—Direct Election of Senators," 19 *George Washington Law Review* 216 (1950).

Sawer, Geoffrey, "Political Questions," 15 *University of Toronto Law Journal* 49 (1963).

Scharpf, Fritz W. "Judicial Review and the Political Question: A Functional Analysis," 75 *Yale Law Journal* 517 (1966).

Schattschneider, E. E. "Urbanization and Reapportionment," 72 *Yale Law Journal* 7 (1962).

Schnorr, Martin A. "Constitutional Law: Due Process: Validity of Nominating Petition Regulation," 34 *Cornell Law Quarterly* 620 (1949).

Schwartz, Warren F. and Wayne McCormack: "The Justiciability of Legal Objections to the American Military Effort in Vietnam," 46 *Texas Law Review* 1033 (1968).

Sheiner, Leo. "Constitutional Law: Congressional Districts: Creation by 'Legislature'." 17 *Cornell Law Quarterly* 466 (1932).

Sindler, Allan P. "Baker v. Carr: How to 'Sear the Conscience' of Legislators," 72 *Yale Law Journal* 26 (1962).

Sommer, William E. "Constitutional Law: Right of Voter to Equality of Voting Power in Congressional Elections," 35 *California Law Review* 296 (1947).

Stone, David O. "Equality of Voting Power as a Constitutional Right: The Georgia County Unit Case," 2 *Syracuse Law Review* 73 (1950).

Strumpf, Harry P. "Congressional Response to Supreme Court Rulings: the Interaction of Law and Politics," 14 *Journal of Public Law* 377 (1965).

Symposium—"One Man-One Vote and Local Government." 36 *George Washington Law Review* 689 (1968).

Taft, William Howard. "Can Ratification of an Amendment to the Constitution be Made to Depend on a Referendum?" 29 *Yale Law Journal* 821 (1920).

Taylor, William L. "Legal Action to Enjoin Legislative Malapportionment: The Political Question Doctrine," 34 *Southern California Law Review* 179 (1961).

Tigar, Michael E. "Judicial Power, the 'Political Question Doctrine,' and Foreign Relations," 17 *University of California-Los Angeles Law Review* 1135 (1970).

Tollett, Kenneth S. "Political Questions and the Law," 42 *University of Detroit Law Review* 439 (1965).

Tucker, Emmett E., Jr. "Constitutional Law—Application of Political Question Doctrine in Suit to Enjoin Discriminatory State Election Procedure," 8 *Washington and Lee Law Review* 190 (1951).

Velvel, Lawrence R. "Suggested Approaches to Constitutional Adjudication and Apportionment," 12 *University of California-Los Angeles Law Review* 1381 (1965).

———. "The War in Viet Nam: Unconstitutional, Justiciable, and Jurisdictionally Attackable," 16 *Kansas Law Review* 449 (1968).

Walter, David O. "Reapportionment of State Legislative Districts, 37 *Illinois Law Review* 20 (1942).

Weiss, Jonathan. "An Analysis of Wesberry v. Sanders," 38 *Southern California Law Review* 67 (1965).

Williams, Henry N. "Legislative Apportionment in Tennessee," 20 *Tennessee Law Review* 235 (1948).

Wright, J. Skelly. "Professor Bickel, the Scholarly Tradition, and the Supreme Court," 84 *Harvard Law Review* 769 (1971).

INDEX OF CASES

184 INDEX OF CASES

GENERAL INDEX